Advance Praise fo
YOUR GREEN HO

I'm often asked by homeowners if there is a single, definitive guide I
would recommend for building a house that's truly earth-friendly.
Well, folks: this is it. This is the book we've all been waiting for,
from Alex Wilson, the best author I know for delivering unbiased,
practical and up-to-the-minute information on all things Green.
It's a must-read for anyone wanting a new home that's
good for themselves AND the planet.

— Sarah Susanka, author, *The Not So Big House*

Alex Wilson is the dean of green building in this country, the
go-to guy for saving the planet (not to mention cutting down on
your electric bill). This book synthesizes a lifetime of research
and experience into an invaluable toolkit for anyone
with a home or plans to get one.

— Bill McKibben, author, *The End of Nature*

Your Green Home does more than provide a wealth of practical
guidance from one of the most trusted names in the green building
business; it also makes clear how design choices can make all the
difference in how your green home performs in terms of
environmental impact, budget and comfort.
This is a terrific resource.

— Christine Ervin, past President & CEO,
US Green Building Council

Alex Wilson was preaching the gospel of green building long before $3-a-gallon gasoline, and long before global warming became a movie starring Al Gore. I can think of no better guide through the murky claims and requisite compromises of this nascent science. In *Your Green Home*, Wilson is staunch without being strident, explaining the terms, outlining the choices, and most important, clarifying the priorities for anyone contemplating the construction of a green home.

— Kevin Ireton, editor, *Fine Homebuilding*

Building green homes is one of the most important steps we can take to protect the health of our environment — not to mention the health of our families. In *Your Green Home*, Alex Wilson clearly and thoroughly explains the principles of green building and how to put them into practice in home design and construction. This book is an invaluable resource for homeowners, designers, and builders alike, and should be required reading for anyone preparing to build a new home.

— Rick Fedrizzi, President, CEO and Founding Chair, US Green Building Council

YOUR GREEN HOME

A Guide to Planning a Healthy, Environmentally Friendly New Home

ALEX WILSON
FOREWORD BY JOHN ABRAMS

NEW SOCIETY PUBLISHERS

Cataloging in Publication Data:
A catalog record for this publication is available from the National Library of Canada.

Cover design by Diane McIntosh. Cover credit: Photo Wood frame construction: Getty Images, Photodisc Red, photographer David Buffington. Kitchen photo by Randi Baird of a home designed and built by South Mountain Company.

Printed in Canada.
Second printing February 2007.

Paperback ISBN-13: 978-0-86571-555-4
Paperback ISBN-10: 0-86571-555-6

Inquiries regarding requests to reprint all or part of *Your Green Home* should be addressed to New Society Publishers at the address below.

Disclaimer: Any improvements or alterations outlined in this book are done at your own risk. Local or national codes and manufacturer's instructions take precedence over any advice given in this book. The author or publisher cannot be held responsible for accidents or other trouble arising from any information contained in this book.

To order directly from the publishers, please call toll-free (North America) 1-800-567-6772, or order online at www.newsociety.com

Any other inquiries can be directed by mail to:
New Society Publishers
P.O. Box 189, Gabriola Island, BC V0R 1X0, Canada
1-800-567-6772

New Society Publishers' mission is to publish books that contribute in fundamental ways to building an ecologically sustainable and just society, and to do so with the least possible impact on the environment, in a manner that models this vision. We are committed to doing this not just through education, but through action. We are acting on our commitment to the world's remaining ancient forests by phasing out our paper supply from ancient forests worldwide. This book is one step toward ending global deforestation and climate change. It is printed on acid-free paper that is 100% old growth forest-free (100% post-consumer recycled), processed chlorine free, and printed with vegetable-based, low-VOC inks. For further information, or to browse our full list of books and purchase securely, visit our website at: www.newsociety.com

NEW SOCIETY PUBLISHERS   www.newsociety.com

For my daughters Lillian and Frances—
and the Earth they will inherit.

Books for Wiser Living from
Mother Earth News

Today, more than ever before, our society is
seeking ways to live more conscientiously.
To help bring you the very best inspiration
and information about greener, more sustainable
lifestyles, New Society Publishers has joined
forces with *Mother Earth News*. For more than
30 years, *Mother Earth News* has been North
America's "Original Guide to Living Wisely,"
creating books and magazines for people
with a passion for self-reliance and a desire to
live in harmony with nature. Across the
countryside and in our cities, New Society
Publishers and *Mother Earth News* are leading
the way to a wiser, more sustainable world.

Contents

Acknowledgments

I OWE IMMENSE GRATITUDE to the many people I have learned from and received inspiration from over the past quarter-century as I've pursued a career of teaching and writing about more sustainable buildings. Some of these individuals are among my closest friends, including John Abrams, Marc Rosenbaum, Michael Totten, Gail Lindsey, Bob Berkebile, David Eisenberg, John Hayes, Mark Kelley, Peter Yost, Steve Loken, Larry Sherwood, and Terry Brennan, to mention a few. Others, I've spent less time with over the years, but enough time to absorb some of their wisdom: Amory Lovins, Paul Hawkin, Ray Anderson, Edward Wilson, John Knott, Bill McDonough, David Orr, Joe Lstiburek, Joe Van Belleghem, Joel Ann Todd, Hillary Brown, and Bill Browning.

A few of my mentors have sadly passed away: Dana Meadows, Bill Yanda, Keith Haggard, and my parents, Conrad and Barbara Wilson.

I owe tremendous gratitude to my coworkers at BuildingGreen, Inc. in Brattleboro, Vermont, especially my business partner Nadav Malin. Nadav and I have worked and learned together in our adventure with *Environmental Building News,* since it was just an idea over fifteen years ago. We've built on each others strengths and skills — struggling at first as we sought to make a business out of a fledgling green building movement and now struggling to keep up, as our business has grown to more than 16 employees.

Our other editors at BuildingGreen — Jessica Boehland, Mark Piepkorn, Tristan Roberts — have helped hone my writing skills, while ensuring that our resources are both useful and readable. During the many times when my plate has been too full, they have helped to ensure that we keep up with our publishing deadlines and maintain the quality our readers depend on.

I am grateful to those who have read this manuscript and provided valuable comments, especially the aforementioned John Abrams and Nadav Malin, as well as Tony Grassi, a relatively new green homeowner as well as past Chair of The Nature Conservancy, whom I got to know through my involvement with that organization. Their comments have been greatly appreciated, though I take full responsibility for any mistakes and omissions in this book.

I am grateful to BuildingGreen's art director, Julia Jandrisits, who provided all of the illustrations for this book. In an age when so much is transitioning to electronic format, Julia's skills with pen and ink are much appreciated. And thanks to Ethan Goldman, BuildingGreen's webmaster, for creating the fuel cost comparison chart and for his work on the companion website (www.BuildingGreen.com/YourGreenHome).

I am grateful for the careful attention and tremendous care the editors and production staff at New Society Publishers afforded this book in its gestation and production. Most importantly, Chris and Judith Plant encouraged me to finish a manuscript that I had begun several years earlier, but set on the back burner. They saw a need for this book and inspired me to update and complete what I had earlier written. I am grateful for the superb copyediting that Gayla Groom did on this manuscript — despite the long hours required to satisfy her requests for clearer explanations, additional detail, and sometimes new information. In an age when most publishers consider a manuscript good enough as-is, New Society invests time and effort to make their books better, which benefits us all. And I am grateful to Ingrid Witvoet and the production staff at New Society. I am particularly thankful for New Society's patience in waiting for corrected manuscripts, missing illustrations, captions, and the seemingly endless stream of details that I was always too busy to provide in a timely fashion.

Thanks too to my cousin, architect Morris Tyler, who loaned me the use of his Maine cabin for a week so that I could devote a concentrated time to the final chapters of this book. Distractions and interruptions being what they were, I really needed to get away from the meetings, e-mail, and phone calls that dominate my work week!

Finally, and most importanty, I am grateful to my wife, Jerelyn, and daughters, Lillian and Frances, for putting up with my long hours of work for many years — on this book and many other projects — including the all-too-frequent evenings and weekends that found me (and still find me) pecking away on my computer keyboard. My older daughter tells me that the sound of a computer keyboard helps her fall asleep, since it reminds her of time at home when I would pull out the computer after her bedtime.

Thank-you, thank-you all.

— Alex Wilson
Dummerston, Vermont

Foreword

by John Abrams

ABOUT 35 YEARS AGO I moved, with my wife and child and a small collection of friends, to undeveloped land in Guilford, Vermont. We were headed back to the land with plenty of passion and no plan. We camped on the land, cleared it, planted vegetable gardens, and prepared to build a house. We had, among us, almost no money, but we had the energy of youth. We found barns in the area that were falling down, and local farmers who were happy to see them go. We laboriously dismantled them and hauled the materials back to our land in beat-up trucks. Unskilled but undaunted, we erected shelter from the ruins of the past. This was the first building I ever built from scratch *and* my first "green" building, all rolled into one. It was the beginning of a romance with design and building that has remained with me through the decades.

The lessons we learned back then, as we first left the gate — salvaging and marshalling resources, using materials in inventive ways, and fearlessly (and sometimes foolishly) trying new approaches — are still reflected in the work of my design-build company. But as our skills, our practices, and our buildings became more refined, we grew conscious of the environmental implications of our activity. We began to concentrate our efforts on "solar" houses. Over time we learned that a house must be so much more than that. "What are *good* houses?" I asked myself. The English architect Charles Voysey once said, "Simplicity, sincerity, repose, directness, and frankness are moral qualities as essential to good architecture as to good people." We tried to embed those qualities in our houses. We tried to push our craft forward. At the same time, we tried to make houses that are easy on the land, durable, energy-efficient and productive, resource-conserving, and healthy. As we hunted for information to help us learn, Alex Wilson played an important role.

Alex's involvement with renewable energy and green building goes way back. He worked with the New Mexico Solar Energy Association in the late seventies when it was essentially a hotbed of grassroots solar experimentation and activity. He became the executive director of the Northeast Sustainable Energy Association in Vermont, and created a new hotbed. When his tenure as NESEA's director ended, he joined the board, and our paths crossed there when I joined that board in 1990. I'm glad for the crossing. It led to an association which became a friendship that has lasted many years.

For the past 15 years the newsletter Alex founded, *Environmental Building News,* has been the single strongest voice for residential and commercial environmental building. The consistent in-depth research, no-nonsense, unbiased reporting, and long reach has provided practitioners like me with information we could not possibly get elsewhere. With a biologist's trained eye and skeptical sensibility, Alex and his cohorts provide impeccable information. For all those years, I have served on the newsletter's advisory board. Although my contributions have been minor, the honor of the service has been great.

Along with the newsletter, Alex's company, BuildingGreen, Inc., has developed an array of other important tools for professionals. Now, with the publication of *Your Green Home,* Alex has turned his attention to the general public, to people who are building homes for themselves, or having them built. People like you.

That's a good thing for all of us. When I read the manuscript I was almost embarrassed to find out how much I learned. Wait a minute — this is my field, this is what I do, and this book was written for homeowners, not for professionals like me. But I was delighted, too. I found a wealth of information carefully explained, relentlessly organized, and neatly sorted out to make it readable and comprehensive. You will share my delight if the topic piques your curiosity, or if you are about to build or renovate a new home. I look forward to sharing this book with all of our clients, *and* with our designers as well. A single source of information, being read by those on both sides of the table, will enhance communication and help us to make better buildings.

This book will not teach you how to make a good house, or a green one. It will teach you how to learn. It will teach you how to find the help you need, and how to ask the right questions, of yourself and others. It will help you to think — about where, how big, what kind of structure, energy use, materials, systems, indoor environment, water, waste, landscape, and even about how to live well in your new home. It will teach you how much there is to know and how little possibility there is that you (or I) could know it all.

Not to worry. What I particularly like about this book is that it unpacks all the tools and concepts and unwraps all the mystery. Although it covers an exceptional range of green building topics and issues, it is not overwhelming. The message is that it's not necessary to knock yourself out to do everything green at once, but that it's better to do something — whatever aspects you can manage, as much as you can, and do it well—than it is to do nothing.

My decades of design and building have convinced me that making a house, although it is an immense undertaking with attendant stresses and difficulties, can also be — and should also be — a joyous adventure. One thing I have learned is that it is the buildings that are loved that endure. Buildings that people care about are maintained and adapted to new uses over time. Are you getting ready to build or renovate a house? If so, read this book. It will help you find your way down a path that is likely to produce a home that will stand the test of time in that way. Remember to enjoy the ride!

John Abrams is cofounder and CEO of South Mountain Company, a widely respected, employee-owned, design-build company on Martha's Vineyard, Massachusetts. His 2005 book, *The Company We Keep: Reinventing Small Business for People, Community, and Place* (Chelsea Green), traces the history of South Mountain and explores the role of business as a potent force for cultural, social, and ecological progress.

CHAPTER 1

So You Want to
Build a Green Home

THERE ARE MANY REASONS to build a green home. Perhaps you want to provide a safe, healthy place for your children to grow up. Or maybe you're concerned about rising energy costs. Your priority might be comfort, or durability — knowing that the house will last a long time with minimal maintenance. For a growing number of us, building a green home is about doing our part to protect the environment, helping to make the world a better place for our children and grandchildren. A green home is all of this, and often much more.

This book is written to help you understand what green building is all about, and then show you what's involved in applying these ideas to your home — whether you are having that home custom-built, looking for a house built by a speculative builder, or building a home yourself.

WHAT IS GREEN BUILDING?

The term green building is used to describe design and construction of buildings with some or all of the following characteristics:

- Buildings that have minimal adverse impacts on local, regional, and even global ecosystems;
- Buildings that reduce reliance on automobiles;
- Buildings that are energy-efficient in their operation;

🏠 Buildings and grounds that conserve water;

🏠 Buildings that are built in an environmentally responsible manner from low-environmental-impact materials;

🏠 Buildings that are durable and can be maintained with minimal environmental impact;

🏠 Buildings that help their occupants practice environmentalism, e.g. by recycling waste; and

🏠 Buildings that are comfortable, safe, and healthy for their occupants.

Quite often, when people think of green building, what comes to mind is the use of recycled-content building materials — insulation made from recycled newspaper, floor tiles made out of ground-up light bulbs, and so forth. Materials are indeed an important component of green construction, but this way of building goes much further.

Green building addresses the relationship between a building and the land on which it sits; how the structure might help to foster a sense of community or reduce the need for automobile use by its occupants; how to minimize energy use in the building (energy consumption being one of the largest environmental impacts of any building); and how to create the healthiest possible living space. These priorities, from a broad

FIGURE 1.1—*In today's cohousing communities, houses are clustered and compact, and vehicles are kept separate so as to create pedestrian-friendly spaces where children can feel safe.*

FIGURE 1.2—*In the 1970s, solar house designs often focused on solar heating with little regard to anything else, and the aesthetics were often too different to appeal widely.*

environmental standpoint, are usually far more important than whether or not the floor tiles in the entry hall are made out of recycled glass.

A SHORT HISTORY OF GREEN BUILDING

Green building can trace its origin, in part, to builders of solar homes during the 1970s and '80s. Many of the architects, designers, and builders who were involved with solar energy back then had gotten involved because of concerns about energy shortages and the environment. Since solar energy is a clean, *renewable energy* source, designing and building homes to make use of solar was a way to reduce impacts on the environment, creating homes that required less fossil fuel or electricity.

These designers and builders began to realize, however, that their focus was too narrow, that reducing conventional energy use was just one part of a much bigger picture of resource efficiency and healthy building. Sure, those solar pioneers could build a house that used solar energy to keep its occupants toasty on cold winter nights, thus saving money and helping the environment at the same time. But what about *where* these houses were being built? What about their durability? What about the materials used in construction? Was the wood coming from clear-cut old-growth forests in the Pacific Northwest? What about the

FIGURE 1.3—*Our travels into space in the 1960s and '70s gave us a new perspective on our own Earth: It is finite and needs to be cared for.*

alarming increases in asthma among children? What about ozone depletion? And what about comfort? Some of those houses with extensive south-facing glass overheated or experienced glare problems during the day.

Environmentally aware designers and builders began to broaden their focus. They recognized that North America's buildings accounted for a huge percentage of its energy use, greenhouse gas emissions, ozone depletion, resource use, and health problems (see figure 1.4). And instead of simply being part of the problem, these pioneers wanted to be part of the solution. A few professional organizations, including the American Institute of Architects and the Urban Land Institute, formed new committees or divisions to address environmentally responsible building. New organizations were created, including the US Green Building Council. New publications were launched addressing green building, such as *Environmental Building News.* Even the mainstream industry magazines, such as *Builder* and *Architectural Record,* began running feature articles on green building. A shift began that will forever change the way we design and build.

Homebuyers and commercial building owners are also encouraging the green building movement. People want to live or work in buildings that are healthier and better for the environment. Opinion polls regularly show that the public is willing to spend more for something that's better for the environment; it only makes sense that this concern extends to our homes and workplaces. In commercial buildings, research shows that people working in green buildings (with features like natural daylighting, healthy air, and operable windows) are more productive; they get more done in less time, whether manufacturing widgets or processing insurance forms. Because the labor costs of running a business dwarf the costs of operating a building (see figure 1.5), improving the productivity of workers can yield tremendous financial returns.

Similar studies are showing that students learn faster in classrooms that have natural daylighting. A highly detailed 1999 study of hundreds of classrooms in the San Juan Capistrano School System in southern California, for example, correlated the rate of learning with the presence

FIGURE 1.4

Energy and Environmental Impacts of US Buildings	
Share of primary energy consumption from buildings – 2003	40%
Share of electricity consumption from buildings – 2003	72%
Total carbon dioxide emissions from buildings – 2003	2.5 billion tons
Share of carbon dioxide emissions from buildings – 2003	39%
Share of sulfur dioxide (SO_2) emissions from buildings – 2002	52%
Share of nitrogen oxide (NOx) emissions from buildings – 2002	19%
Total energy expenditures for buildings – 2003	$305 billion
Total energy expenditures for houses – 2003	$177 billion
Total value of new residential construction – 2003	$353 billion
Total value of home improvement and repairs – 2003	$177 billion
Avg. annual energy expenditure, single-family detached homes – 2001	$1,780
Number of new single-family houses completed in 2003	1,386,000
Average size of new single-family house in 2003	2,330 square feet
Average lumber use in average new single-family home – 2000	13,800 board feet
Total construction waste from home construction	6.6 million tons
Total annual building-related construction and demolition waste	30-35 million tons
Construction & demolition waste as percent of municipal solid waste	24%
Total number of households in U.S. – 2003	112 million

Data from 2005 Buildings Energy Databook, *August 2005, US Department of Energy.*

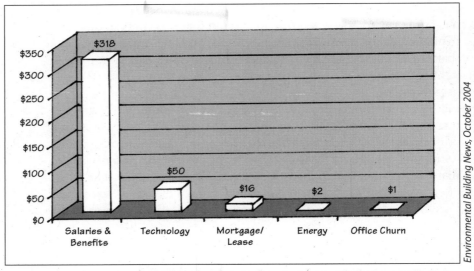

FIGURE 1.5—*In a typical office building, more than a hundred times as much money is spent on people as on energy. Boosting productivity can yield tremendous economic returns.*

or absence of natural daylighting. The researchers found that learning progressed 20% faster in math skills and 26% faster in verbal skills in classrooms with the most natural daylighting compared to classrooms with the least daylighting.

While much of the green building movement is very new, there are also aspects that have been around for a long time. Many of the ideas being advanced by environmentally concerned designers and builders are drawn from the past. Landscape architects in the American Midwest are studying how Native Americans managed the tall-grass prairies using fire and are using those practices at some large corporate office parks. Ideas from pioneering individuals — such as Frederick Law Olmstead, 19th-century designer of New York City's Central Park, Frank Lloyd Wright in the early 1900s, and landscape architect Ian McHarg beginning in the 1950s — are referenced widely in the green building field today. Some of the underlying principles of passive solar design date back to prehistoric cliff dwellings.

Green building is still in its infancy. Not only does the building industry not yet have all the answers about how to build green, it often doesn't even know the right questions to ask. There have been tremendous strides made since the early 1990s in understanding the environmental impacts associated with building (for example, scientific studies of the *life-cycle impacts* of building materials), but we still have a very long way to go. Some of the ideas presented in this book will probably become obsolete as the green building movement matures over the coming years and decades. But we now know enough to provide clear guidance to someone who wants a home that will have a lower impact on the environment, and that is the purpose of this book.

HOW TO USE THIS BOOK

Your Green Home is written primarily for people planning to build a home. Whether you'll be involved with the actual design and construction yourself or hiring professionals, this book will guide you in the process of ensuring that your home is designed and built in an environmentally friendly and healthful way. This book is also relevant to those looking to buy an older home or renovate an existing home; many of the same issues apply, although you generally have far less control over the outcome.

FIGURE 1.6—*Some aspects of green design have their origins prior to European settlement in North America. The Anisazi cliff dwellings in the American Southwest were built into south-facing cliffs. Overhangs gave protection from the high summer sun, but allowed the lower winter sun to warm their homes.*

Your Green Home introduces a great many issues to consider; on first blush, you might even find it overwhelming. But realize that this book is not meant to be a prescriptive guide to building a green home. Think of it as a smorgasbord from which you can pick out some strategies and design features to incorporate into your home. I certainly hope that you will take some of these ideas to heart and incorporate them into your house, but it is very unlikely that you'll be able to accomplish everything I describe. Even if you can only implement a small percentage of the ideas that are in this book, you will have helped to protect the environment — and you'll likely end up with a house that's safer to live in and less expensive to operate. Your home doesn't have to be a demonstration building that shows off the state of the art in green home building. But if you at least consider the ideas here and act on some of them, you *will* make a difference.

If you're not involved with building, there will no doubt be a lot of terms in this book that are new to you. I've highlighted in italics those that I thought could use some explanation and included them in a glossary. You'll find that on page 211.

While this book is packed with design ideas, it is not really a design book. It is not a book that you can take to your builder and say, "Here, build this." Nor is this a construction manual; it doesn't provide recommended construction details, or engineering guidelines. While you will find recommendations for particular types of materials, don't expect to find guidance on exactly how those materials should be installed; that's where the manufacturer or designer or builder comes in. What this book provides is guidance on the many considerations that come into play when planning a new home — where to build, general design priorities, energy design strategies, indoor air quality considerations, and so forth.

Perhaps most importantly, *Your Green Home* tells you where to turn for the help you need in building a healthy, environmentally responsible home. An accompanying web site (<www.BuildingGreen.com/ YourGreenHome>) provides a wealth of resources — books, periodicals, product directories, software resources, and other web sites — that you and the building professionals working for you can turn to for more detailed information.

CHAPTER 2

Finding the
Help You Need

Very often, the biggest challenge in building a green home is finding professionals who understand green building and can provide you with what you want. Hopefully, this will be different in a few years as more designers and builders become skilled in green building, but for now it's a reality. So how do you find the help you need?

The first step you have in your hands. To find design and building professionals who can create the green home you want, you have to know what you want. You have to understand, at least to an extent, what green building is all about. Reading this book from cover to cover will help you understand what is involved with green building, and it will enable you to evaluate the suggestions and ideas presented by the designers and builders you talk with.

At the same time, reading this book does not make you an expert. If you want a green home that sits lightly on the land, requires very little energy to operate, and is functional, durable, and attractive enough to stand the test of time, you probably need to hire a professional to design it. One of the biggest differences between conventional building and green building is that green building requires a larger investment in upfront design, particularly if such energy features as passive solar, daylighting, and natural cooling are planned. Taking the time to find a qualified designer and builder will make all the difference in your new home.

FIGURE 2.1—*Finding designers and builders who are knowledgeable about green building is a challenge in many locations.*

HIRING A DESIGNER

There are several ways to hire a home designer. The traditional approach is to hire an architect to design your house, then hire a builder to construct it. With this arrangement, the architect typically stays involved with the project from start to finish, helping to find the builder and making sure that the house is built as specified. You usually pay the architect a fixed percentage of the total project cost to cover the design work. Depending on the specific contract, you might pay extra for project management if the architect provides that function.

Another approach is to hire a *design-build firm* that will handle both design and construction. This can be a huge advantage with a green home, because you can be confident that these functions will be integrated. The design will be done with careful attention to how easily and efficiently it can be built. When it comes to building the home, any modifications that appear necessary can be dealt with easily since the designers and builders are part of the same company. For design work, design-build firms either charge by the hour, or they charge a fixed percentage of the total project cost. For construction work, they typically charge on a *cost-plus basis,* charging you the actual cost of materials and labor, plus a fixed profit level. Most design-build firms are small, with fewer than 25 employees.

An architect can be drawn from a wide geographic region (and it may be necessary to range far to find one highly knowledgeable about green building). Design-build firms, on the other hand, generally have to operate closer to home, so until green building is widely accepted, you may have trouble finding such a firm in your immediate area. However, if a design-build firm is available locally with expertise in green design, that will generally be your best option.

Yet another approach is to hire just a builder who will handle the design. Many builders work from stock plans they purchase — perhaps making a few modifications along the way — and thus eliminate the "middleman" expense of a designer. This can be a way to save a lot of money, but there are several problems with this approach. First of all, there aren't many stock plans available for green homes, let alone plans that are optimized for your particular climate. Second, as you will learn by reading this book, green building involves elements that are not conducive to the use of stock house plans, such as a close examination of the building site and a careful tailoring of the design to make the home fit the site.

Evaluating the expertise of an architect or designer when it comes to green building can be difficult. After you become familiar with what's involved with green building, talk to prospective designers about what you would like to do. Listen to the ideas they suggest. Evaluate their priorities and suggestions relative to what you've learned about green building. Ask about energy-efficient and green homes they have designed. Find out if you can call past clients as references; ideally, designers will arrange for visits to several homes they designed. Ask if the designer will bring additional experts to the team, such as an energy specialist or landscape designer.

The importance of good energy design cannot be overemphasized. Hopefully, the architecture firm or design-build company will have the in-house expertise needed to create a very low-energy house. If not, the designer should have a good working relationship with an energy expert who is skilled in energy-efficient construction detailing, *passive solar heating* design, *daylighting,* computer modeling of energy performance, advanced mechanical equipment, and state-of-the-art electric lighting.

FIGURE 2.2—*Make sure that the design firm you choose has expertise in green design — or is willing to learn.*

The design team should also include expertise in landscape design and land-use planning, to address how the house fits onto the land and is integrated into the community. If at all possible, the designer should add a landscape architect, designer, or planner onto the team, at least during the earliest planning meetings. People often think of landscape design as something that's done after the house is completed, or nearly completed, choosing which shrubs to plant and where. But, as will become clear as you read through this book (especially Chapters 3 and 12), the landscape plan should be addressed at the earliest stages of planning and design.

HIRING A BUILDER

As noted above, design-build firms provide both design and construction services. If you don't opt for such an approach — or if a design-build firm with expertise in green building is not available locally — your architect should be able to recommend an appropriate builder or general contractor, and perhaps take care of the whole process for you. As commonly used, builder refers to someone who handles all aspects of building, while general contractor refers to someone who manages the project but contracts out most of the work. These two terms are often used interchangeably, though.

As when selecting a designer, try to evaluate how open prospective builders are to green building ideas. Have they ever heard of it? Are they familiar with *Environmental Building News,* other green design magazines, or any books on green building? Do they sound skeptical? Do they argue that you shouldn't try to do anything out of the ordinary, or are they open to what you have in mind? How do they respond when you ask about energy efficiency and renewable energy?

Just because builders don't have experience with green building is not a reason to rule out hiring them. Remember, this is a fairly new field. But you should expect to find an interest in learning about green building. Offer to provide prospective builders with a copy of this book, then check back to find out what they think after reading through parts or all of it. Also, look into how long they've been in business and try to gauge their reputation. Ask for references of past clients and call or visit several of them. If possible, have prospective builders take you around to see several houses they have built.

With builders that subcontract out a significant portion of the construction work, ask about the subcontractors they will use. Will insulation contractors use care in sealing all gaps and ensuring that insulation

FIGURE 2.3—*A builder who is committed to green building will probably sort waste materials on the job site to separate out those that are recyclable.*

will be placed behind wires and in hard-to-reach corners? Are drywall hangers willing to minimize waste and collect scrap for recycling or grinding as a *soil amendment?* Will the electrician undo all the hard work in sealing the *building envelope* by leaving large gaps and unsealed cracks? Is the floor finishing contractor or painting contractor open to using less-toxic *waterborne finish* or at least willing to ventilate the space during finishing? These seemingly minor considerations can make a big difference in ensuring that your house will be as green as possible. It will be the responsibility of the general contractor or builder you hire to oversee the work of these subcontractors, so the most important priority is to find someone who buys into your green agenda.

SERVING AS YOUR OWN GENERAL CONTRACTOR

If you have some background in building and are highly organized, you might want to consider being your own general contractor. You would serve as the overall project coordinator, ordering all building materials, hiring all the subcontractors (excavation contractors, framers, electricians, plumbers, drywall contractors, etc.), and making the day-to-day decisions that are required even with the most carefully drawn plans. The general contractor, whether a professional or yourself, is also the one who must make sure that the green building agenda is followed, including that all subcontractors stay green. Being your own general contractor can save you a lot of money.

Don't fool yourself, though. It isn't easy to be your own general contractor. It can take a huge amount of time; it can be frustrating, especially if you're not used to the building industry; and it isn't even certain that you'll save any money. Professional builders or general contractors already have relationships with subcontractors and local building supply yards. They know when to schedule different tasks so that the whole project moves ahead on schedule, and they carry enough weight to get the subcontractors to show up when they say they will. (Because subcontractors depend on getting business from the builder in the future, they're likely to show up when they said they would, while they might not be as responsive to homeowners serving as general contractors.) Chances are that builders or general contractors will be able to get a better discount on materials than you can, since they do a large volume of business with the supply company, although many building supply yards will extend contractor discounts to homeowners. But, if you're aware of these difficulties and ready to take on the challenge, being your own general contractor can be highly satisfying — putting you right in the center of transforming an idea and a design into a real house.

BUILDING YOUR OWN HOUSE

If you're skilled in the building trades or really adventurous, you might even want to build your home yourself. For those with enough background in building or who take the time to learn building, the gratification of living in a product created by your own hands can be tremendous. All of the concerns noted above relative to being your own general contractor, however, are multiplied several-fold for the potential *owner-builder*. You shouldn't even consider this unless you have a very good idea of what you're getting into — and have at least a year to devote to it.

There are several excellent owner-builder schools around the country where you can pick up many of the skills you need to build your own house; search online to learn more about these. Taking a few courses at an owner-builder school is highly recommended, but you'll still face many challenges in building your own house. These courses cannot

FIGURE 2.4—*Some of the "alternative" construction techniques, such as strawbale, are very popular among owner-builders.*

begin to provide the level of experience and know-how a professional builder brings to a house-building project. (Couples considering building their own homes might also want to budget some money for marriage counseling!)

There's a lot to think about as you plan a new house. Getting good support is critically important. As you read through the rest of this book, consider the advice and support you will need to put all the pieces together. Then plan to invest the time needed to find that help. The right architect or design-build firm can turn your dreams into reality. Don't forget to visit this book's companion web site (<www.Building Green.com/YourGreenHome>) to track down additional information.

CHAPTER 3

Where to Build

YOU MAY ALREADY HAVE A SITE in mind for the house you're planning to build, but let's assume, for the time being, that you don't. What should you look for? What considerations should come into play as you seek a building site? Is building a new house really the way to go, and what are the alternatives? If you decide on a *greenfield* (previously undeveloped) site, how should you analyze that site and figure out where to build on the property? These are the types of questions this chapter will examine, seeking a place and a context for your green home.

As you begin to answer these questions, it will be very beneficial if you already have your designer and builder in place. They can play a lead role in this process, guiding you in the decision-making.

BUILDING A NEW HOUSE VS. FIXING UP AN OLD ONE

The discussion of where to build should include a discussion of whether you really want to build in the first place. From an environmental standpoint, every building project has environmental impacts. Green building is, really, an issue of trying to keep those impacts as small as possible. Before launching into your building project, you should at least consider whether your needs might be served just as well by renovating an existing house, instead of building from the ground up.

FIGURE 3.1—*Before deciding to build a new house, consider whether it might be possible to buy an older house and fix it up. While not covered in any detail in this book, green remodeling is generally preferable, from an environmental standpoint, to building a new house.*

The environmental impacts of excavating for foundation walls and erecting structural walls and roof are considerable. If you start with an existing building — even if you carry out an extensive *gut-rehab*, where almost everything is removed down to the structural frame, then rebuilt — you will eliminate many of those impacts and can create a greener home. To keep the home's total environmental burdens low, however, you have to achieve high levels of energy performance, and that can be a challenge when walls are already in place. For the remainder of this book, we will assume that a decision has been made to build a new house from the ground up.

YOUR HOME AS PART OF THE COMMUNITY

Green building is not only about a particular building; it is also about the relationship between that building and the larger community. Decisions you make in planning your home can help to foster a strong, healthy, cohesive community.

Such a community is environmentally beneficial because less driving will be necessary. Residents are more likely to shop and use services locally instead of driving somewhere else; close neighbors are more likely to share trips to the supermarket, or keep an eye on each other's homes and children.

Transportation comes into play in other ways at the neighborhood or community planning level. Along with doing what we can to ensure that neighbors form connections that might lead to shared automobile trips, consider access to other forms of transportation. Examine whether there are any regional bicycle paths or walkways that would be accessible from your new home. How easy would it be to walk to the nearest bus stop or, in more urban areas, a light-rail stop? Take a look at commercial and retail space nearby where you might work or shop — is it walking distance? Bicycling distance?

While most zoning in the United States forces us to keep different types of development separate (e.g. residential, commercial, retail) there are very good reasons to do just the opposite. So-called *mixed-use development,* in which different uses are allowed to coexist, has significant benefits. For instance, allowing residential apartments to be located above commercial and retail storefronts benefits both the businesses and residents. For the businesses, there will be more walk-in traffic. Residents will be able to just walk down a few flights of stairs and down

FIGURE 3.2—*Mixed-use development is conducive to bicycling and walking, so it can reduce the use of automobiles.*

the block for the Sunday paper and a cappuccino; they might also be able to walk to work. And everybody benefits because the area won't be deserted after working hours and thus crime rates are likely to be lower.

These broad land-use planning issues may not come into play with every building project, but they should always be considered. After all, even if we do everything in our power to build a super-green, low-energy home, if we then climb into our cars to commute 10 or 20 miles to work or to shop for groceries, our total environmental impacts will still be pretty high. Driving two 20-mile roundtrips per day in a car getting 25 miles per gallon will use about 600 gallons per year. That's more energy, and more carbon emissions, than a well-insulated green home will use annually for heating.

BUILDING ON PREVIOUSLY DISTURBED LAND AND URBAN INFILL LOTS

Even if you are building a house from the ground up, consider looking for a site that has already been impacted by development in some way. Building on a degraded site is an opportunity for restoration and environmental improvement — and it allows the most pristine, undeveloped land to be left in its natural state.

Cohousing: A New Model for the 21st Century?

Some of these ideas about the importance of community are being addressed through an innovative development pattern first brought to the US from Europe during the 1980s. In *cohousing*, a group of families cluster their homes together on commonly owned land. While each family owns its own home, the group as a whole typically owns a common house, which may include a large kitchen and dining area so that community members can dine together a few nights a week, a childcare room and playground, guest rooms that residents can sign up for when family or friends are visiting (allowing members' homes to be smaller), and perhaps a workshop or hot tub room. Community members may also share little-used pieces of equipment, such as lawn mowers and a pickup truck or van.

Cohousing communities can range from a handful of homes or apartments up to 30 or 40. Larger communities can be organized into individual cohousing neighborhoods to keep the scale appropriate. Cohousing is typically designed with a pedestrian focus; for example, buildings might surround a central green, with cars restricted to the outside perimeter. As of 2005, there were about 80 cohousing communities up and running in North America and several hundred more in the planning stages.

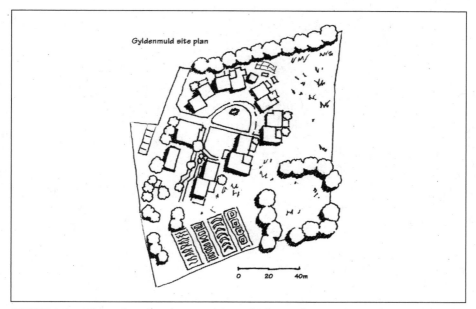

Gyldenmuld site plan

0   20   40m

FIGURE 3.3—*With cohousing communities, vehicles are kept to the perimeter in order to create a pedestrian-friendly central area. The large building is the common house, which is owned by the entire community; houses are privately owned.*

Urban *infill sites* — empty or abandoned lots between existing buildings — can be ideal for a green home. Sometimes a house or apartment building has burned or been torn down; other times, a lot was established but a house was never built on it. Building on infill sites instead of greenfield sites concentrates development in areas that are already developed, while keeping open land more natural and pristine.

EVALUATING GREENFIELD SITES

Most people who are ready to build the green home they have been dreaming about will be building on previously undeveloped land. Although building on these greenfield sites may not be ideal from an environmental standpoint, it is the reality. So what should you look for? How do you find the right property? On a given property, how should you decide where to build your house?

The first step should be a careful evaluation of any site you are considering. If possible, hire a landscape architect or environmental scientist to carry out such an assessment, or at least to help you do it. A

FIGURE 3.4—*Consider choosing a degraded site to build on, leaving the pristine, undeveloped sites open.*

comprehensive site assessment offers a number of important benefits: It will identify any fragile or ecologically important areas on the property that should be protected; it will guide the siting of your house in a location that will result in minimal disturbance to the land and ecosystems; it will help you fit the house and driveway into the landscape with minimal visual impact; and it will guide you or your designer in creating a climate-responsive building that minimizes energy use.

A site assessment should examine the following:

🏠 Topography. How steep is your site? Where are the flat areas that may be best left for agriculture, or parking, or septic system drainage fields? Topographical information is important in determining the risk of erosion from building sites and driveway construction.

🏠 Soils. What types of soils are found on your site? What are the drainage and fertility characteristics? How deep are the soils, both to bedrock and to the water table? With rural sites, understanding the soils will guide the placement of a septic system and show whether some land might most appropriately be left undeveloped for future use in farming, for instance.

🏠 Surface waters. Any streams, springs, ponds, and wetlands on the property should be carefully mapped. Wetlands can be difficult to map, because they may not be immediately obvious to the untrained eye; they are often signified by soil type or specialized vegetation.

🏠 Groundwater. On rural sites where you don't have access to municipal water, you will want to know about the underground aquifers. How deep will you have to drill your well? Is the groundwater contaminated or at risk of contamination?

🏠 Vegetation. What vegetation types are found on the site? Are there any unusual or threatened species present? Carefully examining and mapping the vegetation on your site will help you or a landscape architect find appropriate building sites. It will also identify areas or even individual plants that need special protection.

🏠 Wildlife habitat. Is there important wildlife habitat on your property? What about on neighboring properties and in wildlife corridors that span multiple properties? Fragmentation of habitat is a major problem in many areas. Understanding the type and extent of wildlife habitat on your site will help you devise a strategy for protecting it.

🏠 Temperature. How cold is your area in the winter? What is the maximum frost depth? How hot is it during the summer? Are there pockets where cold air will collect on cold winter nights? In your energy planning, become familiar with such temperature information as reasonably expected extremes (heating and cooling *design temperatures*) and the magnitude of heating and cooling requirements averaged over time (heating and cooling *degree days*).

🏠 Humidity. What's the typical relative humidity in your area? With low summertime humidity, you may be able to use an energy-efficient *evaporative cooler* instead of a conventional air conditioner. In areas with high humidity, special construction details may be called for to prevent moisture problems.

🏠 Wind. Are there areas on the property that are particularly exposed to cold winter winds and should be avoided? Are there locations where cool summer breezes can be channeled into the house, helping to reduce air conditioning requirements? To design a climate-responsive house, you should have an understanding of the characteristics of wind on your site.

- Precipitation. How much rainfall does your site receive? Does it arrive in small storm events spread out over the course of the year, or is it primarily seasonal or dumped in a few deluges? What's the typical snow depth in the winter? This sort of information can guide your landscape design relative to *stormwater* runoff, and it can guide your house design when it comes to foundation drainage, or special measures to prevent ice dams on roofs. Understanding snowfall can help you design your driveway for ease of snow plowing. Low precipitation or frequent droughts may argue for such measures as *xeriscaping* (low-water-use plantings), rainwater catchment, or separation of *graywater* (shower, bathtub and laundry wastewater) for landscape irrigation.

- Solar energy. How sunny is it where you plan to build? Is there adequate sunshine for space heating or water heating? Does your building site offer reasonable solar access (a generally unobstructed view to the south)? While shading on the south is a problem, shading on the west and east can be an energy benefit, helping to reduce air conditioning requirements.

- History of the land. When examining the physical, ecological, and climatological aspects of sites, consider how the land has been used by humans in the past. We can learn a lot from our predecessors, whether Native Americans, early settlers, or recent inhabitants. What stories do the early stone walls and ancient apple trees tell? What can you learn from the old cellar holes that might help you choose the placement of your house?

- Toxics. Are there any nasty surprises awaiting you? Many an old farm dump or bank-side junk pile has become a hazardous waste site through leakage of agricultural chemicals or fluids from abandoned vehicles or equipment. Old apple orchards often have soils with very high arsenic and lead levels from the lead arsenate pesticides that were used for pest control. Examine your land carefully. If a quick survey of the property finds areas of potential contamination, bring in an environmental engineer to carry out a more comprehensive assessment. It's better to find out before you build than after you move in.

- Aesthetics and views. Green building is, in part, about celebrating nature. You should situate and build your house so that you can appreciate that which is around you. Consider how you can design outdoor spaces that will put you closer to nature. Spend some time on the land getting to know it. While seeking a building location that puts you in touch with nature, consider also that the house will interfere with nature; finding the right balance of these contradictory motivations can be a challenge.

- Impact on neighbors. Also think about the impact your home might have on your neighbors. Respect the views of others, who may appreciate the natural beauty of your land as much as you do. On smaller sites, consider whether your house might block solar access of a neighbor to the north.

REGULATORY CONSTRAINTS

As you examine potential properties for the ideal building site, you should also take a look at the land-use regulations that govern what can and cannot be done in the municipality where you are considering building. Some of the best green building strategies — such as clustering several homes together or building close to the corner of a property and leaving the rest of the land undeveloped — may not pass muster with zoning bylaws. You may be able to appeal for a variance to outmoded regulations, but first you need to research what the existing regulations are.

FIGURE 3.5—*Clearly presenting any new or unusual development plans is key to gaining approval by a municipal planning commission or development review board.*

If you need to get a variance for the home or development you are considering, make sure you follow the proper procedures. The local zoning administrator or the staff at the local planning office can be a big help to you in interpreting regulations. Depending on where the property is, this office may be part of a town, county, or city department. In smaller towns and counties, it may be a volunteer committee that meets monthly. It often makes sense to hire the services of a landscape architect, civil engineer, or land-use lawyer to guide you through the regulatory hurdles.

If you are interested in something that is highly unusual and likely to be unfamiliar to planning staff or committee members, such as a cohousing development, offer to meet with the staff, planning commission, or development review board early in your planning process to educate officials about the development strategy and outline what you hope to do.

SITING YOUR HOME

After making your decision to acquire a piece of land, following careful examination of what the site has to offer, the next step is to decide where on the land to build. On an urban lot or a small suburban lot, your options will be very limited. On larger suburban lots and rural properties, house siting is a very important consideration. From an environmental standpoint, house and driveway siting are among the most important choices you will make; don't rush into your decisions. If possible, seek the advice of a landscape architect who understands and respects your green building priorities.

For some people planning a new home, where to build won't be a point of discussion; you have a building lot and that's that. But whenever possible, it makes a great deal of sense to give the issue of siting your full attention. Before you sign on the dotted line to purchase a building site, think about what the implications of building in that location will be down-the-road. If you're out in the country, what will happen if the price of oil doubles or triples? If you're planning to stay in the house until retirement, how will the location work if you have trouble getting around? Is there a café or market within walking distance? These sorts of questions can only be addressed before you buy that property. By thinking them through carefully and selecting your building site with care, your new home will likely serve your needs very well. The checklist below provides a starting point for planning the siting of your home.

Checklist – Rural Site Selection

Build on disturbed portions of a site	Build on previously developed, damaged, or disturbed portions of a site, and protect more pristine areas. With sites that are damaged over a larger area, consider incorporating ecosystem restoration into your landscaping plans.
Minimize the impact area on a site	Limit building impact to as small a portion of a site as possible. Rather than building in the center of a parcel, locate the house in one corner, and keep most of the land undeveloped. Keep the footprint of your house and construction area as small as possible.
Minimize the visual impact of your house	Consider the visual impact of your house on the surrounding area. Study the site from the vantage point of neighbors and roads, and try to fit the house and any outbuildings discreetly into the landscape. Respect the region's scenic and historical character.
Protect ecologically sensitive areas	Avoid disturbance to wetlands and other ecologically sensitive areas when siting buildings, driveways, utility lines, and other structures.
Protect and celebrate a site's uniqueness	Determine the attributes, qualities, and features that make a site unique, and work to protect and celebrate them through careful siting of your home.
Help protect wild areas beyond your property borders	Work with neighboring landowners to protect wildlife corridors and any contiguous areas of significant wildlife habitat. Examine your land within the broader context of habitat that extends across property borders.
Avoid building on agricultural land	Prime agricultural soils, whether or not in current agricultural use, should be protected from development whenever possible.
Allow landforms and vegetation to inform siting	Lay out buildings and driveways only after carefully mapping and studying the land and the vegetative cover. Try to fit the development onto the land in a low-impact and non-obtrusive manner.
Minimize distances from utilities	Site homes to minimize the distance from available utilities (power, sewer, water), to minimize driveway length, pavement area, impacts of trenching for buried utilities, etc.
Minimize driveway impact	Along with reducing the length of a driveway, look for opportunities to share driveways, and minimize erosion by not cutting driveways into steep slopes.
Optimize solar orientation	Select a building site that will permit passive solar and daylighting design appropriate to the climate. In most areas, the ideal orientation is to the south or southeast, with minimal shading from trees, hills, and structures to the south.
Choose sites that provide natural shading	Particularly in warm climates, look for a building site where natural shading is provided by trees or other vegetation on the west and east—solar gain contributes the most to summertime air conditioning loads on these orientations.

(continued)

Checklist – Rural Site Selection *(continued)*	
Choose sites that are protected from wind	Particularly in cold climates, situate buildings so that landforms and existing vegetation will help to shield the buildings from winter wind. This generally means avoiding ridgetops and hilltops as building sites (a strategy that also reduces the home's visual impact on the landscape).
Choose sites with a moderate grade	It is not always wise to build on flat land. Buildings can accommodate relatively steep slopes—sometimes as high as 25–30% (11-14 degrees), depending on soils and other conditions. Leave the precious level land for other uses that more acutely need it (agriculture, parking, play). Sloped sites also provide better drainage.
Plan for sewage disposal in the site selection process	If a conventional on-site wastewater system is planned, select the building site accordingly. If soils do not drain properly for a conventional in-ground wastewater system, find an alternate building site, or consider an alternative system, such as a recirculating sand filter or composting tolet/graywater disposal system.

FIGURE 3.6—*Use these suggestions as a starting point for planning the siting of your home.*

CHAPTER 4

General Issues
in House Design

O NE OF THE MISTAKES that home designers — yes, even *green* home designers — make is failing to step back and look at the big picture. Instead, they quickly get into specifics about materials, construction details, and which appliances to buy. A better idea is to begin your design process by considering a number of broad, overarching issues. Whether you have hired a designer or are designing your home yourself, begin with the big issues, then zero in on the details. This chapter examines a few of these general issues, focusing on those that can help to make your home environmentally friendly.

IS A STAND-ALONE, SINGLE-FAMILY HOUSE WHAT YOU REALLY WANT?

Since the 1940s, the American dream has been the single-family home. Billions of dollars in advertising, countless television shows, and a wide range of government policies have fueled our desire for that brand-spanking-new, single-family suburban home. For many, this image is rounded out by a shiny SUV parked in the driveway out front, a Sunday afternoon on the riding lawnmower, and a backyard deck looking out on their own "little piece of paradise." Indeed, there is much to be said for owning a single-family home on its own lot. You have privacy. You and your family make the decisions about how your house looks, how it's landscaped, and the protection provided by your little oasis. You're in charge.

But let's take a look at some of the alternatives. As was noted in the last chapter, green building is partly about building strong, vibrant communities. We are seeing more and more housing projects today in which the goal is *not* the single-family, stand-alone home located as far away as possible from neighboring homes. We're rediscovering that closer association with neighbors can be a good thing. We're hearing about cohousing and other developments where homes, or multi-family housing units, are clustered together on just a small portion of the site, and most of the land is kept as open, undisturbed land.

Clustering buildings is environmentally beneficial for many reasons. More land can be kept open and available for natural vegetation and wildlife, the area devoted to driveways can be reduced, less disturbance is required for buried utilities (sewer pipes, underground cables, etc.), and direct site impacts during construction can be reduced because a single staging area can serve a number of houses. With more people living closer together, public transit and shared transit are more feasible. As you begin to think about your dream home, at least give some thought to whether you really want a house all by itself, or

FIGURE 4.1—*The American image of an ideal suburban home is quite different than the ideal green home.*

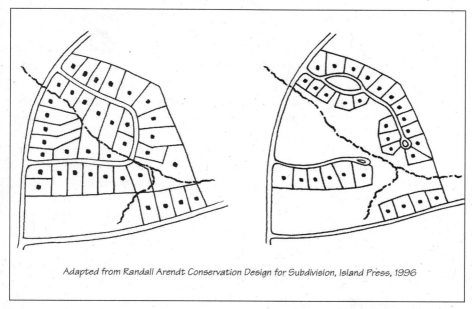

Adapted from Randall Arendt Conservation Design for Subdivision, Island Press, 1996

FIGURE 4.2—*By clustering houses, driveways can be shared, excavation costs for utilities can be reduced, and open space can be protected.*

whether a house that creates or contributes to a sense of community might be part of your vision.

HOW BIG A HOUSE DO YOU NEED?

The bigger the better, right? Isn't that a part of the American dream? The average US home has more than doubled in size since 1950, growing from about 1,000 square feet to 2,340 square feet in 2004. This has happened even as the average family size has shrunk by one-fourth, from about 3.4 in 1950 to 2.6 in 2004. Today's homes provide, on average, three times as much square footage per family member (290 in 1950, 900 in 2004). In fact, some of the largest homes being built today are for empty nesters, couples whose children have left the home and who are at the top of their money-earning potential.

What's wrong with this picture? Plenty. The bigger a house, the bigger its environmental impacts. Almost all building materials, even those we call green, have environmental costs associated with manufacture and shipping. And energy consumption is, to a significant extent, proportional to house size. So building smaller is better.

Early in the design process, carefully consider how big a house you need. Try to design the house to use space efficiently. This may mean investing more money in design, since it's a challenge to create smaller spaces that work well. Chances are, however, that any extra investment you make in design to optimize space in your house will more than pay for itself, since a smaller, more compact house usually costs less to build and operate. Downsizing the house allows you to incorporate higher-quality products, additional amenities, and a higher level of craftsmanship. Wouldn't you rather have hardwood flooring with natural finish instead of plywood subflooring and petroleum-based wall-to-wall carpeting, or ceramic tile flooring in the bathroom instead of sheet vinyl?

Some people decide to build a large house to provide for future expansion: in-laws moving in, for example, or a home office. While it certainly makes sense to design for *planned* family expansion (a recently married couple planning for children, say), when it comes to unplanned but possible down-the-road space needs, it usually makes more sense to keep the house smaller — sized to your current needs — but design it to facilitate easy expansion.

DESIGN FOR DURABILITY

No matter what type of house you build, there will be substantial environmental impacts associated with its construction — from the *embodied energy* in the materials, to the solid waste generated on the construction site. The longer your house lasts, the longer the period of time over which those impacts will be amortized, or spread out.

How do you design a house to be durable? First and foremost, the house should hold up well to the elements. This means choosing designs and construction details that are resistant to rainfall, humidity, heavy snowfall, flooding, intense sunshine, or other conditions that may be experienced in your climate. In climates with more than 20 inches of rainfall annually, it means designing with special attention to water management — for example, sizeable roof overhangs; ground sloping away from the house; and capillary breaks on the foundation footings and exterior foundation walls, and beneath floor slabs. It means choosing materials that will hold up for a long time, sometimes even if those materials aren't what would be considered the greenest (see Chapter 8).

Another requisite for a durable house is a durable design — the idea of timeless architecture. Try to create a house whose style will hold up well over the decades, or even centuries. Avoid trendy styles that are likely to lose popularity when the next fad comes along. Some of the trendy designs from the 1960s, for example, did poorly on several counts when it came to durability. You won't find many 30-year-old geodesic domes or yurts; most of those that didn't rot out due to poor detailing have been torn down to make way for more traditional — durable — designs.

DESIGN FOR ACCESSIBILITY AND ADAPTABILITY

Like it or not, most of us are getting older. In designing houses for the long term, consider providing handicapped accessibility. Creating entries, kitchens, bathrooms, and other spaces that can be used by wheelchair-bound individuals is referred to as *universal design*. If the home you're planning is likely to be the one you retire in, universal design is a high priority.

Needs change in other ways, too. Families grow larger, or the kids may grow up and leave the nest. You might start a home business that requires significant space. Houses that are designed to be adaptable to the evolving needs of their occupants are likely to be around longer.

FIGURE 4.3—*Accessible design calls for wider doors, a way to get into the house without stairs, key services on the first floor, and sinks that can be used by someone in a wheelchair.*

If interior spaces can be reconfigured easily with little actual construction, you'll save money, and environmental burdens will be lower. Perhaps a less-used part of the house can be closed off and require less heating and air conditioning. Some houses are being built today with moveable partitions or room dividers, so that some reconfiguring of spaces can be done with almost no effort. Providing a moveable partition between a small dining room and a family room, for example, might allow the space to be opened up on those rare occasions when large family gatherings or neighborhood get-togethers are held.

If an addition is likely down the road, pay special attention to the layout of the kitchen and other key rooms. Some starter homes are designed so that they can be added onto very easily with only minimal disruption to the house layout.

To reduce the cost and impacts of future additions or modifications, have your builder keep careful photographic records as construction proceeds. If your builder doesn't want to do this, bring a camera yourself during construction. Take photos, for example, of open wall cavities after plumbing and wiring have been run, but before drywall has been installed. Key all of the photos to specific locations on the house plans so that you will know exactly what you're looking at. Keep the photos, photo key, and house plans together in a binder. Down the road, when you need to cut an opening through a wall or modify the plumbing for a new bathroom, you can refer to these photos and figure out exactly where you need to open up the wall with minimal disturbance. If a leak develops in a wall, such photos can be invaluable in finding and repairing it.

HOUSE CONFIGURATION

What should the basic shape of your house be? Should it be tall and boxy? Low and spread out? Long and narrow, or roughly square? These are fundamental questions that will have very significant ramifications as to how your house is designed, what resources go into building it, how well it fits into its site, whether passive solar heating can play an important role in heating it, and how easy it will be to keep cool. Thinking about the house configuration early in the design process makes a lot of sense.

As the examples in Figure 4.4 demonstrate, a fairly tall, boxy house has less surface area for a given volume of space and thus won't lose heat as quickly in cold weather — since there is less wall area to lose that heat through. A tall, boxy house also has less roof area to absorb sunlight, leading to savings in air conditioning bills. The boxy house will also use less material in its construction.

FIGURE 4.4— *A tall, boxy house has less surface area relative to the square footage of floor, so it will require less heating and air conditioning.*

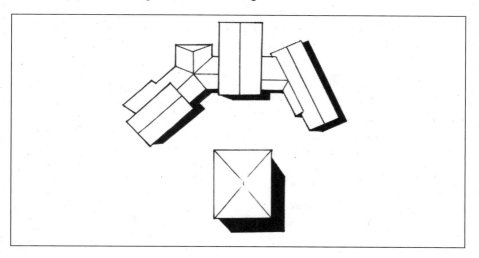

FIGURE 4.5— *To optimize passive solar heating, the longer axis of the house should be oriented east-west, providing more area for south-facing windows.*

On the other hand, the low house with more complex geometry may be better suited to passive solar heating and natural daylighting, and it may be a more interesting house visually. It can also lend itself better to outdoor living space (patios, decks, porches), thus providing inexpensive additional living area, especially in temperate climates where such spaces can be enjoyed over a long season. In the American Great Plains, a low house also has the advantage of being more protected from heavy winds and tornadoes.

From a solar heating standpoint, a long, narrow house, with the long dimension running east-west, usually makes the most sense. This way, there is more room to put windows on the south side of the house, to help heat it during the winter months. And because east and west windows transmit significantly more *solar gain* (net heat from sunlight) during the summer months than south-facing windows, they contribute more to overheating. Thus, having less east- and west-facing wall area can help to control air conditioning costs. (See Chapters 6 and 7 for more on energy design.)

WHAT ABOUT AN ATTACHED GARAGE?

If you plan to build a garage, should it be an integral part of the house, as is the case with most suburban houses? Should it be attached but with just one common wall? Or should it be kept totally separate?

FIGURE 4.6—*From an indoor air quality standpoint, a garage should be separate from the house; if that's not possible, the common walls must be extremely well-sealed.*

This is one of the many areas where green building requires a careful trade-off between conflicting issues. The integral garage is the most resource-efficient choice, since it requires the least additional material to build, but it also results in the greatest risk to homeowners from an air quality standpoint. Automobile exhaust leaking into the house from an attached garage is one of the most significant indoor air quality problems in many homes.

If the site allows it, a totally detached garage is usually the best option. In a climate with inclement weather, consider an open, covered walkway between the house and garage, but try to keep the garage separate. If that just isn't possible, try to have just a single common wall between the house and garage, and provide a very tight air seal in this wall. Avoid designs in which the house surrounds the garage, as it will be much harder to keep fumes out of the house. (See Chapter 9.)

OTHER DESIGN ISSUES

Some general design issues that should be considered early in the design process are not covered in this book, for example, the style of house. Many of these issues relate to personal tastes and the local real estate market. *Your Green Home* will not debate the relative merits of a raised-ranch vs. a Prairie style vs. a New England saltbox. That's up to you and your designer.

Other broad design issues will be covered in other chapters of this book, particularly Chapters 5, 6, and 7, which address the structural building system, energy-efficient design, and renewable energy.

As you begin getting into the more detailed design strategies in the following chapters, keep in mind the broad issues covered in this chapter. By controlling the overall house size, for example, you may be able to pay for higher-cost green features such as solar power. By thinking about the relationship between the house and garage early on, you can save a lot of time further along in the design process. Start with the big-picture issues, then move to the specifics.

CHAPTER 5

The Structural
Building System

W HAT TYPE OF BUILDING SYSTEM are you planning for your house? The vast majority of new homes are framed out of 2x4s or 2x6s, but this certainly isn't your only option. This chapter takes a look at some of the basic building systems that you, your designer, and your builder can consider. For each option, we take a look at such considerations as energy, climatic or regional limitations, suitability for owner-builders, and cost.

If you've already selected a builder, his or her input on this question is key. Most builders work with just one basic system. This is what they're comfortable with. Trying to convince a conventional stick builder (someone who builds out of 2x4s or 2x6s) to build your house out of adobe bricks or structural insulated panels rarely makes sense. If you're convinced that you must have a house built out of one of the less common building materials, find a builder who has experience with that system.

CONVENTIONAL WOOD FRAMING (2x4, 2x6)

Roughly 80% of new homes in North America are built using conventional wood framing, also called *platform framing*. With this system, walls are constructed out of 2x4s or 2x6s, either on a concrete slab or on a wood deck that is built on top of the foundation. At the top of this wall, a second platform is built that serves either as the second floor or attic floor, depending on whether a one-story or two-story house is being built. The roof is framed either with solid wood rafters or, more commonly, roof trusses. The outside of the frame is covered with *sheathing* panels, usually plywood or *oriented-strand board* (*OSB*). The walls are insulated, usually with fiberglass or cellulose insulation (see Chapter 6), and then covered on the inside with drywall.

If you've decided on a conventional wood framing system, 2x6s are preferable to 2x4s, because they provide more space for insulation. One of the most important goals of green building is to minimize energy consumption. Energy use for both heating and air conditioning can be reduced by providing more insulation in the walls, foundation, and attic or roof. Even in a mild climate, the extra insulation of a 2x6 wall can easily be justified compared with a 2x4 wall.

Wood doesn't insulate as well as insulation, so using less wood and more insulation improves the wall's overall energy performance. In a wall made out of wall studs and insulation, the wood studs cause *thermal bridging* (heat flows through the wood more quickly than it moves

FIGURE 5.1—*Advanced framing techniques save energy by reducing the amount of wood in a wall, leaving more room for insulation.*

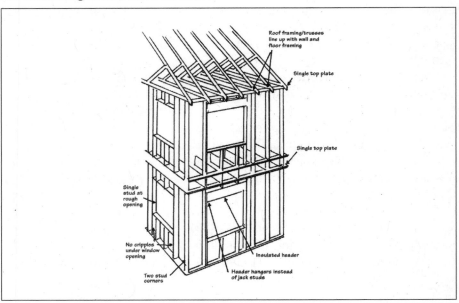

through the insulation). A standard 2x6 wall framed 16 inches *on-center* (wall studs spaced with 16 inches from the center of one to the center of the next) and insulated with R-19 fiberglass insulation achieves an average insulating value, or *R-value,* of R-15.1; in other words, the wood framing degrades the insulation performance by over 20%.

Using an *advanced framing* technique, many builders install the wall studs farther apart — 24 inches on-center, vs. 16 inches. Other advanced framing techniques include building corners out of just two studs, eliminating double studs at windows (*cripple studs*), installing a single (rather than double) *top plate* on stud walls to support trusses, and aligning the roof trusses with the wall studs. Used together, advanced framing techniques allow more of the wall area to be comprised of insulation and less of wood — so the average insulating value of the wall is higher. Using the example above of 2x6 walls with advanced framing, the average insulating value is R-16.0 (compared with R-15.1 with standard framing).

CONVENTIONAL WOOD FRAMING
WITH RIGID FOAM INSULATION

Rigid foam insulation provides more insulating value (R-value) per inch of thickness than standard insulation and thus helps keep highly insulated walls from being too thick. Most commonly, one or two inches of rigid foam is added to the outside of the wall framing. In fact, if adequate provision has been made to reinforce the wall with bracing or plywood at corners, in most regions this rigid foam can be used *in place of* the structural plywood or oriented strand board (OSB) sheathing. The type of rigid foam insulation with a shiny foil facing on it provides the highest R-value per inch (see Chapter 6).

Instead of putting the rigid foam insulation on the outside of the walls, some builders install it on the interior, then cover it with drywall. Either location can help ensure a tight house. Building science experts generally prefer exterior placement to reduce the risk of moisture problems in the wall cavity, although if properly installed, either placement can perform well.

The downside of rigid foam insulation, from an environmental standpoint, is that it is made out of petrochemicals. Some types of foam insulation are made using potentially toxic chemicals, risking pollution of the environment during manufacture, and most require the addition of flame retardants — some of which have their own health concerns (see Chapter 8). Also, one type of rigid foam insulation, *extruded polystyrene,* (*XPS*)

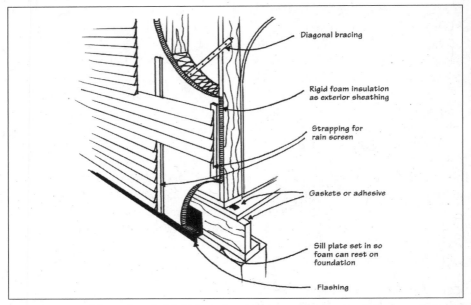

FIGURE 5.2—*Adding a layer of rigid foam insulation outside of a wood-frame wall signifi-cantly boosts the wall's R-value. The wall system shown, with 2x6 advanced framing and one inch of polyisocyanurate insulation, provides an average insulating value of about R-23.*

is still made using *HCFC* (*hydrochlorofluorocarbon*) blowing agents that damage the Earth's protective ozone layer (see Chapter 6).

HIGH-TECH WOOD-FRAMING SYSTEMS

For homeowners willing to invest in thicker walls, petrochemical-based foam insulation can be avoided. There are several options involving building thicker walls and insulating the wall cavity with just fiberglass or cellulose.

One alternative is a *double wall* of 2x4s, with the walls held apart from one another by several inches. A 2x4 is 3-1/2 inches deep, so two 2x4 walls provide 7 inches of depth, plus any additional space between the walls. The downside of this system is the loss of interior floor space.

You could also build a structural wall (2x4, 2x6, or *timber frame,* discussed in next section), then attach non-structural wall trusses (some-times called *curtain trusses,* or "Larson" trusses after a Canadian builder who developed the system) to provide lots of thickness for insulation. These wall trusses are made using a minimum of wood (usually thin pieces of plywood or OSB spanning 2x2s) so as not to significantly reduce the performance of the insulation. If 8-1/2-inch-deep wall trusses are attached to a 2x4 wall and the entire cavity is insulated, a total of 12 inches of insulation can be installed. When wall trusses are used on the outside of a timber frame, the timbers are often left fully exposed on the interior; all of the insulation is installed between the wall trusses.

To keep the walls from feeling oppressively thick with these high-tech wood-framing systems, window and door openings can be splayed (angled) inward, as shown in Figure 5.4. This way, the windows won't feel so tunnel-like, and more light can get into the room. Splaying does involve more complicated carpentry, however, so keep that in mind. The wide windowsills that result from either of these framing systems can serve as planters, display areas, or even seats.

TIMBER FRAMING

Timber framing (sometimes called *post-and-beam construction*) was widely used by early settlers in the northeastern US, then died out as less expensive framing using 2x4s and other small-dimension lumber

FIGURE 5.3—*Non-structural curtain trusses allow a maximum amount of insulation to be added to a structural wall; fiberglass or cellulose insulation can be used.*

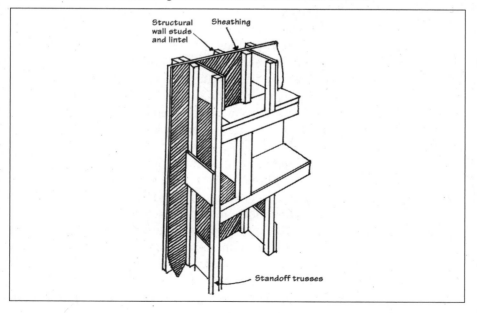

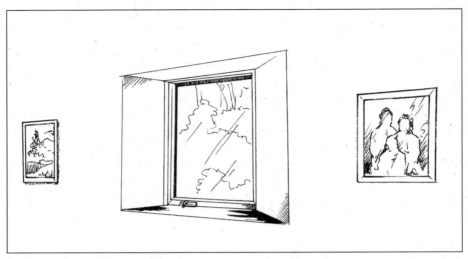

FIGURE 5.4—*By splaying the window opening and providing a wide windowsill, the thick walls of many alternative building systems won't be so apparent.*

was developed. Timber framing had a resurgence in popularity, however, beginning in the 1960s, and today there is a small but very active segment of the building industry devoted to this beautiful and highly durable building system.

From an environmental standpoint, there are both disadvantages and advantages to timber framing. Timber-frame houses use considerably more wood than houses built using conventional wood framing, and this wood comes from large, mature trees. Sometimes, in fact, most of the timber frame is redundant, as some timber framers erect the frame out of large-dimension members, then construct insulated infill walls out of 2x4s or 2x6s. A better technique is to wrap the timber frame with a non-structural system of lightweight curtain trusses or insulated panels. With this approach, the entire timber frame remains in view, with the non-structural insulation layer hung outside the frame.

A key advantage of timber framing is durability. There are timber-frame houses in the US that are more than 300 years old. If proper care is given to protecting the frame from moisture and rot, a timber-frame house built today should last hundreds of years — probably a lot longer than a conventional 2x4 house. Even if the timber-frame house uses twice as much wood to build, if it lasts four times as long, it may be more resource-efficient over the long term — over its entire life cycle.

Furthermore, timber-frame houses are often built out of locally milled wood from an under-utilized species, such as eastern hemlock, or they can be built out of salvaged timbers that have been removed from old buildings or bridges that are being torn down. Indeed, some leading timber framers use *only* salvaged timbers in their work. Thus, even though timber framing is usually significantly more resource-intensive (and more expensive) than conventional platform framing, there are ways to make it environmentally attractive.

Timber frames today are most commonly insulated with *stress-skin panels* or *structural insulated panels* (*SIPs*). Stress-skin panels have a thick layer of foam insulation (either expanded polystyrene (EPS) or *polyurethane foam*) with a layer of drywall on the interior face and a layer of OSB on the exterior. Because the timber frame provides all the structural strength needed for the wall, these panels do not need to be structural. When wrapped around a timber frame, the stress-skin panels provide the finished interior layer of drywall, the wall insulation (uninterrupted by wood studs), and the exterior sheathing. Because the panels do not require wood or steel for strength, there isn't the same thermal bridging that we find with frame walls. Structural insulated panels (SIPs) are just like stress-skin panels, except that they have OSB on both faces; when used on timber frames, an interior layer of drywall still has to be added.

STRUCTURAL INSULATED PANEL (SIP) CONSTRUCTION

Although structural insulated panels (SIPs) were originally developed for enclosing timber frames, manufacturers quickly realized that, because these panels had oriented strand board on both interior and exterior faces, they could be used in building houses *without* a separate structural timber frame. As noted previously, SIPs have a thick insulation core surrounded by skins of OSB.

SIPs are typically connected with plywood *splines* that fit into pre-routed grooves in the panel edges, although some use special locking connectors. At wall penetrations, such as for windows and doors, the foam is typically routed out, and pieces of framing lumber (sized appropriate to the panel thickness) are inserted to create solid edges. Wall and roof panels are often prefabricated at the factory to exact dimensions, with window and door openings cut to specification. The panels are installed using cranes, and an entire house frame can be erected in just a day or two.

As noted earlier, SIPs are made with either EPS or polyurethane foam insulation as the core. Thickness ranges from about 4-1/2 inches to as much as 12 inches. Because there is very little framing in the panels aside from the spline connectors, SIPs provide very close to their rated insulation level. (The R-value of fiberglass or cellulose insulation in conventional frame walls, on the other hand, is always lower than its rated R-value based on thickness, because of thermal bridging through the wood studs. When installed properly — usually with expanding foam sealant in special grooves between the panels — SIPs result in a very airtight home, thus improving energy performance.

SIPs are very resource-efficient; they use a relatively small amount of structural wood — the OSB skins — to achieve optimal strength. The environmental downside is that the foam insulation used in the core, whether EPS or polyurethane, is derived from petrochemicals. Various pollutants may be released during the manufacture of these foam insulation materials. More significantly, from a homeowner standpoint, small quantities of residual chemicals in the foam, as well as significant quantities of *formaldehyde* from the OSB, may be emitted

FIGURE 5.5—*Structural insulated panel (SIP) construction eliminates the thermal bridging that occurs with conventional frame construction. SIP houses are very tight and insulate extremely well.*

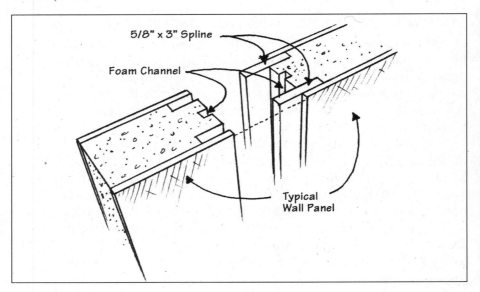

5/8" x 3" Spline

Foam Channel

Typical
Wall Panel

from SIPs into the home. While polyurethane insulation used to be made with an HCFC *blowing agent,* that is no longer the case.

The biggest concern with SIP construction is long-term durability. This construction system has only been around since the 1970s, so we really don't know how long SIP houses will last. We don't know how long the adhesive bonds will last or whether the OSB or foam will begin to deteriorate after a number of decades. In some parts of North America, there have been significant problems with air and moisture leaking through SIP panel joints and causing decay and even structural failure. Careful detailing is absolutely critical to ensure long life with this construction system.

STEEL FRAMING

Steel framing has often been suggested as an environmentally responsible alternative to wood framing for houses. Indeed, steel is more easily recycled than wood. Steel framing is lighter (for a given structural capacity) and easier to ship. It is resistant to insects. It is made, in part, from recycled steel; light-gauge steel framing is typically 20 to 25% recycled content. And, proponents argue, it doesn't require cutting down forests to produce.

While steel has some attractive environmental features, it also has significant drawbacks. First, while steel framing does contain recycled steel scrap, it also contains *a lot* of virgin material. Iron and zinc ores (zinc is the primary component of *galvanized coatings*) are non-renewable, and their extraction can be ecologically damaging. Wood, on the other hand, is ultimately a renewable resource. Carbon dioxide is converted into wood fiber through the process of photosynthesis, which is driven by solar energy. If forests are managed in a sustainable, ecologically responsible manner, wood is a highly attractive building material. The timberlands producing that wood provide wildlife habitat and recreational land for us to enjoy (*see* chapter 8).

A second drawback is that steel framing takes more energy to produce than wood framing; it has higher embodied energy. The difference between the embodied energy of steel framing and that of wood framing is significant, although it isn't as high as many people once believed. An article in *Environmental Building News* showed that the embodied energy of the steel used in a steel-framed house is about 28% higher than that of the wood in a wood-framed house.

Third, and most important, steel conducts heat far more effectively than wood. When used as framing for insulated walls, the steel studs

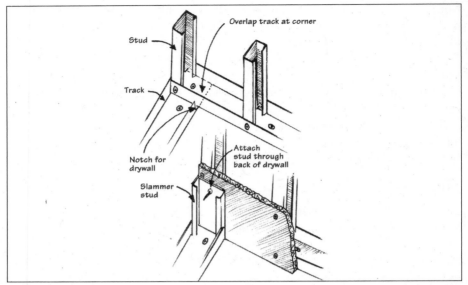

FIGURE 5.6—*Steel framing has some advantages, such as resistance to insects, but the energy penalties are so great that it is not recommended for exterior wall framing.*

become thermal bridges, allowing a large amount of heat to escape, and dramatically reducing the overall R-value of the walls. A 2x4 wall framed with steel studs 16 inches on-center and insulated with R-11 fiberglass insulation will achieve an average insulating value of only R-5.5 (a 50% reduction in the rated R-value of the insulation). A 2x6 wall built of steel studs 24 inches on-center and insulated with R-19 fiberglass insulation will achieve an average R-value of just 8.6. To work effectively as wall framing, steel studs must be covered with rigid foam insulation, and the environmental burdens of that foam insulation should be considered as a part of the overall package.

While the energy penalties argue against steel framing for exterior walls, steel studs do make a lot of sense for interior partition walls, where the high thermal conductivity of steel is not an issue. For non-bearing walls, even lighter-gauge steel can be used. Some green builders are using such a hybrid building system, with wood framing or some other alternative for exterior walls and steel framing for interior walls.

Steel framing can also make sense in very mild climates and where the alternative is framing houses entirely out of preservative-treated wood.

CONCRETE MASONRY UNIT (CMU) CONSTRUCTION

Currently, the second most common building system for houses in the US (after conventional wood framing) is *concrete masonry unit (CMU)* construction. Usually, concrete blocks have two or three cores that are separated by webs (a structural component of the block extending across the width). The blocks are stacked, usually with mortar between the layers. Block walls are sometimes reinforced with wire mesh and rebar, and some of the cores are generally filled with poured concrete.

Perlite or some other type of insulation may be poured or foamed into the hollow CMU cores to improve the insulating properties of the walls, although the thermal bridging through the block edges and webs is significant. The energy performance of concrete masonry construction, even with insulated block, is fairly poor.

Concrete's thermal mass can be a significant benefit in moderate climates where the outside temperature fluctuates widely above and below the inside temperature, such as in the southwestern US. In these climates, a masonry wall can have a *mass-enhanced* or *effective R-value* that is higher than the rated R-value (see Chapter 6).

INSULATED CONCRETE FORMS (ICFs)

Another building system gaining interest and market share in North America is *insulated concrete form (ICF)* construction. ICFs are usually made from *expanded polystyrene (EPS)* insulation. The lightweight forms are stacked and reinforced, and then the cores are filled with concrete, which cures to provide the structural wall system. ICFs may be used just for foundation walls, or for the house walls as well. Some ICFs have polystyrene walls as much as 2-1/2 inches thick, providing a wall system with an average insulating value as high as R-25.

There are a number of alternative ICF materials with significant environmental features. One product is a composite of recycled polystyrene beads and cement; two others are composites of wood fiber and cement. Although these alternative materials are more structural than polystyrene ICFs, their cores must still be filled with concrete.

OTHER MASONRY BLOCK BUILDING SYSTEMS

Another masonry block material that has only recently become available in the US is *autoclaved aerated concrete (AAC)*. Widely used in Europe and throughout most of the world for many decades, AAC is a

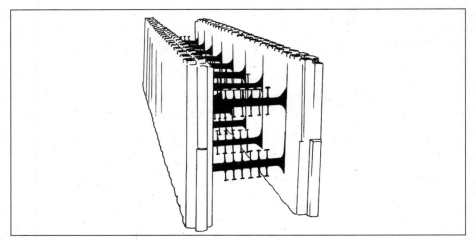

FIGURE 5.7— *Insulated concrete forms (ICFs) have insulating layers on both the interior and exterior. After walls are poured, they are typically finished on the exterior with stucco and on the interior with drywall.*

lot lighter than concrete block. During manufacture, a chemical foaming process uses hydrogen bubbles to create a cellular structure containing tiny air pockets, so AAC blocks are lightweight and insulate quite well. Unlike concrete blocks, the blocks are solid, and they are laid up with thin-set mortar instead of the thick bed of mortar typically used with conventional masonry block. (Thin-set mortar is laid with a toothed trowel, the type used for installing tile.) Because of their light weight, AAC blocks can be fairly large.

Adobe is another type of masonry block. Used for thousands of years in the American Southwest, adobe bricks are made by mixing mud with a small amount of straw, then air-dried. Soil with the right mix of clay and sand is needed to produce strong adobes that won't crack. After walls are built, they are generally plastered on both the interior and exterior — traditionally with a mud plaster, but today usually with a *portland cement* plaster. Both adobe and AAC can be very effective construction systems for passive solar homes calling for significant thermal mass.

With both AAC and adobe construction, 2x4 frame walls are typically used for interior partitions, although light-gauge steel framing can also be used. Interior AAC or adobe walls are too thick to be practical in most cases.

STRAWBALE CONSTRUCTION

Interest in *strawbale construction* has been growing rapidly in the US, especially among owner-builders. A completed strawbale house looks a lot like an adobe house in the Southwest, with thick walls, somewhat rounded corners, and stucco finish. From an environmental standpoint, this building system has a great deal going for it. The thick walls insulate extremely well, and the primary raw material is an agricultural waste product.

Straw is the dried stems that are left after harvesting grain, such as wheat, barley, oats, or rice. It doesn't make sense to plow all the straw back into the soil, because the microorganisms required to break it down rob nitrogen from the soil, and thus more fertilizers need to be added. Until recently, straw was usually burned in fields after harvesting the grain (a practice that in California generated more smog-causing air pollution than all of the state's power plants combined). Traffic accidents caused by burning straw during shifting winds have led to bans on burning in some areas, and pollution-control and safety regulations have greatly curtailed the practice. Using straw as a building material is a great way to make use of this waste product.

The idea of using baled straw as a building material goes back to the late 1800s, just after baling machines were invented. There are

FIGURE 5.8—*With load-bearing strawbale houses, the bale walls carry the full load of the roof. Structural ties generally extend down to the foundation and prevent roof uplift in heavy wind.*

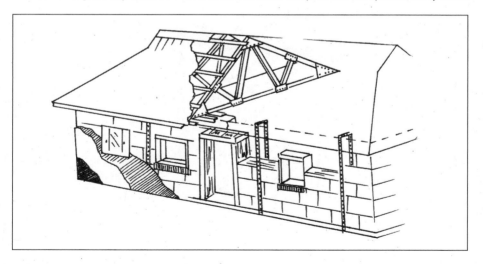

strawbale houses in Nebraska that have held up well for more than a hundred years. A few people resurrected this building system in the 1960s and '70s, and it began really catching on in the '90s.

There are two basic types of strawbale houses. With load-bearing strawbale construction, stacked bales serve as the structural wall system, holding up the roof. With infill strawbale construction, a post-and-beam frame serves as the structural system, and bales are used as infill, non-structural walls.

The load-bearing approach is more resource-efficient, but care has to be taken to ensure that the walls are sturdy enough. Usually, the bale walls are pre-compressed, using cables or threaded rod, before building the roof, so that they won't settle later and cause the plaster to crack or roof to warp. Load-bearing strawbale houses are generally limited to a single story, and a hip roof (in which the roof surface slopes down to all four sides) is usually required, because the weight of the roof is better distributed on the four walls. There are some building code jurisdictions in the Southwest in which load-bearing strawbale houses are now accepted as a matter of course.

FIGURE 5.9—*Strawbale walls can be used to close in and insulate timber-frame houses. The large overhang of the roof protects the bale walls from rain during construction.*

Building officials are generally more accepting of infill strawbale construction. With the infill system, there is more flexibility in house design and wall height, because the strawbale walls do not carry the weight of the roof. Another big advantage in wetter climates is that the roof can be completed before the bales are stacked; if the roof has enough of an overhang, the walls can be kept dry even if it rains during construction. Bales should not be allowed to get wet during construction, because mold growth can ensue, causing indoor air quality problems in the finished house. Even worse, wet bales can rot or even catch fire from the heat generated by the decay process.

With either approach, once the bale walls are completed, wire mesh is secured on both sides. Plaster or stucco is then applied in layers; this helps to strengthen the walls, keeps out rodents and insects, and provides exceptional fire resistance. If you are considering a strawbale house, keep in mind that even though the strawbale walls may go up quickly, there is a lot of work involved in plastering them. If you are contracting out the work, plastering can be very expensive.

DECIDING AMONG THE BUILDING SYSTEM ALTERNATIVES

As we've seen, there are a lot of options for a building system, each with various advantages and disadvantages. How do you decide which to use? While the answer is not always obvious, the following considerations may help you make your decision.

Familiarity of Your Builder with the System

The familiarity of your builder with the building system to be used is very important. There is a learning curve involved with any building system, and particularly with one that is new or uncommon, such as strawbale, SIPs, or ICFs. If your builder has already built several houses using such an approach, that will be an advantage.

On the other hand, builders are inherently conservative and leery of trying new ideas. Sometimes it takes a client who is willing to say, "Let's just go for it," and accept a certain amount of risk that mistakes will be made or that construction will not go as smoothly as it would if the builder's usual building system were being used. This is what moves the building industry forward: customers looking for something better — better in terms of the environment, energy consumption, and long-term durability. Try to settle on a system that your builder is comfortable with. But try to push your builder a little further than he or she might ordinarily go in making your house more environmentally friendly.

Cost

Any time a builder ventures into a new construction system, costs can be expected to rise. This is due in part to uncertainty about working with a new system and the need on the builder's part to reduce financial risk. It is important to understand this if you are considering a non-traditional building system — and be upfront in discussing it with your chosen builder. Sometimes the high costs are due to specialized and hard-to-find skills required with the construction system. AAC and plastered strawbale construction both require plastering of interior and exterior walls; skilled plasterers are hard to find, and the labor rates are often quite expensive. To contain costs, consider reducing the overall size of your planned home (see Chapter 4).

Vernacular Styles and Building Systems

What are the traditional, or *vernacular,* housing styles in your area — not the styles you typically see in large subdivisions, but the styles and building systems in older houses? If you are in the Southwest, stuccoed, flat-roofed adobe is probably the vernacular. In New England, common styles are Cape Cod, colonial, and *salt-box.* In the Great Plains, the vernacular is likely to be low houses, even *earth-bermed,* to afford protection from high winds and intense storms. In urban areas, the vernacular is very different, often with taller, multi-family brick or stone buildings.

Choosing a style and building system that looks at home in your region is important down the road, when you consider possible sale of your house or its use a generation or two hence. Remember, part of building a green home is producing a home that will be around for a long time. While you might be enamored of plastered strawbale in Maine, will you find a buyer for that house if you decide to move in 15 years? Will your home's style remain popular enough that it will be maintained properly and live to celebrate its centennial? Not too many geodesic domes from the 1960s are still standing....

Balancing Environmental Choices

Some of the choices we need to make between different building systems or building materials come down to our own values. In building a green home, which is a higher priority: saving trees or avoiding foamed plastic insulation? If your top priority is saving trees, then steel framing might be the way to go. If the priority is to avoid the use of foam insulation in exterior walls, wood framing is preferable over steel.

Also think about whether you are willing to sacrifice energy performance for an all-natural, locally available earthen building system. For some people, the highest priority is sourcing all of the materials for a house from a 50-mile radius, and in this case strawbale or adobe might be the building system of choice. Sacrificing optimal energy performance might be considered acceptable for people living in the country with a fully sustainable supply of fuel wood. (Although, given the increasing concerns about global climate change caused by carbon dioxide emissions, energy conservation should always be a high priority — see Chapter 6.)

We will come back to this sort of environmental choice in the discussion of building materials in Chapter 8 and throughout the book. But the key point here is that there often is not a single right answer. Green building choices depend on the values we each hold. Diversity is okay; it's all right if the values of one individual differ from the values of another.

Energy-Efficient Design

E XTREMELY LOW ENERGY CONSUMPTION should be a top priority for any green home. Among the many environmental impacts of buildings, energy consumption is one of — if not the — most significant. With the notable exception of most renewable energy systems (see Chapter 7), the energy consumed in operating our homes carries very significant environmental impacts at every stage of resource extraction, use, and waste disposal.

WHY REDUCE USE OF FOSSIL FUELS?

Carbon dioxide (CO_2), a greenhouse gas that traps heat in the Earth's atmosphere, is the primary combustion product given off when fossil fuels (coal, oil, and natural gas) are burned. Scientists now almost universally believe global warming is occurring as a result of carbon dioxide and other greenhouse gas emissions. The reductions in CO_2 emissions associated with various energy conservation practices are shown in Figure 6.1.

In addition to CO_2, such pollutants as sulfur dioxide (SO_2), nitrous oxides (NOx), carbon monoxide (CO), and particulates are emitted from the burning of most fuels and the generation of electricity from fossil fuels. Plus, significant pollution results from the extraction of fossil fuels and from the disposal of waste products, including ash from coal-fired power plants and spent radioactive fuel from nuclear power plants.

Reductions in CO_2 Emissions from Energy Conservation

Energy Conservation Measure	CO_2 Savings (tons per year)			
	Nat gas (1)	Oil (2)	Elec (3)	Gasoline
Replacing 10 75-watt incandescent light bulbs with 23-watt CFLs (4)	–	–	0.78	
Replacing typical 1980 refrigerator with a 2005 ENERGY STAR model (5)	–	–	0.72	
Replacing 65% efficient furnace or boiler with 90% efficient model (6)	2.6	3.5	–	
Replacing double-glazed windows with "superwindows" (7)	1.0	1.4	3.7	
Planting shade trees around house and painting house a lighter color (8)	–	–	0.9–2.4	
Installing a solar water heater (9)	1.0	1.6	3.4	
Boosting energy performance of house when built from standard insulation levels to superinsulation (6, 10)	5.3	7.4	19.8	
Reducing automobile use by two trips per week (11)				7.8
Replacing average vehicle with hybrid car (12)				26.6

1. Assumes CO_2 emissions of 117 lbs CO_2/million Btus (U.S. EPA data).
2. Assumes CO_2 emissions of 161 lbs CO_2/million Btus (U.S. EPA data).
3. Assumes average U.S. generation mix for electricity, which generates 1.64 lbs CO_2/kWh (U.S. EPA data).
4. Assumes lights on five hours per day.
5. Assumes 1,300 kWh/yr for 1980 refrigerator; 490 kWh/yr for 2005 ENERGY STAR model.
6. Assumes 2,350 ft^2 house, heating load of 6.95 Btu/ft^2·°F-day, northern climate (6,300 degree-days).
7. Assumes 350 ft^2 window area (15% of 2,350 ft^2 house); replacing double-glazed, aluminum-frame windows (unit U-factor 0.63) with triple-glazed, dual-low-e, argon-filled superwindows (unit U-factor 0.20). Assumes natural gas and oil burned at 90% efficiency or electric resistance heat.
8. Data from Lawrence Berkeley National Laboratory, Berkeley, CA; based on computer simulations for various locations around the country.
9. Assumes two-panel solar system delivering 14.25 million Btus per year (75% of demand); natural gas water heating using demand system at 82% efficiency; oil water heating at 70% efficiency; electric resistance water heating at 100% efficiency.
10. Boosting energy performance from 6.95 Btu/ft^2·°F-day to 1.37 Btu/ft^2·°F-day (from standard 2x6 construction to "superinsulation" performance); assumes natural gas and oil heat at 90% efficiency, electric-resistance heat at 100% efficiency.
11. Carpooling, bicycling, or use of public transportation to eliminate two 20-mile round-trip commutes per week; assumes vehicle getting U.S. average light-duty-vehicle (model-year 2005) fuel economy of 21.0 mpg; CO_2 emissions of 157 lbs CO_2/gallon for gasoline (U.S. EPA data).
12. Replacement of average 2005 model-year vehicle getting 21.0 mpg with a hybrid car getting 40 mpg; assumes vehicle driven 15,000 mile per year.

FIGURE 6.1—*Energy conservation practices reduce carbon dioxide emissions. Shown here are the CO_2 savings that result from a number of energy conservation activities.*

On top of these direct environmental impacts, the supply of fossil fuels is limited. In a span of time measured in decades, oil and gas reserves that took hundreds of millions of years to produce during prehistoric times are being depleted. The United States, the world's leading oil producer until relatively recently, has already used up well over half of the oil that ever existed here, and the world is expected to reach the halfway point on oil consumption early in the 21st century — if that peak was not already reached in 2005 or 2006, as some experts believe.

Here's another way to think about it: More than 90% of all the oil that's been consumed since the dawn of the petroleum age (in the mid-1800s) has been consumed during the past 50 years — about the length of time *Leave It to Beaver* and its reruns have aired on television. Sure, the estimates of petroleum (and other fossil fuel) reserves may change, but the fact is that we are in the middle of a once-in-a-lifetime (the Earth's lifetime) blow-out party of gluttonous consumption, without regard to the petrochemical needs of our offspring a few generations down the road. And, as noted above, by releasing all of that stored carbon into the atmosphere, we're dramatically altering the global climate. Any way you look at it, reducing energy consumption in your house is beneficial for the environment.

The environmental impacts from energy consumption in operating our houses are all the more significant, because they go on and on. Decisions we make today to boost the energy efficiency of a new house will go on helping the environment for decades to come, for the life of the house.

This chapter takes a quick look at some of the many opportunities for reducing energy consumption in a new home. Consider this a starting point in learning about the basics of saving energy. Resources in the companion web site provide much more detail on energy-efficient home design and equipment selection.

INTEGRATION IS KEY

Efforts to minimize energy use in a home are most successful when an *integrated design* process, bringing together various experts, is used. Exactly who will be part of this process depends on how you are going about designing and building the house (see Chapter 2). The architect or designer's firm may bring the necessary skills — for instance, energy modeling, mechanical system design, lighting, landscape design — or may invite in outside experts.

Rather than bringing in experts only after the basic house design is complete, all this expertise should be assembled at the very beginning of the design process, during the scoping sessions. This early in the process, many significant opportunities for saving energy may emerge, opportunities that might not be realized with a more traditional design process.

The extra cost of integrated design can more than pay for itself through long-term energy savings and, in some cases, upfront savings during construction. For example, by designing highly insulated walls and roof, specifying the highest performance windows, and incorporating passive solar into the design, it might be possible to eliminate a central heating system altogether. Sure, you will spend more to *superinsulate* the walls and buy the super-windows, but that extra cost may be paid for by eliminating a whole-house heating system, saving $6,000 or more. If just a tiny amount of backup heating is required, it may make more sense to supply it with an inexpensive through-the-wall-vented gas space heater, a small wood stove, or even a few sections of electric baseboard heater.

A SUPERINSULATED, AIRTIGHT ENVELOPE

Providing a highly insulated, airtight building envelope (the insulated walls, roof, and floors that surround the living space) is the number-one priority in designing an energy-efficient home. Many different structural building systems can be used to achieve superb energy performance (see Chapter 5). While a few of these building systems, such as strawbale and ICF construction, provide integral insulation as part of the wall system, most entail the addition of insulation. To make wise decisions about insulation, it helps to understand some of the basics of heat flow (see sidebar).

Insulation Materials

There are many kinds of insulation, ranging from the most widely used fiberglass batts to blown-in cellulose, sprayed foam, and rigid foam boards. Common insulation materials are compared in Table 6.3, which lists R-values (insulating performance), typical uses, various properties, and how well the materials perform relative to health and the environment.

In considering different insulation materials and the energy performance of those materials, keep in mind that the insulation is part of a system that includes the insulation material as well as the structural support, such as 2x4 wall framing. As you saw in Chapter 5, the wood studs in a frame wall degrade the insulation performance, since wood insulates to about R-1 per inch of thickness, while fiberglass insulates to about R-3.3. By accounting for the relative area of wood and insulation in a wall and the R-values of the two materials, we can arrive at an average or *whole-wall R-value*. Instead of R-11, that wall system only provides about R-9. With steel studs, the difference is even greater, and the whole-wall R-value is half or even less of the insulation material's rated R-value.

Differences between expected and actual energy performance can also result if the insulation material is not installed properly. If fiberglass batts do not fill the wall cavities completely, for example, or if they are compressed to fit behind wires, the energy performance of the wall can be significantly compromised.

Understanding Heat Flow

Heat flows by three mechanisms: conduction, convection, and radiation. Conduction is the molecule-to-molecule transfer of kinetic energy; one molecule becomes energized, and in turn energizes adjacent molecules. A cast-iron skillet handle heats up because of conduction through the metal. Convection is the transfer of heat by physically moving the energized molecules from one place to another — for instance, hot air rising, or a forced-air heating system that uses fans to push heated air around a house. Radiation is the transfer of heat through space via electromagnetic waves (radiant energy); a campfire can warm you even if there is wind between you and the fire, because radiation is not affected by air.

With buildings, heat flow is measured in a number of different ways. R-value describes a material's or a building component's resistance to heat flow. The higher the R-value of a material, the better it is at resisting heat loss or heat gain. U-factor is a measure of how much heat actually flows through a material in a given amount of time and given a certain difference in temperature from one side of the material to the other — heat always flows from the warmer to the cooler side. R-value and U-factor are the inverse of one another: $U = 1/R$. For example, if a wall system has an average R-value of 15, the U-factor for that wall would be 1/15, or 0.067. That U-factor tells us how many Btus of energy will move through one square foot of that wall for every one degree Fahrenheit difference in temperature across the wall (0.067 Btu/ft²·°F·hr). Materials that are very good at resisting the flow of heat (high R-value, low U-factor) can serve as insulation materials.

FIGURE 6.2—*Heat flows through three mechanisms: conduction, convection, and radiation.*

Thermal Mass and Mass-Enhanced R-Value

It is important to clear up some confusion about the insulation performance of *thermal mass* materials, such as concrete block, adobe, or log walls. Manufacturers of high-mass materials often make the claim that their materials have an effective R-value that is a lot higher than the material's laboratory-measured R-value. The argument is that the high-mass material heats up during the day and only slowly releases that heat at night, and thus the material behaves as if it had a much higher R-value.

Indeed, this mass-enhanced R-value is real and *can* boost the energy performance of high-mass materials. The problem is that this thermal mass effect is only significant in certain climates, primarily those with moderate temperatures that fluctuate widely between daytime and night, such as are found in the American Southwest and Rocky Mountain states. In these areas, the mass-enhanced R-value of a high-mass material can be as much as 50% higher than the material's laboratory-measured R-value. But when we use that same material in a different climate, such as the Northeast or the Southeast, where the day-night temperature cycling is far less pronounced, there will be little if any added benefit to the mass. This is important to understand

Insulation Materials – Environmental and Health Considerations

Type of Insulation	Installation Method(s)	R/inch	Raw Materials	Pollution from Manufacture	Indoor Air Quality	Comments
FIBER INSULATION						
Cellulose	Loose-fill, spray-applied (damp-spray), dense-pack	3.0 – 3.7	Old newspaper, borates, ammonium sulfate	Vehicle energy use and pollution from newspaper recycling	Fibers & chemicals can be irritants, should be isolated from interior spaces	Contractor-installed; high recycled content, very low embodied energy
Fiberglass	Batts, loose-fill, semi-rigid board	2.2 – 4.0	Silica sand, limestone, boron, recycled glass, PF resin or acrylic resin	Formaldehyde emissions and energy use during manufacture	Fibers can be irritants, should be isolated from interior spaces; formaldehyde a carcinogen	Most widely used insulation material
Mineral wool	Loose-fill, batts, semi-rigid or rigid board	2.8 – 3.7	Iron-ore blast furnace slag, natural rock, PF binder	Formaldehyde emissions and energy use during manufacture	Fibers can be irritants, should be isolated from interior spaces; formaldehyde a carcinogen	Good fire resistance; rigid board superb as foundation drainage and insulation material
Cotton	Batts	3.0 – 3.7	Cotton and polyester mill scraps (especially from denim)	Negligible	Considered very safe	Also used for flexible duct insulation
Perlite	Loose-fill	2.5 – 3.3	Volcanic rock	Negligible	Some nuisance dust	Used for filling masonry block

(continued)

Type of Insulation	Installation Method(s)	R/inch	Raw Materials	Pollution from Manufacture	Indoor Air Quality	Comments
FOAM INSULATION						
Polyiso-cyanurate	Foil-faced rigid board, nail-base with OSB sheathing	5.0 – 6.5	Fossil fuels, some recycled PET, pentane blowing agent, chlorinated flame retardant, aluminum facing	Energy use during manufacture	Potential health concerns during manufacture, negligible emissions after installation	Phase-out of HCFC blowing agents now completed
Extruded polystyrene (XPS)	Rigid board	5.0	Fossil fuels, HCFC-142b blowing agent, brominated flame retardant	Energy use during manufacture, ozone depletion	Potential release of residual styrene monomer (carcinogen) and brominated flame retardant	Only insulation material made with ozone-depleting blowing agents
Expanded polystyrene (EPS)	Rigid board	3.6 – 4.4	Fossil fuels, pentane blowing agent, brominated flame retardant	Energy use during manufacture	Potential release of residual styrene monomer (carcinogen) and brominated flame retardant	
Closed-cell spray polyurethane	Spray-in cavity-fill or spray-on roofing	5.8 – 6.8	Fossil fuels, ozone-safe HFC-245fa blowing agent, non-brominated flame retardant	Energy use during manufacture, global warming potential for HFC blowing agent	Quite toxic during installation (protection required), allow several days of airing out prior to occupancy	Contractor-installed
Open-cell, low-density polyurethane	Spray-in cavity-fill (typically open cavities)	3.6 – 3.8	Fossil fuels, water as blowing agent, non-brominated flame retardant	Energy use during manufacture	Quite toxic during installation (protection required), allow several days of airing out prior to occupancy	Contractor-installed; excellent air sealing

(continued)

Type of Insulation	Installation Method(s)	R/inch	Raw Materials	Pollution from Manufacture	Indoor Air Quality	Comments
Air-Krete	Spray-in cavity-fill	3.9	Magnesium oxide from seawater, ceramic talc	Negligible	Considered very safe	Contractor-installed; Highly fire resistant, inert, remains friable
RADIANT BARRIER						
Bubble back	Stapled to framing	Depends on installation	Aluminum, fossil fuels	Energy use during manufacture	Minimal offgassing from plastic	Exaggerated R-value claims common
Foil-faced polyethylene foam	Stapled to framing, requires air space to benefit from radiant barrier	Depends on installation	Aluminum, fossil fuels, recycled polyethylene	Energy use during manufacture	Minimal offgassing from polyethylene	Exaggerated R-value claims common; recycled content from some manufacturers
Foil-faced paperboard sheathing	Stapled to framing, requires air space to benefit from radiant barrier	Depends on installation	Aluminum, fossil fuels, recycled paper	Energy use during manufacture	Considered very safe	High recycled content, structural sheathing products available (e.g., Thermo-Ply®)
Foil-faced OSB	Most common as attic sheathing	Depends on installation	Wood fiber, formaldehyde binder in OSB, aluminum	Energy use and VOC emissions during manufacture	Formaldehyde emissions	Primary benefit reduced heat gain

Sources: *From Environmental Building News, Vol. 14, No. 1, January, 2004. Used with permission.*

FIGURE 6.3

Credit: Environmental Building News, January 2004 (Vol. 14, No. 1).

when examining performance claims from manufacturers of some of the masonry building systems described in Chapter 5.

Airtightness

How airtight a house is can be almost as important as how well-insulated it is. It's not unusual for older houses to lose as much heat through air leakage as they do by conduction through the house envelope. How airtight a building envelope will be depends on the methods and care with which it was constructed. Some building systems, such as structural insulated panels, are inherently more airtight than standard wood-frame building systems. But workmanship can play an even greater role in determining airtightness. For example, careful use of foam gaskets between framing assemblies or installation of a continuous polyethylene *air barrier* or *vapor retarder* can create a wood-framed house that is every bit as tight as a SIP house.

Moisture Control

In planning the construction details that will be used in a house, it is very important to consider moisture control. Too much moisture in a house, or moisture that gets trapped in wall or ceiling cavities, can cause significant problems, ranging from structural deterioration to degraded insulation performance, to some of our most serious indoor air quality problems, such as mold (see Chapter 9). Strategies for moisture control vary significantly depending on where you live; a strategy for controlling moisture in Miami may not be at all appropriate in Minneapolis.

Proper moisture control requires preventing plumbing leaks inside the house, stopping water from leaking into the house from precipitation, preventing condensation from occurring on surfaces inside the house, blocking air leakage through the building envelope, and slowing down the diffusion of water vapor through permeable materials in the building envelope.

The first of these, preventing plumbing leaks, may seem pretty obvious, but leaks in houses are remarkably common. This is one reason why it makes a great deal of sense to photograph walls before they have been closed in, so that you or a contractor can figure out exactly where a leak is likely to have occurred, and limit damage to the wall in repairing it.

Keeping precipitation out of the house is an obvious function of the building envelope, especially the roof. But *flashing* details are often done improperly, in which case they can contribute to, rather than prevent, moisture problems. Moisture also gets into a house through *capillary forces,* via a concrete floor slab, foundation walls, or siding. On walls, you can use a *rainscreen* detail (see Figure 6.4) to provide an air space behind the siding to block the capillary flow of moisture into the building envelope.

Condensation inside the house can occur in two different situations. In cold weather, condensation can develop on the inside of poorly insulated windows when the window surface is cold. The droplets of water will run down the window and soak the window frame and sill, potentially causing decay. Condensation can also occur in the warmer months when very humid indoor air comes in contact with cooler surfaces such as cold-water pipes and a toilet tank. This latter scenario is

FIGURE 6.4—*Rainscreen detailing on walls helps prevent moisture from migrating through the wall system via capillary action. It also increases the life of siding and the paint on the siding, by allowing it to dry out more quickly.*

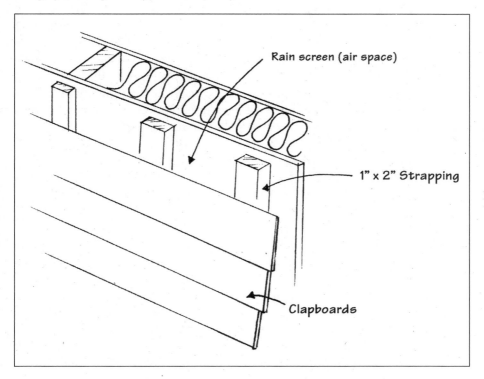

primarily a concern in areas with high humidity, such as most of the eastern United States and the Pacific Northwest. Strategies for dealing with condensation include eliminating water vapor sources in the home (see Chapter 9), installing high-performance windows, wrapping water pipes with insulation, and choosing pressure-assist toilets that prevent condensation by separating the water vessel from the ceramic toilet tank (see Chapter 10).

Air leakage can introduce moisture into a wall or ceiling cavity, where that moisture can condense and cause serious problems. The best defense against air leakage is to provide an air barrier in the wall system. This is a layer that blocks airflow through the wall. It can be the layer of drywall if the drywall panels are sealed at joints and at connections to framing members (*airtight drywall*), or it can be a layer of rigid foam insulation with edges and joints sealed, or it can be a continuous layer of polyethylene that is overlapped and carefully sealed at penetrations. Note that stopping air leakage is both an energy conservation strategy and a moisture-control strategy.

Finally, if we've dealt with air leakage, we can address *vapor diffusion* by installing a continuous low-permeability layer in the building envelope (a vapor retarder). Some materials, such as a layer of polyethylene in northern climates, can serve as both the air barrier and vapor retarder. In other situations, it makes more sense to separate these functions, with sealed drywall providing the air barrier function and a layer of vapor-retarder paint blocking moisture diffusion. In cold northern climates, the vapor retarder should be close to the inside surface (warm side) of the walls and ceiling. In hot climates, the less permeable surface should be closer to the *outside* of the building envelope (because the inside of the house is likely to be cooler than the outside, and as moisture cools off it is able to hold less water and condensation may occur).

Can a House Be Too Tight?

With energy-efficient houses, the question often asked is whether the house can be too tight. Are we risking creating an unsafe house by limiting the natural flow of outside air through it?

Most building science experts today argue that making a house loose does not mean that it will have fresh air flowing through it. The natural flow of fresh air through a house depends on there being a pressure difference between the inside and outside of the house. A pressure difference will exist on a windy day or when there's a significant difference in temperature between the inside and outside. But on a calm day that is relatively mild, the inflow of fresh air may be close to zero even in a fairly loose house. To guarantee adequate fresh air in a house, most experts agree that mechanical *ventilation* of some sort is needed (more on this in Chapter 9).

Creating an airtight envelope and providing mechanical ventilation let you control *where* the air enters and exits the building. Fresh air entry and stale air exhaust occur through controlled points rather than coming through the building envelope at uncontrolled locations where they can cause comfort and condensation problems.

SELECTING WINDOWS

Windows serve several very different roles in a house: They provide views to the outdoors, they allow sunlight to enter, they can provide fresh air, and they block the flow of heat. The relative importance of these functions varies by climate and by location of the windows in the house. For example, Minnesotans will most likely be interested in passive solar heat gain and will thus want windows that transmit a lot of

FIGURE 6.5—*Windows are tremendously important for controlling energy flow into and out of buildings. The best window glazings today very effectively block heat loss, while appearing fully transparent.*

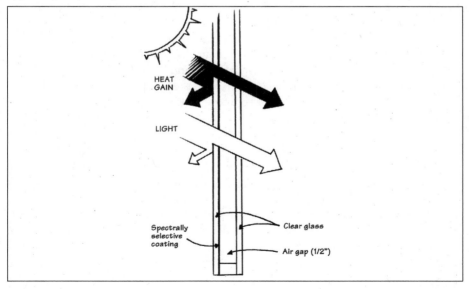

solar heat, especially on the south side of the house. Florida residents, though, will probably be more concerned with blocking solar heat gain (*see* Chapter 7 for more on passive solar heating).

Next to the amount of insulation in the house envelope and the home's airtightness, selection of windows and doors has the greatest impact on energy use for heating and air conditioning. Fortunately, this is where some of the most significant advances have been made in building technology over the past several decades. The best windows today have up to four times the insulation value of the best windows from the early 1970s.

These dramatic improvements in window energy performance have been made possible by several major technical developments, the most important of which was transparent, low-emissivity (*low-e*) coatings on window glass or on plastic films suspended between the layers of glass.

NFRC and the Need for Consistent Reporting of Window Energy Performance

As the energy performance of window glazings improved over the past few decades, the way that energy performance was reported became more and more confusing and (in some cases) deceptive. As the glazings got better, window frames began accounting for a larger share of the heat loss, and thus the old way of advertising the energy performance of a window — the R-value at the center of the window glazing — was no longer an accurate representation of the energy performance of the whole window.

To deal with this issue and ensure more consistent reporting of the energy performance of windows, the National Fenestration Rating Council (NFRC) was formed in 1989. NFRC developed standards for measuring and reporting the unit energy performance of windows, which is reported as the U-factor, or the number of Btus of heat flowing through a square foot of window per hour for each degree-Fahrenheit difference in temperature across the window ($Btu/ft_2 \cdot °F\ hr$). Unit energy performance values account for heat flow both through the glazing and through the frames, and they are reported for industry-standard window dimensions.

On most windows today, you will find NFRC labels that show the U-factor energy performance in a consistent manner so that different products can quickly be compared with each other. Also included on these labels is information on solar heat gain, which tells you how much sunlight is transmitted through the glass. This information is useful with passive solar heating designs and when concerned about air conditioning loads. NFRC publishes a Certified Window Products Directory, which lists the energy performance of several thousand windows on the market.

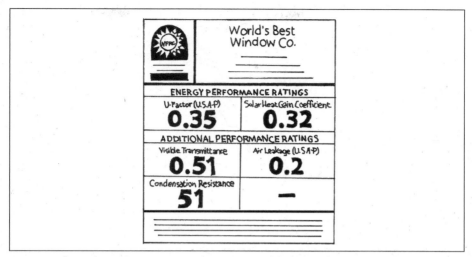

FIGURE 6.6—*To help buyers fairly compare the energy performance on windows, the National Fenestration Rating Council (NFRC) created a standardized method for reporting U-factors and solar heat gain.*

These extremely thin layers of metal transmit sunlight and visible light fairly well, but they block the escape of longer-wavelength heat radiation. In this way, they significantly slow down the loss of heat through a window.

Another important development was the introduction of special low-conductivity gasses into the space between panes of glass in sealed, insulated units. The most common gas fill, argon, has an insulating value 40% higher than that of air (R-7 vs. R-5 per inch). Krypton, used in the highest-performance windows, has an insulating value 2.4 times that of air (R-12 per inch). By combining *low-conductivity gas fill* in windows with two or more low-e coatings and accounting for solar heat gain, it is now possible to buy windows that, in effect, insulate as well as a fiberglass-insulated 2x6 wall.

It can make a great deal of sense to "tune" glazings to the window's orientation. This means using one type of glazing on one wall of a house, and other types of glazings on other walls. For example, with a passive solar house in a cool northern climate, it can make sense to install south-wall windows that transmit a lot of solar energy, but on the east and west orientations — where solar heat gain in the summer is more of a problem — install windows that block more of the solar

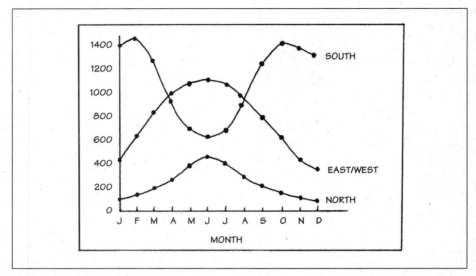

FIGURE 6.7—*South-facing windows transmit much more solar heat in the winter than they do in the summer because the summer sun is much higher in the sky, so more of the sunlight reflects off of it. East- and west-facing windows transmit much more solar heat in the summer than do south-facing windows. Shown here is data for 40° North latitude (Philadelphia, Denver.)*

energy. On the north, maximizing the insulation performance of windows is most important, since there is little direct solar gain to worry about. Some, but not all, window manufacturers offer different glazing options for their windows, although there may be an additional charge to order a non-standard glazing.

Figure 6.7 shows the relative amount of sunlight transmitted through vertical, unshaded glass at different orientations throughout the year.

SELECTING HEATING EQUIPMENT

How good a job you do with energy design largely determines how much energy your house is going to use for heating. If you go far enough with insulation and airtightness (often referred to as superinsulation), and if you incorporate some solar features (see Chapter 7), it may be possible to actually eliminate central heating systems, even in quite cold climates. It will certainly be possible to dramatically downsize heating equipment.

In this section, we'll address some of the most important considerations in selecting heating equipment. (Passive solar heating is covered in Chapter 7.) We will cover heat distribution, fuel choices, efficiency, and combustion safety.

Heat Distribution Systems

In choosing a heating system, the first decision you should make is what type of heat distribution system you want. The most common options are forced-air, baseboard hot-water, radiant-floor, baseboard electric, and individual space heaters.

Forced-air heating, in which air is heated in a *furnace* or heat pump and distributed throughout the house using a blower and network of sheet-metal ducts, is the most common type of heat. It has the advantage of allowing the heat distribution system (ductwork) to also be used for air conditioning and fresh air delivery. Furnaces can be gas-fired (most common), propane-fired, oil-fired, or electric. Some homeowners dislike forced-air heating, saying that it dries out the air or results in temperature stratification in their homes, but these are usually symptoms of other problems, such as a leaky building envelope. A properly designed and installed forced-air heating system in a well-insulated house should be very satisfactory.

Baseboard hot-water heating (often called *hydronic heating*) is quieter than forced-air heating; it requires less energy to move the heat from the b*oiler,* where it is heated, throughout the house; and it allows relatively easy zoning (in which different parts of the house are kept at different temperatures). Most boilers are gas-fired, propane-fired, or oil-fired. Radiators (which work more by convection than by radiation, as air is heated by the radiator fins and rises into the room) are installed along the baseboards in each room, and hot water is circulated through copper pipes to the radiators. Hydronic heat distribution systems are generally more expensive to install than forced-air systems.

Radiant-floor heating is a very comfortable form of heat distribution, and is quite common in green homes. With this system, specialized tubing (typically *cross-linked polyethylene (PEX)*) is usually embedded in a poured concrete floor, and hot water is circulated through the tubing to warm the floor slab.

For a number of reasons, radiant-floor heating is usually not the best choice; it's a great heating option for a poorly designed house. If a house is up to the energy performance standards one should expect with

FIGURE 6.8—*With a highly insulated passive solar house, one or two through-the-wall-vented, high-efficiency gas space heaters should be able to keep the house just as comfortable as a distributed heating system costing thousands of dollars more.*

a green home, radiant-floor heating is actually not a good fit. For the radiant-floor system to provide enough heat to feel warm underfoot (the feature everybody likes with this system), it's going to be cranking out more heat than the well-insulated house can use, and so it will likely cause overheating. A radiant-floor heating system also has a very long lag time between when heat is supplied to the floor slab and when the slab begins radiating heat to warm the room. If there is a significant component of passive solar heating in the home, radiant-floor heating will often cause overheating, because you can't turn off the slab when the sun comes out. Finally, radiant-floor heat distribution systems are expensive, often $8,000 or more for a moderate-size house.

Because a superinsulated house requires very little heat, it may be hard to justify the cost of an expensive heat distribution system. If you spend a lot of money to create a super-efficient building envelope, it makes sense to benefit from that investment by installing a less expensive heating system. With R-25 walls, R-40 ceiling, triple-glazed, low-e windows, tight construction, and passive solar design, you should be able to heat the house and obtain high levels of comfort using just one or two through-the-wall-vented, high-efficiency gas space heaters cost-ing $1,000 to $1,500 apiece (see Figure 6.8), and skip the heat distribution system altogether. Or you could put in a small *fan-coil* (heating element) in the ventilation system so that the ventilation sys-tem can supply the small amount of heat needed.

Electric Heat

There are two primary electric heating options that might apply to a green home: electric-resistance heat and heat pumps.

With *electric-resistance heat,* baseboard electric radiators or radi-ant-electric ceiling panels are installed in each room and typically operated by thermostats right in those rooms. Heat is generated by converting electricity directly into heat using electric-resistance wire. The radiators or ceiling panels are fairly inexpensive, and the cost of heat distribution (ducts or pipes) is avoided. With individual room thermostats, zone control is very easy and inexpensive. The downside is that electric heat is expensive, significantly more expensive than gas in most parts of the country. But in green homes with extremely small heating loads — so-called three-toaster homes — electric-resistance heat can be a reasonable option. The reality is that it just doesn't make sense to put in a $10,000 heating system to provide $100 worth of heat per year.

If electric heat is desired in houses with larger heating loads, a better option is a *heat pump,* which delivers a lot more Btus of heat for each *kilowatt-hour (kWh)* of electricity consumed. Heat pumps are like furnaces in that heat is delivered through a system of ducts. Unlike furnaces, though, they are also used for air conditioning in the sum-mer, extracting heat out of a house's air just like most air conditioners.

Air-source heat pumps use the outside air as the heat source and *heat sink* (the place where unwanted heat is dumped). Since heat can be extracted from outside air only down to about 30° or 40°F, air-source heat pumps shift over to electric-resistance heating in colder tempera-tures; thus, they make the most sense in mild climates. *Ground-source heat pumps* use the more uniform temperature of the ground as the heat source and heat sink, so they operate at higher efficiency than air-source heat pumps in colder climates.

In a superinsulated green home, the same arguments presented above on the economics of radiant-floor heating apply to heat pumps, as well. With very small heating loads, putting in a low-cost heating system, such as electric-resistance heat or a through-the-wall-vented gas heater, often makes the most sense.

Comparing Fuels

Fuels commonly used in houses include electricity, natural gas, propane, oil, and wood. Costs and environmental impacts of these fuels differ widely. Electricity is generally the most expensive in terms of cost per delivered *Btu,* and natural gas and wood the cheapest, although there are large regional differences. It is difficult to accurately compare the costs of different fuels, however, because they are sold in different units, those units contain different fuel values, and the fuels can be burned or used at different efficiencies. Figure 6.9 helps you compare the actual costs of different fuels on a standard heat-output basis.

In recent years the costs of natural gas, propane, and heating oil have risen dramatically. While some suggest that this is a temporary phenomenon, many others believe that it is a long-term trend that is due to the peaking of world oil production and US natural gas production. Rising oil demand in China and India has contributed to this. According to this peak-oil school of thought, the drop in oil and gas production that will occur after the peak has been reached will inevitably result in higher prices. Some believe that the peak in world oil production occurred around 2005; many others project this point will be reached before 2010.

From an environmental standpoint, wood heat is generally the most damaging of the common fuels in terms of air pollutants that contribute to smog. Environment Canada reported in 1999 that wood burning accounts for nearly 50% of fine particulate pollution in the Province of Quebec and 25% of *volatile organic compounds (VOCs)*; nationwide the figures are 25% and 15%, respectively. An older (non-EPA-certified) wood stove releases as much fine particulate pollution in nine hours of burning as does driving a mid-size automobile 11,000 miles. Other pollutants include carbon monoxide, unburned hydrocarbons, nitrous oxide, and sulfur dioxide. As for emissions of carbon dioxide — considered the most significant greenhouse gas that contributes to global climate change — wood heat is okay as long as the fuel-wood is produced sustainably; the CO_2 released by combustion is more than compensated for by the CO_2 pulled out of the air by the replacement trees.

Natural gas and propane are generally the cleanest-burning fuels. Along with fuel oil, however, these fuels are significant net contributors of carbon dioxide.

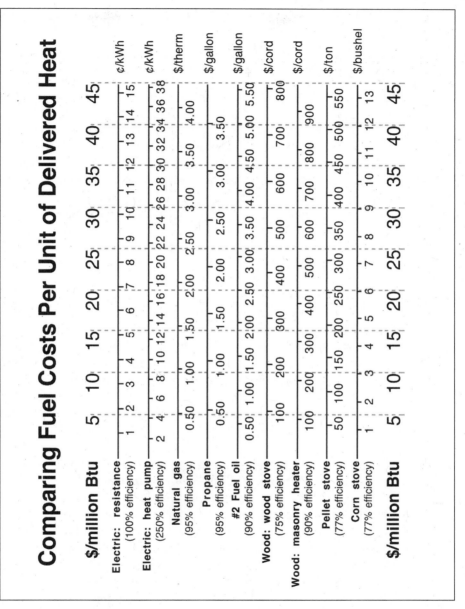

FIGURE 6.9—*To fairly compare the costs of different fuels, you need to convert the different units of fuel (gallons, therms, cords, etc.) to units of* delivered *energy. This chart compares fuels used at various efficiencies on a dollars-per-million-Btu basis.*

Electricity varies widely in environmental impact, depending on which fuel or energy source is used to generate the electricity at the power plant. *Hydropower, photovoltaics (PV)* (solar electricity), and *wind power* result in virtually no pollutant emissions, while coal-fired power plants are very significant polluters. When coal, oil, or gas are burned in a power plant to generate electricity, roughly two-thirds of the energy is lost as heat during generation and through transmission, whereas burning gas or oil directly in a home furnace or boiler typically converts more than 80% — with some equipment, more than 95% — of the energy into usable heat. Nuclear power plants do not generate air pollutants as long as they are properly operating, but they generate radioactive waste that will remain highly toxic for thousands, or even hundreds of thousands, of years. They also carry the risk of malfunctions that could accidentally release radioactivity into the surrounding environment, or terrorist attacks that could result in intentional release of radioactivity.

Heating System Efficiency

A heating system's efficiency is a function not only of the *combustion efficiency,* but also of the *heat distribution* efficiency. Baseboard hot-water distribution heating is generally quite efficient, largely because there can't be any leaks without your knowing it, while forced-air distribution can be very inefficient because duct leakage commonly degrades overall efficiency by 30% or more.

The more efficient a given type of heating system, the better. A 96%-efficient gas furnace is a lot better than an 80%-efficient model, because that much more of the gas is converted into usable heat, and less is converted into pollutants and waste heat. Heating system efficiencies are typically listed as *Annual Fuel Utilization Efficiency (AFUE)* ratings, and they should be listed on the *EnergyGuide* labels that are required on new furnaces and boilers.

It is worth noting, however, that heating system efficiency is most important when that equipment has to crank out a lot of heat. In a highly energy-efficient house, where the heating system is only going to be on for short periods and may only consume a few hundred dollars worth of fuel in an entire heating season, investing in that top-efficiency model isn't as important. You should still pay attention to efficiency, but efficiency does not need to be as much a driver of your decision-making as it should be when replacing a heating system for an older home.

Combustion Safety

Proper ventilation is extremely important when burning any type of fuel for heat in a house, whether gas, oil, or wood. Not only must the equipment be properly installed to prevent an accidental fire, but it should be installed to prevent the accidental spillage of combustion gasses into the home. From an indoor air quality standpoint, the safest furnace, boiler, or space heater is one that has *sealed combustion,* where outside air feeds directly into the *combustion chamber,* and exhaust gasses are vented directly outdoors. With sealed-combustion equipment, there is almost no chance for spillage of combustion gasses into the house (see Chapter 9).

COOLING YOUR HOUSE

As with heating, cooling requirements can be dramatically reduced through careful building design. In addition to high levels of insulation and tight construction, consider measures to reflect or block sunlight. *Reflective roofing* can reduce air conditioning costs by keeping your roof cooler — although, with a highly insulated ceiling or roof, the benefit won't be as great as in a poorly insulated building. Window glazings can have a huge impact on cooling loads; some glazings are specially designed to block most of the solar heat gain (see previous discussion on selecting windows). These glazings make a lot of sense in hot climates; even in moderate and cooler climates, they should be considered for large areas of east- or west-facing windows and on skylights or roof windows, where unwanted solar heat gain often contributes most to air conditioning loads.

Also think about how to keep the sun from reaching your windows. Simple overhangs, awnings, or slatted exterior shutters are fairly easy ways to reduce summertime heat gain through windows. Overhangs work best on south-facing windows; the high summer sun will be blocked, while the lower winter sun can still reach the windows. For east- and west-facing windows, plantings are often more effective for shading, because they are low enough to the ground to block the low morning sun in the east and the low afternoon sun in the west. Protect trees on the building site that will provide natural shading, or plant new trees, shrubs, annuals, and trellised vines that are appropriate for your climate.

Ventilative Cooling

Natural or forced ventilation is a cooling strategy that can be used in a green home, particularly at night, when the outside air is cooler than

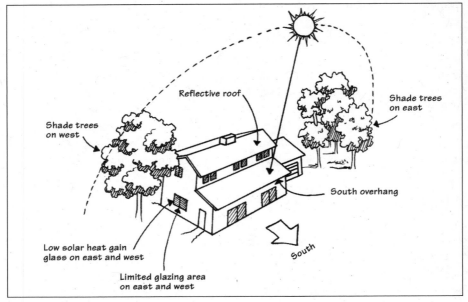

FIGURE 6.10—*The first and most important strategy in cooling your house is to reduce cooling loads; a number of strategies are shown here.*

the indoor temperature. The idea is to bring lots of air into the house at night when it's cool outside, then close up the house during the daytime, keeping the hot outside air from entering. Even in warmer climates, reliance on nighttime ventilative cooling can shorten the season during which air conditioning is required, but be aware that high humidity levels can make this strategy impractical — because an air conditioner has to work harder to remove excess moisture. If the outdoor temperature at night is higher than about 65°F or if the outdoor air is very humid, nighttime ventilation probably isn't appropriate. But in many situations, nighttime cooling makes a great deal of sense.

This nighttime ventilation strategy can be accomplished simply by opening windows to allow nighttime breezes to flow through the house. Another strategy is to install a whole-house (attic) fan on the top floor of your house and operate that fan at night with the windows open on the first floor. The whole-house fan allows you to quickly cool the entire house; it uses electricity, but far less than a standard air conditioner. If you install a whole-house fan, install a model with a tight-fitting, insulated lid to prevent excessive air leakage and heat loss during the winter months.

Increasing Comfort without Cooling the Air

With air conditioning, keep in mind that comfort is what you're after, not a specific air temperature. To reduce air conditioning needs, one strategy is to raise your comfort threshold. Dressing in light clothing can help to some extent during warm weather. More importantly, ceiling-mounted paddle fans or portable room fans can provide airflow that evaporates moisture from your skin so that you will be comfortable at a higher air temperature. With the airflow generated by a paddle fan, the comfort threshold for many people can be increased from about 75°F to as much as 82°F. Note that fans don't actually lower the air temperature; in fact, they raise the temperature slightly from the motor's waste heat. So turn off fans when you leave a room.

Mechanical Air Conditioning

When you can't maintain adequate comfort by blocking sunlight, ventilating at night, and using fans to raise your comfort threshold, the last resort is mechanical air conditioning.

Most mechanical air conditioners function a lot like your refrigerator, except that part of the unit is located outside your house. These

FIGURE 6.11—*Fans can significantly reduce cooling needs by making you comfortable at warmer air temperatures.*

units use a *refrigerant* cycle in which a special refrigerant fluid is alternately compressed and evaporated to extract heat from inside your home and dump it into the air outside.

With a *whole-house (central) air conditioner* or heat pump, there is an outside compressor where the refrigerant is compressed from gas to liquid in a process that raises its temperature and allows that heat to be transferred to the outside air. Inside the house is an evaporator where the refrigerant changes phase from liquid to gas, cooling off in the process. A blower connected to the evaporator circulates cooled air throughout the house. With a window-mounted or through-the-wall *room air conditioner,* these two components are more closely connected, but the basic operation is the same.

Unfortunately, refrigerant-cycle air conditioners require quite a lot of energy to keep your house cool. Most of them also contain a refrigerant that damages the Earth's protective stratospheric ozone layer. These HCFCs are slated to be phased out over the next several decades. Some air conditioners with ozone-safe refrigerants are already on the market.

When selecting a refrigerant-cycle air conditioner, look for an energy-efficient model. The energy efficiency of whole-house air conditioners is listed as the *seasonal energy efficiency rating (SEER)*; look for a model with a SEER of at least 14. The energy efficiency of room air conditioners is given in an *energy efficiency rating (EER)*. Look for a model with an EER of at least 10.5. In humid climates, when choosing an air conditioner, also consider how effectively the model removes moisture. Ask a salesperson or your air conditioning contractor about the moisture removal capacity of different models and what you need for your climate.

In dry climates, an evaporative cooler (*swamp cooler*) can be a great alternative to a conventional, refrigerant-cycle air conditioner. By evaporating tiny droplets of water in an airstream, an evaporative cooler uses far less energy to cool the air than standard air conditioners, although most models do use a significant amount of water. This approach is not effective in humid climates.

WATER HEATING

Water heating usually accounts for the third-highest energy consumption in American homes (after heating and cooling). In a very high-efficiency home, water heaters may be the single greatest energy consumer.

The most common water heaters are storage models; water is heated by electric heating elements or gas combustion (or sometimes by oil), and the water is kept hot in an insulated tank. The performance of storage-type water heaters is determined largely by the amount of insulation surrounding the tank, although with gas and oil models the combustion efficiency and the heat exchanger configuration in the tank also affect performance. With most storage-type water heaters, energy consumption can be reduced by wrapping the tank with additional insulation, although with combustion water heaters precautions must be followed.

In homes with baseboard hot-water heat or radiant-floor heat, the same boiler that supplies heat can be used for water heating. The most common approach for doing this is a *tankless coil* inside the boiler. This solution is not recommended, because the boiler has to come on whenever hot water is needed; in summer months especially, this on-off cycling wastes energy. A better approach is an *indirect water heater.* With this option, hot water from the boiler is circulated through a *heat exchanger* in a separate, insulated storage tank. The water heater is treated as a separate zone (most boilers deliver heat separately to different parts of a house, called zones). Thus, the boiler is used in the summer to heat water, but it does not have to come on every time hot water is drawn.

Another option for water heating is an *instantaneous* or *demand water heater.* These models, widely used in Europe, turn on only when hot water is drawn. Small electric models are sometimes used for sinks, but for most residential applications, gas-fired models make the most sense, because they are better able to supply the amount of hot water needed for showering or clothes washing. (An electric demand water heater large enough to supply a whole house may require 40 to 60 amps at 220 volts.) Choose a high-efficiency, electronic-ignition model that doesn't require a pilot light. A half-dozen manufacturers offer these systems.

An even better option for a green home is a solar water heater, which relies primarily on solar energy rather than electricity, gas, or oil (see Chapter 7).

Hot Water Distribution

A discussion of water heating cannot be complete without addressing how that hot water is distributed. Tremendous waste of water occurs from people waiting for hot water to reach sinks and showers that are

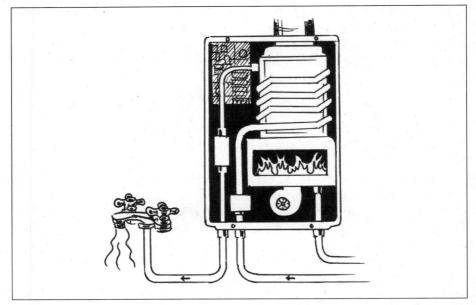

FIGURE 6.12—*Demand water heaters are growing in popularity in North America. High-efficiency models with electronic ignition provide significantly better energy performance than storage-type water heaters, largely because standby heat loss through the tank is eliminated.*

located some distance from the water heater. This wait for hot water has gotten longer in the last few decades as our houses have gotten bigger and more sprawling, as the water use of showers and faucets has dropped, and as plumbing codes have mandated larger-diameter piping.

An increasingly common, but far from ideal, household solution is the type of water distribution system used in hotels: a continuous circulation system that pumps hot water around the house all the time. It wastes a huge amount of energy, because it acts like a low-efficiency radiator that operates 24/7.

Two solutions are emerging to the problem of hot water distribution. One is an *on-demand circulation* system, in which the homeowner, using a button or occupancy sensor in the bathroom or kitchen, activates a small pump to quickly bring hot water to that location. (Instead of the cooled-off water sitting in the hot-water pipe going down the drain, it flows back to the water heater.) The other solution is a *home-run plumbing system,* in which small-diameter plastic tubing (usually PEX) is used to deliver hot water from the water heater or a central *manifold* right to the fixture. Because the tubing is dedicated to the end-use fixture, it can be sized accordingly; 3/8-inch-diameter tubing will deliver hot water to a bathroom faucet far more quickly than 3/4-inch copper pipe, which is standard today. Larger-diameter tubing is used for the bath-tub to fill it quickly.

HOME APPLIANCES

There have been very significant advances in a number of home appliances in recent decades. The energy consumption of refrigerators has dropped by about two-thirds since the mid-1970s, even while more convenience features have been added. With clothes washers, *horizontal-axis* (front-loading) machines are now widely available that use half as much water

Understanding EnergyGuide Labels

Federal law requires that EnergyGuide labels be placed on water heaters, refrigerators, freezers, dishwashers, clothes washers, furnaces, boilers, heat pumps, room air conditioners, and whole-house air conditioners. For most appliances and water heaters, the bold yellow label shows the expected energy consumption under "standard" operating conditions, as defined by the U.S. Department of Energy. As with the mileage ratings on cars, your actual energy use may vary, depending on how the appliance is used. Energy consumption is listed in kilowatt- hours (kWh) per year for electric appliances and therms per year for gas-fired appliances. The expected annual cost to operate the appliance is shown near the bottom of these labels. This cost estimate is based on the average cost of electricity or natural gas in the United States. Keep in mind that energy costs in your area may be significantly different from the national average. EnergyGuide labels for heating and air conditioning equipment list the energy rating for the appliance rather than its energy consumption. For furnaces and boilers, the Annual Fuel Utilization Efficiency (AFUE) is shown. For air-source heat pumps, both the Heating Season Performance Factor (HSPF) and Seasonal Energy Efficiency Rating (SEER) are provided, showing performance during the heating season and cooling season respectively. For room air conditioners, the Energy Efficiency Rating (EER) is listed. And for central air conditioners, the SEER is shown.

An EnergyGuide label provides a useful comparison of how that particular model compares with other products on the market. This information is presented on a linear scale, as shown in the illustration. Be aware that these scales are not updated regularly, so a particularly energy-efficient appliance might be off the scale.

FIGURE 6.13—*An EnergyGuide label helps you compare the energy performance of the model you are looking at with others you might be considering.*

and energy as conventional *vertical-axis* (top-loading) machines. Better controls and sophisticated designs have significantly reduced the water and energy consumption of some dishwashers, even while improving cleaning performance and reducing noise.

Most appliances are sold with EnergyGuide labels that show the expected annual energy use and cost for operating the appliance (see sidebar). These EnergyGuide labels will help you compare different models when shopping. With most major appliances, you should also look for ENERGY STAR models. ENERGY STAR is a program of the US Environmental Protection Agency (EPA) and the US Department of Energy (DOE). These standards were designed to recognize the most efficient models of a given appliance type. To learn more about ENERGY STAR criteria and to find listings of ENERGY STAR products, visit <www.energystar.gov>. For more on selecting energy-saving home appliances, including features to look for in specific appliance categories, consult the *Consumer Guide to Home Energy Savings,* which is updated every few years and includes lists of the most energy-efficient appliances on the market.

LIGHTING

Since the dawn of the electrical age over a hundred years ago, nearly all electric lighting in homes has been provided by *incandescent light* bulbs ("lamps" in the lighting industry jargon). The light quality from incandescent lamps is excellent, but they provide far more heat than light. In fact, about 90% of the electricity they use is converted into heat, only 10% into usable light.

In commercial buildings and some spaces in the home, such as garages and workshops, *fluorescent lighting* came into use in the 1950s and '60s. Fluorescent lamps provide three to four times as much light per unit of electricity consumption as incandescents. Until recently, however, the light quality from fluorescent lamps was quite poor; colors did not look natural under fluorescent light, the lamps often flickered, and the ballasts hummed or buzzed. In recent years, the light quality from standard, straight-tube fluorescent lamps has improved dramatically, and new electronic ballasts have eliminated the hum and flicker. As a result, fluorescent lighting has become a much more reasonable lighting option for the home, especially for indirect lighting, such as hidden cove lights.

An even more significant development was the development of *compact fluorescent lamps (CFLs)* in the 1980s. Most CFLs have screw-in bases and can simply be substituted for incandescent bulbs. Others are designed for special fixtures that can only use CFLs. Typical CFLs with flicker-free, silent, electronic ballasts last 10 times as long as incandescent lamps and use one-quarter to one-third as much electricity. Some homeowners still object to CFLs because they cost more to buy, because some of them take up to a minute to reach full brightness, or because of bad experiences with early versions failing or being too large to fit into their light fixtures, but generally CFLs are finding far greater acceptance in the residential marketplace.

Another advance in lighting is the development of LED (light-emitting diode) lights. LEDs are extremely long-lasting (30,000 to 50,000 hours), and their efficacy (in lumens of light output per watt of electrical consumption) has improved dramatically. LEDs have been used for years as indicator lights in electronic equipment (such as the small red and green lights on your stereo), in exit signs in commercial buildings, and in outdoor traffic signals. Recently, they have become available in white for general illumination purposes. Recessed downlights, pendants, wall sconces, and other common residential light fixture styles are now available with LED lamps.

FIGURE 6.14—*A wide range of compact fluorescent lamps is available, so there should be a product for most applications where incandescent lamps have been used. Products shown have integral ballasts and can be screwed into standard light bulb sockets.*

With the improvements in traditional fluorescent lamps, the widespread availability of CFLs, and now the introduction of LED lighting options, there should be few or no incandescent lamps in a green home — with the exception of decorative lights, appliance lights, and outside lights that are controlled by motion sensors. The latter are on for such short periods of time that energy consumption is not so significant, and in outdoor applications CFLs take even longer to reach full brightness.

ENERGY IMPROVEMENTS ON THE HORIZON

The rapidly rising costs of energy since around 2000 show no signs of reversing, and many experts project a continuing upward trend. A good way to protect yourself from uncertain energy costs in the future is to invest in state-of-the-art energy-conserving designs and equipment whenever you build or renovate a home.

While there have been dramatic improvements in energy efficiency and conservation in recent years, there is still plenty of room for further advances. We will see more energy-efficient construction details, better window glazings, and more energy-efficient heating and cooling equipment, appliances, and lighting. There may be breakthroughs in the coming years and decades that we can't even imagine today. When upgrading equipment or considering an addition to your house, it pays to look at what's new out there.

Once you've done everything practical in designing a house to reduce its energy consumption — through high insulation levels, proper construction detailing, high-performance windows, and high-efficiency heating equipment, appliances, and lighting — it makes sense to look at how some (or all) of the remaining energy needs can be met using renewable energy. That's what will be covered in the next chapter. But far too often, people interested in creating green homes turn first to renewable energy and don't pay enough attention to the building envelope and all the other issues covered in this chapter. Think of renewable energy as the icing on the cake. Make sure you deal with the issues covered in this chapter first!

CHAPTER 7

Making Use of Renewable Energy

N O MATTER HOW GOOD a job you do in designing and building a tight, energy-efficient house, you will still need to use some energy for heating, water heating, electrical appliances, lighting, and (maybe) cooling. With a green home, the goal should be to minimize your use of fossil fuels and electricity generated with either fossil fuels or nuclear power.

As explained in the previous chapter, fossil fuels such as natural gas, propane, and fuel oil all produce air pollution in varying amounts, and they all release the greenhouse gas, carbon dioxide (CO_2).

Generating electricity from nuclear power can satisfy our energy needs without producing net CO_2 emissions and thus doesn't contribute to global warming, but nuclear power has a unique set of serious problems associated with it, especially the safe storage of radioactive waste.

Renewable energy is the other way to satisfy our energy needs without producing net CO_2 emissions. This chapter will address several categories of renewable energy use: passive solar heating, natural daylighting, solar water heating, photovoltaics, and wood energy. We will also touch on wind power and the purchase of green electricity.

PASSIVE SOLAR HEATING

Passive solar heating is one of the most direct and elegant ways to make use of renewable energy, but that doesn't mean it's simple. A passive

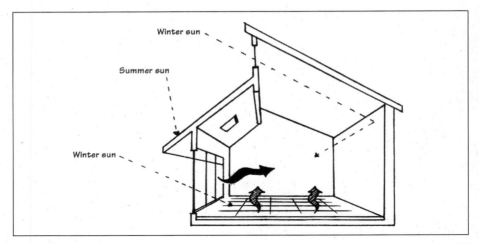

FIGURE 7.1—*With direct-gain passive solar designs, south-facing windows and skylights collect sunlight, and the heat is stored in high-mass materials in the living space.*

solar house has to be carefully designed, and while it will save a lot of energy and money over time through lower heating bills and may even cost less to build than a conventional house (because of downsized heating equipment), a passive solar house will cost more to design. That's where you will have to make the additional investment.

The most common type of passive solar design is known as a *direct-gain system*. The basic idea is to design your house so that sunlight warms the space directly during the day, with some of that heat being absorbed into the house walls and floor (high-mass materials are best), and then released over time to keep the house warm at night. These high-mass materials can be a concrete-slab floor, brick interior wall facing, plaster walls, etc. The house itself becomes the solar collection, heat storage, and distribution system. No fans or pumps are needed to move heat from one place to another, thus the term "passive."

A less common type of passive solar heating system is the *thermal storage wall* or *Trombe wall*. A high-mass wall is positioned between the south-facing glass (glazing) and the living space. Sunlight shines through the glazing and heats up the wall's outer surface (which should be dark, so as to maximize solar absorption), and the heat slowly moves through the wall to the interior. If carefully designed, the thermal storage wall will deliver most of its heat to the living space in the evening when direct-gain solar heat is not available.

A third type of passive solar heating system is a *sunspace*, which is a separate room on the south side of a house, with lots of south-facing glass. The sunspace heats up during the day, and windows, a door, or vents between the sunspace and house can be opened to allow that warm air to circulate into the house. At night, the sunspace will drop in temperature, and the openings between the house and sunspace are closed. Some refer to this type of passive solar system as an isolated-gain system, because the solar-heated space can be isolated from the living space.

Even if you don't plan a full-blown passive-solar house — in which the glazing area, placement of thermal-storage materials, and air circulation patterns are all carefully planned to provide a significant amount of heat for the house — it is possible to benefit from sunlight simply by orienting the house so that a longer wall with more windows faces south. This design strategy is referred to as *suntempering*.

With suntempering, nothing special is done with the design, other than orienting the building with the long wall facing south and putting a few more of the windows on the south side of the house than on east, west, or north. A suntempered house doesn't collect enough heat to warrant special considerations for heat storage, but a suntempered house also will not provide as significant a portion of the home's heating requirements.

FIGURE 7.2—*Thermal storage walls capture and store heat in a masonry wall between the glazing and the living space. These are less common than direct-gain systems.*

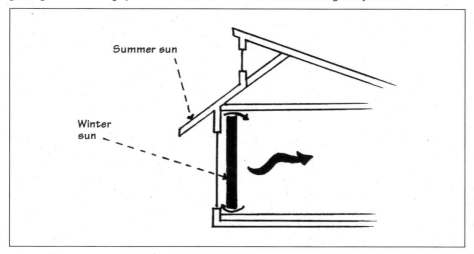

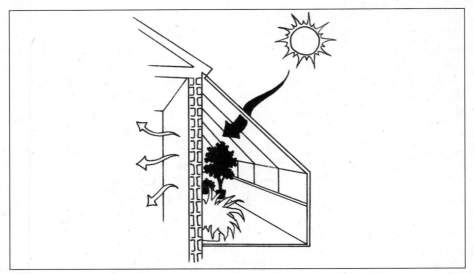

FIGURE 7.3—*Sunspaces have the advantage of providing additional living space, or space to grow plants, in addition to providing heat to the house.*

To avoid overheating with a suntempered house, the south-facing glass area (windows) should equal no more than 7 to 10% of the floor area in those rooms. Suntempered designs can often reduce heating costs up to 10%. By reducing the area of east- and west-facing windows, even greater savings in air conditioning costs can be realized.

Making Passive Solar Systems Work

Careful design and computer modeling are critically important to the successful performance of a passive solar house. Fortunately, we now have superb computer design tools available to help with this. One of these is *Energy-10,* available from the Sustainable Buildings Industry Council. The designer enters information about the house location, square footage, window orientations and area, glazing types, wall and floor materials being planned, etc., and the program generates information on annual and peak heating loads, temperature fluctuation in the house, and so forth. By varying the passive solar design features, the designer can *tune* the design to get the energy performance sought.

New window glazings that have emerged since the early 1980s have greatly benefited passive solar designers. With low-e coatings and special low-conductivity gas fills (see Chapter 6), we can now provide more glazing without as much impact on nighttime heat loss. In other words, the windows insulate better, so we can add glass area for views to the outdoors and for passive solar heating, without as much of a penalty in nighttime heat loss. We can include east- and west-facing windows with less concern about overheating by specifying special glazings that result in little solar heat gain. (Remember, in the summer months, much more sunlight is transmitted through east- and west-facing windows than through south-facing windows, so overheating is a greater concern.) In general, glazings with a high *solar heat gain coefficient* (*SHGC*) should be used on the south, while lower-SHGC glazings make more sense on the east and west. Of the coatings available, the *hard-coat* (*pyrolytic*) *low-e* glazings offer higher SHGC values than the more common *soft-coat low-e* glazings.

Thermal storage materials haven't changed all that much since passive solar first began appearing in the 1970s, but designers today have a better understanding of how much is needed to even out the temperature fluctuations in a house and provide warmth at night. Some early passive solar houses were adding too much mass, or thermal mass components that were thicker than needed for optimal performance.

The most important strategy with passive solar heating is to invest in a designer who has experience with passive solar and can create a successful design. While the concepts of passive solar heating — and especially direct-gain passive solar — are pretty straightforward, the details of making it work well can be challenging. Hire someone with knowledge and experience, including computer modeling skills and software tools to optimize designs. Yes, you will spend more, but if done right, the investment will be returned many times over during the coming years and decades.

NATURAL DAYLIGHTING

An easy, inexpensive way to make use of solar energy is to provide for natural daylighting, so that you use sunlight instead of electric lights during the daylight hours. This can be done with windows, traditional skylights, and a relatively new type of *tubular skylight* (see figure 7.4).

Natural daylighting may seem like common sense and hardly something you'd have to plan for, but that's not the case. To get the most benefit from daylighting, care needs to be given to building geometry (how rooms are configured), window and skylight locations, and the arrangement of furniture and internal spaces within rooms. For example, if you are a morning person who likes to read the paper in the kitchen, it may make sense to design the house with the kitchen on the

FIGURE 7.4—*Tubular skylights provide a simple way to bring daylighting into houses. The round tubes are highly reflective on the inner surface to reflect light downward. On a sunny day, a typical 14-inch-diameter tubular skylight will provide the light output of several 100-watt incandescent light bulbs.*

east side of the house where it will get lots of morning light. If you have kids who will be playing in the family room after school, locating that room on the west side of the house will allow it to benefit from afternoon light. On the other hand, if family members will rarely be home during the daytime, perhaps it doesn't make as much sense to deal with daylighting design; focus your efforts elsewhere.

In making effective use of natural daylight, be aware that design conflicts may come up. For example, skylights or roof windows can be ideal for daylighting, but they can also lead to significant heat gain during the summer months, particularly when mounted on south-facing roofs; they can thus significantly increase air conditioning costs or reduce comfort. If you plan to include skylights in your house design, carefully consider what type of glazing they should have. High-performance, low-solar-heat-gain glazings are available that will reduce the energy penalty of skylights significantly. *Clerestory windows* work very well for both daylighting and passive solar. These are vertical windows extending up from the roofline that bring sunlight deeply into a house, and they are particularly well-suited to flat-roof house designs, which are more common in the western US.

The newest development in residential daylighting is the introduction of tubular skylights. These are round skylights mounted on a roof and connected to living space with large-diameter reflective tubes. The tubes can extend through attics, providing light to bathrooms, hallways, or bedrooms below — even when six feet or more of attic separate the roof from the ceiling. Because most tubes are less than 16 inches in diameter, they can easily fit between roof trusses or rafters, so they can be installed without making structural modifications, as is often required when larger skylights are installed. From the room below, you

FIGURE 7.5—*Closed-loop and drainback solar water heating systems are active systems that rely on pumps and sensors. The hot water is stored remotely from the collection.*

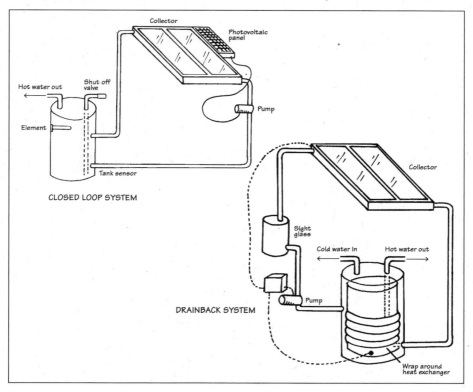

only see the *diffuser;* it looks like a ceiling light fixture. Some tubular skylights more effectively control heat loss than others.

SOLAR WATER HEATING

In an energy-efficient home, water heating is often the second largest energy consumer; in some cases it can be the largest. It surprises many people to learn that a standard electric water heater is responsible for about half the CO_2 emissions per year of an average car!

Your first water heating priority is to minimize hot water use by using faucet aerators and low-flow showerheads, installing a water-conserving clothes washer and dishwasher, insulating the hot water tank, and insulating hot-water pipes. Beyond this, the biggest difference you can

FIGURE 7.6—*Thermosiphon and batch solar water heaters are passive systems. The hot water is stored where it is heated or close by.*

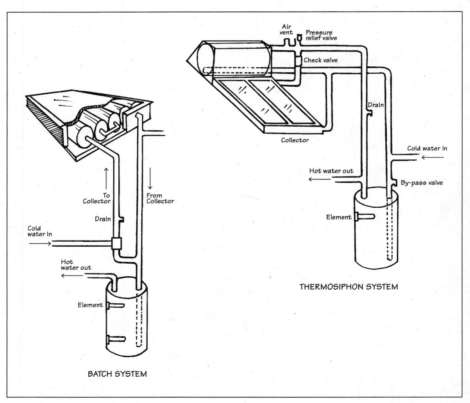

make in reducing the environmental impacts of water heating is to install a solar water heating system.

Solar water heating has been around for many years. In the early 1900s, it was common in Florida and California, but interest dropped after World War II with very low energy costs. The 1970s saw a resurgence in interest and the creation of literally hundreds of companies making, installing, and servicing solar water heating systems. Unfortunately, the vast majority of these companies disappeared following the return of low energy prices and the loss of federal Solar Tax Credits in the mid-1980s. During the 1990s and early 2000s, the solar water heating industry has remained small but steady, experiencing some growth.

There are several types of solar water heating systems, including *active closed-loop, active drainback, thermosiphon,* and *batch.* A full explanation of these systems is beyond the scope of this book, but the basic configurations of these four are shown in the schematics in Figures 7.5 and 7.6.

Two of the systems are active, meaning that pumps are used to circulate water through the collectors and through heat exchangers in the storage tank. In the active closed-loop system, the heat-transfer fluid (usually water with a propylene glycol antifreeze) always remains in the collector and piping. In the drainback system, once sensors tell the system to shut down, the water (or water-antifreeze solution) drains back into a small tank inside the house.

The other two common types of solar hot water systems are passive. That is, they don't need pumps to circulate fluid. The thermosiphon

FIGURE 7.7—*PV cells are elegantly simple in their operation, producing electric current with no moving parts; yet the underlying process is quite complex.*

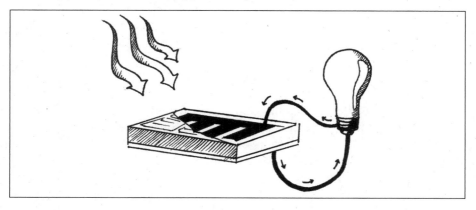

system has a solar collector located below the storage tank. As the fluid in the collector heats up, it naturally rises and circulates through the storage tank (or through a heat exchanger in the tank); this thermosiphon loop naturally transfers heat from the solar collector into the tank. Sometimes such systems use *potable water* and are located inside the heated envelope of the house where they can't freeze, such as in a sunspace.

A batch or *integral collector storage* (*ICS*) solar water heater is the simplest of all. It is usually used as a preheater for a conventional water heater; tap water flows through the collector or batch solar water-heating tank on the way to the conventional water heater. The earliest water heaters were mostly batch systems.

Most solar water heaters serve as preheaters for conventional gas or electric water heaters. Some systems have a separate solar storage tank that feeds into the standard water heater. Other systems serve a single storage tank that also has an electric heating element that kicks in when the solar heating isn't adequate. Advanced gas-fired demand water heaters can be used with solar pre-heaters; if the demand water heater is designed to heat the water up to a prescribed temperature (instead of always providing the same temperature increase), it is an excellent complement to a solar water heating system. When there has been a lot of sunlight and the solar-heated water is quite hot, the demand water heater will do very little supplementary heating, but in the winter or after a long cloudy spell, the demand water heater can provide most of the heating.

Even if you're not planning to install a solar water heating system when you build your new house, it makes a lot of sense to plan for a future installation. Such planning can include providing a south-facing roof with the proper pitch for solar collectors in your location and enough room for the panels, and even pre-plumbing of pipes through the attic. Providing such plumbing when the house is being built doesn't add that much cost, and it can save a lot of money when the solar water heating system is installed.

PHOTOVOLTAICS

Photovoltaics (PV) is the direct conversion of sunlight into electricity. With its origins in the space program of the late 1950s and '60s, this is an exciting way to use solar energy. Interestingly, PV power is the only practical form of electricity production that doesn't make use of a rotating dynamo, the heart of an electric generator. Almost all other forms of electricity production — hydropower, wind power, fossil-fuel-fired

FIGURE 7.8—*With stand-alone PV power systems, batteries are needed to store electricity for use at night or on cloudy days.*

power plants, and nuclear-powered power plants — involve using a strong force to rotate the dynamo, generating electric current. Hydropower uses falling water, wind energy uses wind, and power plants use high-pressure steam produced using heat from fossil fuel combustion or from nuclear fission of a radioactive element.

Photovoltaic cells do not involve any moving parts, only moving electrons. There aren't any turbine blades or bearings or combustion chambers to break down over time. The PV process is extremely simple in its effect, yet quite complex in the actual physics.

With some oversimplification, here's how it works: A *photovoltaic cell* is made of a special material called a *semiconductor,* usually silicon. In a typical PV cell, the two sides of a very thin wafer of silicon have tiny amounts of an impurity (usually boron or phosphorous); this makes one side of the cell want to give up electrons and the other side want to accept them. The layer between these two sides is the cell junction, and the two sides of the cell are connected by wires. When the sun is shining, photons of energy (sunlight) strike the cell and activate the electrons on the electron-donor side of the cell. These electrons want to get across the cell junction to the other side (the electron-receptor side). They do that by traveling through the wire, and an electric circuit is thus created.

By connecting multiple cells together in a *PV module* or panel and connecting multiple modules together into a *PV array*, significant quantities of electricity can be generated — enough to power an outdoor walkway light or your whole house.

Photovoltaic panels generate direct-current (DC) electricity. Some electrical appliances and lights can use DC power just fine, but most of the appliances in our homes are designed to use alternating-current (AC) power. An *inverter* is used to convert DC power into AC power.

Some PV power systems for homes are independent of the utility grid. These are sometimes called *stand-alone power systems*. To provide electricity at night or on cloudy days, stand-alone PV power systems must be able to store electricity. A bank of *deep-cycle batteries* provides this storage.

Other PV power systems for homes are connected to the utility grid. The house draws electricity from the grid when the house needs more electricity than it is producing, and feeds electricity into the grid when the system is producing more electricity than the house needs. Many states now have *net-metering* laws that allow utility customers with PV systems to feed AC electricity into the grid through the same electric meter that measures their electricity use. When they are feeding electricity into the grid, the meter spins in reverse, and each month the customer only pays for the net electricity consumption. The utility company is, in effect, buying electricity from the customer at the same per-kilowatt-hour price as they are charging for it. If the customer supplies more electricity in a particular month than he or she buys, though, the utility generally pays for the difference at a much lower rate.

The decision of whether to install a stand-alone or *grid-connected* PV system can be difficult. If the house is more than a few hundred yards from an existing power line, there will be significant expense involved with getting grid power to the site; in this case it often makes sense to invest that money in the battery bank instead. However, a stand-alone PV system usually has to be larger than a grid-connected system because it has to satisfy 100% of electricity needs, and the batteries cost a lot and have a limited life. If the house is close to power lines, the grid-connected PV system is often more practical (as long as your state offers net-metering); it is also less expensive to install and requires less maintenance. Unfortunately, with most grid-connected PV systems, when the grid goes down, there is no backup power.

The price of PV modules has dropped dramatically since the first applications in the 1960s and '70s. Today, some larger systems can be installed for less than $5.00 per *peak watt*, exclusive of batteries ("peak watt" refers to the rated output in full sunlight; often the actual electrical output will be lower). Prices are expected to gradually drop, but it is unlikely that PV power will be competitive with grid power until the cost of a PV system drops below about $2.00 per peak watt. For now, choosing PV power when conventional grid power is available requires a willingness to spend more for power that's less damaging to the environment.

As with solar water heating, even if you are not including a PV power system in the house you are building, it makes sense to design the house so that a PV system could later be added. This might involve designing the house or garage so that one side of the roof faces south and has the proper pitch for PV modules. Some people even go so far as to install conduit for future PV wiring so as to simplify the PV system installation.

WIND POWER AND GREEN ELECTRICITY

Wind power is another great form of renewable electricity generation. Costs of wind power have dropped, reliability has improved, and wind power now competes successfully against some conventional power-generation technologies.

While wind power can be used for individual home-power systems, the technology is better suited to utility-scale power production due to its very significant economy of scale. Very large windmills are much less expensive, per kilowatt output, than small windmills. In addition, because windmills have moving parts that require specialized maintenance, there is benefit to locating multiple windmills together, on *wind farms*, so that maintenance can be performed more cost-effectively.

To get the benefit of electricity produced from renewable energy sources without having to deal with power-generation systems yourself, see if your utility company offers green electricity or *green power*. You pay a little more per kWh to buy electricity that was generated from a renewable energy source such as wind, but this is an easy, and increasingly common, way to green your home's operation.

WOOD ENERGY

Using wood heat is a mixed bag environmentally. Burning wood in a conventional fireplace or wood stove (even a new, EPA-compliant wood stove) will generate more air pollution per Btu than most other fuels used for heating. Wood is particularly bad in terms of particulates,

FIGURE 7.9— *Masonry heaters burn a small amount of wood at a very high temperature, so are very clean. The masonry absorbs heat and slowly radiates it into the house.*

unburned hydrocarbons, sulfur dioxide, and carbon monoxide. This is why conventional wood burning is banned in some regions or during air pollution alerts. Burning wood also releases CO_2.

On the other hand, wood is a renewable energy source. As long as wood is grown and harvested sustainably (see more on the sustainability of wood in Chapter 8), it can be an attractive fuel source. And even though burning the wood releases CO_2, growing the trees sequesters more carbon dioxide than is released during burning, so heating with wood — from sustainable fuel-wood sources — can be considered *carbon-neutral*.

For cleanest burning, wood should be dry to burn hot. Hardwoods generally have significantly higher Btu content and fewer resins than softwoods, resulting in cleaner combustion.

The bottom line is that in areas prone to atmospheric conditions that trap air pollution in valleys (inversion conditions), burning wood is not a good choice for home heating. But in rural areas where relatively clean-burning hardwoods are available, burning properly seasoned wood can be all right. It might even be preferable to cleaner-burning natural gas and other fossil fuels.

To minimize pollution from wood burning, a very efficient wood stove, *pellet stove,* or *masonry heater* should be used. The most efficient, least polluting wood stoves have *catalytic combustors* that use special catalysts (often containing platinum) to burn up most of the unburned hydrocarbons that would otherwise go up the chimney. Some of the new non-catalytic wood stoves also burn fairly cleanly.

Pellet stoves and masonry heaters generally burn even more cleanly. Pellet stoves have electric blowers that supply extra air, resulting in more complete, and thus cleaner, combustion. The drawbacks to pellet stoves are that specially made fuel pellets usually made out of compressed sawdust must be used, and they don't work during a power outage.

Masonry heaters rely on natural airflow, but they burn at a much higher combustion temperature than conventional fireplaces or wood stoves. Masonry heaters are operated by building a small wood fire that burns at temperatures of 1,500°F or higher, while metal wood stoves and wood furnaces cannot be safely operated at temperatures over 800 or 900°F. Some gasses from firewood don't burn until temperatures as high as 1,100°F are reached, so a hot-burning masonry heater achieves significantly higher combustion efficiency than a wood stove or wood furnace; efficiencies as high as 94% are possible, compared with more like 70% in a good wood stove. Because of the very complete combustion, little creosote is produced (compared to a wood stove) to clog the chimney, and pollution emissions are much lower.

The flue gasses from this intense fire flow through channels built into the masonry heater, transferring heat to the masonry. The large amount of masonry mass heats up and slowly radiates heat into the room. In a very well-insulated, tight house, the masonry heater generally only has to be fired once or twice a day. If the house has passive solar heating, the masonry heater may only be needed on cloudy days.

The primary drawback is cost; most well-designed masonry heaters cost over $5,000. Also, unlike with a wood stove, a new fire is typically built each time the heater is used, which some homeowners will find inconvenient. Most masonry heaters are purchased as kits that a skilled mason assembles in your home.

Wood energy can also be used for water heating. Although the plumbing can get complicated, a wood stove fitted with a heat exchanger can provide an excellent complement to solar water heating in a passive solar home. When there isn't enough sunshine to keep the house warm, such as in the deep of winter or during long cloudy spells in the spring or fall, the wood stove is needed for heat, and that's also when solar energy may be inadequate for water heating. During the warmer months when you wouldn't want to operate a wood stove, the solar water heater should provide most of the hot water needed (some back-up heat may still be required, as described previously).

ZERO-ENERGY AND CARBON-NEUTRAL HOMES

As interest in green and energy-efficient homes has grown, we hear more and more about zero-energy homes and carbon-neutral homes. These labels deserve some discussion. A zero-energy home uses a combination of energy-conserving construction details and renewable energy collected on the site to produce as much energy as it consumes. A zero-energy home may use supplemental energy to operate (it may draw electricity from the power grid during peak consumption periods, for example), but on an annual basis, the power generated by the house (usually with PV panels) should equal the consumption. While it's a worthwhile goal for a green home, achieving zero-energy performance is very challenging.

A carbon-neutral house is similar, but with reference to greenhouse gas emissions, especially carbon dioxide. The goal with a carbon-neutral home is to achieve, on an annual basis, no net carbon dioxide emissions. This can be achieved by avoiding fossil fuels and electricity generated using fossil fuels.

FINAL THOUGHTS ON ENERGY

As evidenced by the space devoted to energy in this book, reducing consumption of fossil fuels and conventional electricity is a high priority for any green home. Because houses are — or should be — built to last a long time, decisions you make regarding energy consumption when designing and building your home will influence its environmental performance for decades to come.

By contrast, the decisions you make in selecting building materials for your home — the subject of the next chapter — primarily affect *upstream* environmental impacts (those that will already have occurred by the time you move into the house). This is not to say that these upstream impacts (where the wood for framing the house comes from, and how much material you use) aren't important, but the ongoing energy impacts are usually more important. So it makes sense to devote time and effort to ensuring that your new house will be as energy-efficient as possible.

CHAPTER 8

Materials and Products
for Green Building

W HEN MANY PEOPLE FIRST THINK about building a green home, it
is the materials and products that come to mind: insulation
made from recycled newspaper and decking made from recy-
cled plastic, for example. Product selection is an important part of green
building, but it is generally not as important as energy performance or
where the house is built (to minimize automobile use and protect natural areas), or measures to ensure a healthy indoor environment.

It is certainly a good idea to select green building products whenever possible, but note that it is possible to build a home that would be
considered green by almost any measure — a compact, healthy, energy-
efficient home close to alternative means of transportation — using few if
any products that are specifically considered green (i.e., products listed
in the book *Green Building Products*). Conversely, a house could be built
almost entirely from these green products, yet not be very green at all
— because it isn't energy-efficient, because it's much bigger than necessary, because it necessitates driving 20 miles to get to work or shop for
groceries, or because building it harmed an ecologically sensitive area.

That said, this chapter addresses materials and products to use in
green building. We will address some general issues related to material
use and environmental assessment of materials, then review the criteria
used to designate building products as "green."

WHY CHOOSE GREEN BUILDING PRODUCTS?

There are really three stakeholders that can benefit from the use of green building products: the people who work with the materials in the factory and on the job site; the homeowners who live with the materials; and the local, regional, and global environments that are protected through the production and use of the materials.

The direct benefits of green building products to workers and homeowners are the easiest to justify. A construction company can save money if its employees don't require protective gear and if they stay healthier, losing less time to sick leave. And that company can build loyalty among its employees if it works hard to maintain healthy working conditions.

Homeowners benefit from green building products by being able to live in a safe, healthy home, the importance of which almost goes without saying. Since we spend more than 90% of our time indoors, it's imperative that our indoor environments don't make us sick. There are thousands of chemicals we introduce to our homes whose health effects we know almost nothing about: *plasticizers* in vinyl siding, *brominated flame retardants* in carpet padding, and *fluoropolymers* in electrical cabling, for example. Some of these chemicals are now showing up in the blood of humans worldwide and are being linked to behavioral and human development problems.

Many green building products provide their benefit in the operation of a home. Some are more energy-efficient or more water-efficient than conventional products; others are more durable, or will require less maintenance. These direct benefits will save homeowners money or time over the life of the home and can easily be justified on those grounds.

Selecting green products because they protect the environment can be more difficult to justify, but is also important. While most homeowners will be sympathetic to concerns about rainforest destruction, or ozone depletion, or toxic chemical releases from manufacturing plants, those impacts are far away and most of them don't directly affect us. However, growing awareness about global warming is helping consumers understand the fact that actions in one place have environmental impacts far away. If, as many scientists believe, global warming is going to become a lot more apparent over the coming years and decades, it may become easier to draw the connection between our purchasing decisions and a wide range of impacts. If that happens, the environment could become a much bigger factor in purchasing decisions.

USE LESS MATERIAL

No matter the product, using less is generally better from an environmental standpoint. This recommendation starts with the overall house design — smaller is better. By reducing the size of your house, you save on the materials used in building it, on the land occupied by its footprint, and on the energy required to operate it. By building smaller, you can also upgrade the quality of materials and finishes within your given budget. You'll end up with a smaller finished product, but a higher-quality, lower-energy, more durable one that costs less to operate.

You can also reduce material use by optimizing dimensions (building on 2-foot or 4-foot modules and planning wall heights to make optimal use of drywall and other panel products), by using advanced framing practices (see Chapter 5), and by combining functions of materials (e.g. using a structural material that also serves as a finish, such as a polished concrete slab that eliminates the need for another floor surface).

Be aware that there are some places you don't want to reduce material use. One of these is insulation; add more, not less, to benefit the environment and reduce your heating and air conditioning costs. Another is structural material, such as bracing, that can provide needed strength to the building and protect it from high winds or earthquake damage. Some other added materials can improve durability, such as rainscreen detailing that allows siding to dry out, thus increasing the life of paint or stain.

CONSIDER THE ENTIRE LIFE CYCLE

In trying to determine whether one product or material is better than another in terms of environmental impact, it is necessary to consider its entire life cycle: where the raw materials came from, how the material was manufactured, what happens during use of the material (*offgassing* of VOCs, for example, or energy consumption), and finally, what happens at the end of its life. This process is referred to as *life-cycle assessment* (*LCA*). Think of it as examining the total *environmental footprint* of a material.

Life-cycle assessment of a building product typically examines four primary phases of that product's life: resource extraction, manufacturing, construction/use, and disposal/reuse. For each phase, life-cycle assessment considers such issues as direct and indirect resource use, energy consumption, pollution emissions, and the creation of by-products.

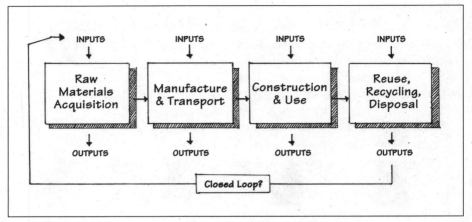

FIGURE 8.1—*Life-cycle assessment considers environmental and health impacts through-out the life of a product, from resource extraction through disposal.*

Assessing a building material's environmental impact can get pretty complicated. Consider the embodied energy vs. *operating energy* of lumber, for example. In producing the lumber, energy is used to operate chainsaws and skidders in the forest, to transport logs to the mill, to operate milling equipment, to dry the lumber, and to transport the finished product to building supply stores and to job sites. These energy inputs are collectively referred to as embodied energy.

Lumber and some other building materials also have a large impact on a building's energy use, or operating energy. A 2x4 is smaller and thus has lower embodied energy than a 2x6, yet when we compare the energy consumption of a house built out of 2x4 walls with one built out of 2x6 walls, we find that there is a significant energy penalty associated with using the 2x4s — because there isn't as much space for insulation. From a life-cycle standpoint, it's better to build the walls out of 2x6s rather than 2x4s.

All of the embodied energy that goes into building a typical house — the embodied energy of each stick of wood, each concrete block, each can of paint — is still usually just a small percentage of the operating energy that the house will consume over its expected lifetime. Because buildings last such a long time — hundreds of years, we hope — it is very important to pay attention to the use phase of any material being considered. In other words, in selecting building materials, we need to consider not only the energy and other environmental burdens that went into producing those materials, but also (and often more importantly) the impact those materials will have during the building's use or operation.

SELECTING BUILDING PRODUCTS

Choosing products is an important consideration in green building. The following guidelines are adapted from the criteria for product selection in this book's companion volume, *Green Building Products.*

Choose Products Made with Recycled, Salvaged, or Agricultural Waste Content

The raw materials used to produce a building product, and where those raw materials come from, are important green criteria, and probably the best known. When many people think of green building products, they think of products made from recycled content. This category also includes salvaged materials and products made from agricultural waste material.

Products with recycled content. Recycled content is an important feature of many green products, indicating that the raw materials were recovered from a waste stream. From an environmental standpoint, *post-consumer* is preferable to *post-industrial (pre-consumer)* recycled content, because post-consumer recycled materials are more likely to be diverted from landfills.

Salvaged products. Whenever we can reuse a product instead of producing a new one from raw materials, we save resources and energy. From an environmental standpoint, a salvaged product is usually better than a recycled-content product, because significant energy did not need

FIGURE 8.2—*This chasing-arrows symbol is used to indicate that the product can be recycled after use. With plastics, the number indicates the type of plastic — high-density polyethylene in this case.*

FIGURE 8.3—*Salvaged materials are especially green, because they divert material from the waste stream and can be reused with little modification.*

to be invested in re-manufacturing it. Many salvaged products used in buildings (bricks, millwork, framing lumber, plumbing fixtures, and period hardware) are available through local or regional salvage yards, although some are marketed nationally. Certain salvaged products are not recommended, including toilets, faucets, and windows, since new products conserve water or energy during the use phase of the building. With salvaged wood products, be aware that lead paint may be present.

Products made from agricultural waste material. A number of building products are considered green because they are derived from agricultural waste products. Various particleboard products are available, for example, that are made from straw (the stems left after harvesting cereal grains). Rice hulls are used for strength in some recycled-plastic decking products, and citrus peels are used to produce the raw material in some natural finishes.

Choose Products that Conserve Natural Resources

In addition to using recycled-content, salvaged, or agricultural waste products, there are a number of other ways that products can contribute to conservation of natural resources.

Recycled Content in Selected Building Materials

Building Material	Environmental Considerations
Fly ash concrete	Fly ash can readily replace about 25% of the cement in concrete (and sometimes up to 50%) while improving some structural and performance properties. Fly ash is a waste product from coal-fired power plants and a significant disposal problem for the utility industry.
Steel framing	Most light-gauge steel framing, which is sometimes used as an alternative to lumber, has 20–25% recycled content. Heavier-gauge steel coming from *mini-mills,* such as rebar and steel I-beams, usually has much higher recycled content.
Fiberglass insulation	Virtually all fiberglass insulation today includes a significant percentage of recycled glass. The glass is primarily post-consumer glass cullet (waste) from window glass manufacturing, although post-consumer beverage containers are also used by some manufacturers.
Cellulose insulation	Made from old newspaper that has been fiberized, with borates and/or ammonium sulfate added as a fire retardant.
Drywall	Most drywall from the major manufacturers is made with 100% recycled paper facings. Some manufacturers also use *synthetic gypsum* instead of virgin gypsum as the core. Synthetic gypsum is a waste product from coal-fired power plants—the scrubbers use calcium carbonate to remove sulfur from the stack emissions, converting that calcium carbonate into calcium sulfate, or gypsum.
Fiberboard panels, such as Homosote®	The Homosote Company has produced wall and subfloor panels out of recycled newspaper since the early 1900s. Natural lignin is the binder; paraffin is added to provide moisture resistance.
Wood-plastic composite decking	Several companies now produce decking made out of wood fiber (sawdust or wood chips) with recycled polyethylene.
Recycled-glass tile	Some floor tiles are made from glass cullet that has been ground and re-melted.
Recycled paint	Partially used cans of latex paint can be collected then re-mixed and modified for use as primer (where color is not as important). Solid waste agencies produce this paint as a way to help keep paint out of landfills.

FIGURE 8.4

Products that reduce material use. These products may not be particularly green on their own, but are considered green because they allow us to reduce the use of other materials. For example, *drywall clips* allow the elimination of corner studs in wood framing (see figure 8.5); *pier foundation* systems minimize concrete use; and special pigments

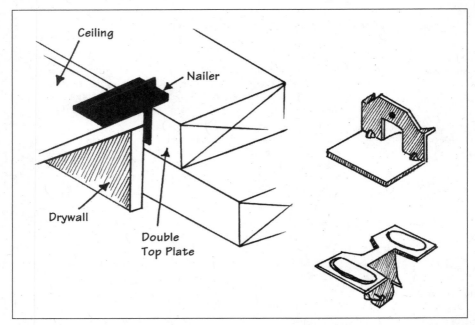

FIGURE 8.5—*These simple drywall clips replace a wood framing member by providing backing for drywall at a ceiling wall corner.*

and concrete polishing systems can turn concrete slabs into attractive finished floors, eliminating the need for conventional finish flooring.

Products with exceptional durability or low maintenance require-ments. These products are environmentally attractive because they need to be replaced less frequently, or because their maintenance has very low impact. Included in this category are such products as *fiber-cement sid-ing,* fiberglass windows, and slate shingles.

Certified wood products. Third-party forest certification, based on standards developed by the Forest Stewardship Council (FSC), is the best way to ensure that wood products come from well-managed forests (see sidebar).

Rapidly renewable products. Rapidly renewable materials are dis-tinguished from wood by their shorter harvest rotation, typically 10 years or less. They are biodegradable, often (but not always) low in VOC emissions, and generally produced from agricultural crops. Examples include natural linoleum, cork, concrete-form-release agents made from plant oils, and natural paints.

Forest Certification

Wood should be one of the greenest building products. After all, the primary energy input in its production is sunlight, via photosynthesis; woodlands provide wildlife habitat and places for humans to enjoy nature; and, as a natural product, wood is totally biodegradable.

Yet wood is often perceived as not being a green product. That's because conventional forestry practices can carry heavy environmental burdens. Many forests are intensively managed as monocultures, planted in just one species and sometimes dosed with herbicides to eliminate others. Extensive clear-cuts and even-aged stands (trees all about the same age) do not provide the varied habitat needed by many plant and animal species. Road construction and logging practices often result in extensive erosion and siltation of streams and rivers. Such practices do not produce forests that support healthy, rich ecosystems.

In an effort to use market pressure to bring about a shift to more sustainable forestry practices, a number of concerned woodworkers formed the Rainforest Alliance in the late 1980s and created the first wood certification program, SmartWood, in 1989. This effort was expanded internationally with other organizations, leading in 1993 to the formation of the Forest Stewardship Council (FSC).

The idea with forest certification is to establish standards for responsible forestry and then have independent, third-party organizations certify that the forestry operations of companies or landowners meet those standards. Wood products derived from those forest operations carry certification stamps. By seeking out certified wood products (and sometimes paying more for them), buyers create incentives for sustainable management of forests.

There are a number of certification systems for forests, but most experts acknowledge that the standards developed by FSC remain the most rigorous. Along with periodically updating these standards, FSC accredits organizations to carry out on-the-ground certifications. In North America there are two organizations, the SmartWood program of the Rainforest Alliance, and Scientific Certification Systems (SCS), that carry out most such certifications. As of January 2006, a total of 60 million acres of timberlands in North America and 170 million acres worldwide were certified under FSC guidelines.

To be sure that you are buying wood products that come from an FSC-certified forest, look for the FSC logo. Wood from these forests can be tracked through processing, manufacturing, and warehousing so that the finished product can carry a certification label. This process is referred to as "chain-of-custody" certification, and it is how you can be sure that wood products you buy indeed came from FSC-certified forests. A wide range of wood products is now available with such designation: lumber, plywood, furniture, even musical instruments and paper.

FIGURE 8.6—*Look for the FSC logo as evidence that the wood came from forests that were managed according to standards of the Forest Stewardship Council.*

Choose Products that Avoid Toxic or Other Emissions

Some building products are considered green because they have low manufacturing impacts, because they are alternatives to conventional products made from chemicals considered problematic, or because they facilitate a reduction in the pollution or emissions from building operations or construction and demolition activities.

Substitutes for conventional products made with environmentally hazardous components may not, in themselves, be particularly green (e.g. they may be petrochemical-based or relatively high in VOCs), but *relative to the products being replaced* they can be considered green. Most of the products satisfying this criterion are in categories that are dominated by the more harmful products.

Natural or minimally processed products. Products that are natural or minimally processed can be green because of low energy use and low risk of chemical releases during manufacture. These can include wood products, agricultural or nonagricultural plant products, and mineral products such as natural stone and slate shingles.

Alternatives to ozone-depleting substances. Included here are products in categories where the majority of products still contain or use HCFCs, such as refrigerants in air conditioners. As HCFCs are phased out, the relative importance of this green criterion continues to drop. For example, *polyisocyanurate* (*polyiso*) insulation is no longer made with HCFC-141b as the blowing agent, so the greater environmental benefit of the competing ozone-safe product, expanded polystyrene (EPS), has disappeared.

Alternatives to hazardous products. Some materials are considered green because they are environmentally preferable to conventional products in a particular application. For example, *polyvinyl chloride* (*PVC* or *vinyl*) products contain a large amount of chlorine that can be converted into hazardous chlorinated hydrocarbons, such as dioxins, if incinerated, and the plasticizers in these products may be *endocrine disruptors,* chemicals that mimic natural hormones and may cause reproductive or developmental problems (see sidebar, Chapter 9). Thus a product may be considered green because it can substitute for PVC. Other examples of such products include fluorescent lamps that contain less mercury, concrete form-release agents (oils that allow the forms to be removed after pouring concrete) that won't contaminate groundwater, and products made without brominated flame retardants.

Products that reduce or eliminate pesticide treatments. Periodic pesticide treatment around buildings can be a significant health and environmental hazard. The use of certain building products can reduce or eliminate the need for pesticide treatments, and such products are therefore considered green. Examples include physical termite barriers, borate- or sodium-silicate-treated building products, and bait systems that eliminate the need for broad-based pesticide applications.

FIGURE 8.7—*An important criterion of a green building product is less pollution during manufacture.*

Products that reduce stormwater pollution. Some paving products are permeable, allowing rainwater to soak into the ground, rather than contributing to stormwater runoff and pollution of nearby streams and other water bodies. Components used in vegetated or green roofs can also reduce stormwater runoff. For areas such as parking lots that generate a lot of pollution in stormwater runoff, there are filtration and oil-separation systems that remove these contaminants.

Products that reduce impacts from construction and demolition activities. Included in this category are various erosion-control products, foundation systems that eliminate the need for excavation, and exterior stains that result in lower emissions of smog-causing VOCs. Low-mercury fluorescent lamps reduce environmental impacts of demolition and renovation.

Good News about Pressure-Treated Wood

Treating wood with chemicals to protect it from decay can be a good thing, because it helps the wood last longer. For decades, the most common chemical used for *pressure-treated wood* was *chromated copper arsenate* (CCA), and tens of billions of board feet of lumber have been treated with this chemical since the 1960s. Due primarily to concern about *leaching* of toxins, however, wood treated with CCA has now been removed from the market for most residential uses. The industry has replaced CCA primarily with two copper-based chemicals, ACQ and copper azole. These are much less toxic, although copper is still quite harmful to aquatic organisms, and they are also moderately corrosive to steel, which can reduce the durability of structures constructed from this treated wood, such as decks.

Borate wood preservatives are also used as a CCA replacement, although they are not generally appropriate outdoors, since they are water-soluble. A newer treatment process using sodium silicate and heat treatment offers a better alternative. In a process somewhat like fossilization, the sodium silicate forms an amorphous glass coating around the wood fibers, rendering the wood inedible.

While there is no longer a lot of CCA-treated wood coming into use, there is a lot coming out of use, and this poses quite a significant disposal problem. In recent years, as much as 17% of all softwood lumber was pressure-treated with CCA, over 5 billion board feet per year. CCA-treated wood removed from service should not be disposed of through incineration; some of the arsenic will be released as air pollution, and most of the arsenic, copper, and chromium will end up in the ash in a highly toxic and highly leachable form. CCA-treated wood should be disposed of in lined landfills.

FIGURE 8.8—*Porous grid-pavers are "green" because they allow rain to infiltrate on the ground where it falls, instead of contributing to stormwater runoff.*

Products that reduce pollution or waste from operations. Alternative *wastewater* disposal systems reduce groundwater pollution by decomposing organic wastes more effectively. Masonry fireplaces and pellet stoves burn fuel more completely with fewer emissions than conventional fireplaces and wood stoves. Recycling bins and compost systems let occupants reduce their solid waste generation.

Choose Products that Save Energy or Water

The ongoing environmental impacts that result from the energy and water used in operating a building often far outweigh the impacts associated with building it. Many products help save energy or water; there are several distinct subcategories:

Building components that reduce heating and cooling loads. Examples include structural insulated panels (SIPs), insulated concrete forms (ICFs), autoclaved aerated concrete (AAC) blocks, and high-performance windows (see Chapter 5).With windows, energy performance can be objectively compared using standards developed by the National Fenestration Rating Council (NFRC) (see Chapter 6).

Equipment that conserves energy. For energy-consuming equipment, such as water heaters, clothes washers, and refrigerators, the US Department of Energy has developed standardized testing procedures so that manufacturers can report energy performance consistently. EnergyGuide labels on most appliances as well as heating and cooling equipment allow you to compare the energy performance of products. ENERGY STAR designations identify products with higher efficiency. In

FIGURE 8.9—*The new generation of horizontal-axis (front-loading) clothes washers save energy by using less hot water than conventional top-loading washers, since the washtub doesn't have to be full of water for effective washing, as it does with a top-loader. They also extract more water in the spin cycle (by spinning faster) so the dryer doesn't have to do as much work.*

most categories, the energy performance criteria used in *Green Building Products* are even more stringent than ENERGY STAR standards. (See Chapter 6 for more on energy performance ratings.)

Renewable energy and fuel cell equipment. Equipment and products that allow use of renewable energy instead of fossil fuels and conventional electricity are highly beneficial from an environmental standpoint. Examples include solar water heaters, photovoltaic systems, and wind turbines. *Fuel cells* can also be considered green, even though they nearly always use natural gas or another fossil fuel as the hydrogen source; as renewable sources of hydrogen become available, fuel cells will help alleviate fossil fuel dependence. (See Chapter 7 for more on renewables.)

Fixtures and equipment that conserve water. To be designated as green in *Green Building Products,* toilets must use at least 20% less water per flush than allowed by the federal water efficiency standards, and they must perform satisfactorily, based on independent, third-party testing. There are also showerheads, faucets, irrigation systems, and other products that are green because they use significantly less water than conventional products. Less common water-saving products, such as rainwater catchment systems and graywater components, are also considered green. (See Chapter 10 for more on water.)

Choose Products that Contribute to a Safe, Healthy Built Environment

Houses should be healthy to live in, and the building products you select will significantly affect the quality of your home's indoor environment. Some products are green because they can enhance community well-being — green is about more than the house. Green building products that help to ensure a healthy built environment are separated into several categories below. (See Chapter 9 for more on creating a safe indoor environment and Chapter 3 for more on community planning.)

Products that don't release significant pollutants into the building. Included here are zero- and low-VOC paints, caulks, and adhesives, as well as products with very low emissions, such as manufactured wood products made without formaldehyde binders.

Products that block the introduction, production, or spread of indoor contaminants. Certain materials and products are green because they prevent the introduction or production of pollutants, especially biological contaminants. Rainscreen products, for example, can help keep moisture out of houses and, thus, prevent mold growth. *Track-off mats* at entryways help to remove pollutants from the shoes of people entering the house.

Products that remove indoor pollutants. High-efficiency ventilation products, certain air filters, and radon mitigation equipment are considered green because they remove pollutants or introduce fresh air.

Products that warn occupants of health hazards in the building. Included here are high-quality carbon monoxide (CO) detectors, lead paint test kits, and radon test kits.

Products that improve light quality. There is a growing body of evidence suggesting that natural daylight is beneficial to our health and productivity. Products that enable us to bring daylight into a building, such as tubular skylights, can thus be considered green.

Products that help control noise. Unwanted noise from indoor and outdoor sources has been shown to cause stress and other health problems.

A wide range of green products are available that absorb or block noise, or mask it with sound-cancellation technologies.

Products that enhance community well-being. Certain green products can directly or indirectly contribute to safer, more pedestrian-friendly communities. Bicycle storage racks, for example, can make bicycling more convenient and, thus, a more viable alternative to cars.

GETTING THE INFORMATION YOU NEED FOR MATERIAL SELECTION

Green material and product selection would be pretty easy if everything were black and white, but the reality is told in shades of gray. Very often when comparing several different materials, we have to consider very

New Classes of "Designer Toxins" Pose Unknown Risks

Concerns about lead, asbestos, PCBs (polychlorinated biphenyls), and numerous other materials have long been understood, and many products have disappeared from use as a result. Now there are growing concerns about several new classes of compounds that are widely used today.

Brominated flame retardants are widely used in products ranging from computer cases to carpet padding and foam insulation. Two forms of brominated flame retardants, penta and octa forms of PBDE (polybrominated diphenyl ether), have been banned in Europe and several U.S. states, and the sole manufacturer has ceased production of them. But other brominated flame retardants, including deca-PBDE, TBBPA, and HBCD, are widely used in the U.S. and worldwide; in 2001, some 450 million pounds of the five most common brominated flame retardants were produced.

Concerns about brominated flame retardants arose after studies found that levels of PBDEs in human breast milk have been rising dramatically in recent years. Some brominated flame retardants are persistent and highly bioaccumulative in the food chain. And more and more studies are showing that they pose a health risk, particularly during fetal development. Impacts of PBDEs in laboratory animals include interference with thyroid function, liver cancer, and changes in learning, memory, and behavior. TBBPA, a brominated flame retardant widely used in epoxy resins and circuit boards, has been identified as an endocrine disruptor (a compound that mimics or interferes with hormones, such as estrogen). HBCD, used in polystyrene, has been found to cause changes in learning, memory, and behavior when mice are exposed to it before birth. Based on these concerns, some companies, such as home furniture supplier IKEA and office furniture manufacturer Herman Miller have been eliminating brominated flame retardants from their products.

different types of environmental impacts. For example, vinyl (PVC) siding has very low maintenance requirements, since you don't need to paint or stain it, as you do with most wood siding. But, as described earlier in this chapter, PVC has other impacts that should be considered, such as disposal and the plasticizers used to make it flexible.

When we try to compare different materials, we need to weigh these conflicting considerations. That can get pretty complex, and it can bog you down. Fortunately, there are a number of excellent sources of information on green building material selection. One of these is the companion volume to this book, *Green Building Products,* which includes 1,600 product listings based largely on the criteria described in this chapter. For more on this book, visit <www.newsociety.com> or <www.BuildingGreen.com>.

Phthalate plasticizers are widely used in PVC and a few other plastics to increase flexibility. Vinyl shower curtains, for example, are typically over 50% phthalate plasticizer by weight. DEHP, a plasticizer that typically makes up about 30% of the weight of vinyl sheet flooring and up to 45% of the weight of PVC electric cable sheathing, has been implicated as a cause of asthma and as an endocrine disruptor. Concerns with endocrine disruptors came into public focus with the 1996 publication of the book, Our Stolen Future, by Theo Colborn, Dianne Dumanoski, and John Peterson. Phthalate plasticizers and other endocrine disruptors have been blamed for falling sperm counts and a variety of other reproductive and developmental problems.

Bisphenol-A, which is used in making epoxies and polycarbonate plastics, is another compound identified by many as an endocrine disruptor. A 2005 paper in the journal Endocrinology showed that when mice were exposed to the compound before birth, breast tissue developed in a way that could increase risk of breast cancer.

More recently, the fluoropolymer PFOA (perfluorooctanoic acid, or C-8) has come under heavy scrutiny. In January 2006, an independent scientific review panel advised the U.S. Environmental Protection Agency that PFOA is a likely carcinogen. Concern has also been raised that the compound may harm the human immune system. PFOAs are used in producing data cable sheathing, and in Teflon® non-stick coating and Gore-Tex® stain-resistant fabric coating. 3M Corporation took its PFOA-containing ScotchGuard® fabric protector spray off the market in 2000, and ceased production of PFOA after learning that the chemical is now found in humans worldwide. Meanwhile, DuPont, the maker of Teflon®, has a warning on its web site that Teflon-coated pans should not be used around pet birds, because the birds may die.

FIGURE 8.10 —*While this chapter has laid out some background on green building products, the companion volume,* Green Building Products, *lists actual products and provides full contact information.*

As you try to find green building materials and products for your house, don't get discouraged. Remember, even though material selection is often considered the defining element of a green home, that is not the case. Material selection is only one part of green design — and a relatively small part at that. Pay attention to the materials used in your house, but not at the expense of carefully addressing such issues as energy efficiency, house size, automobile dependence, and indoor air quality. These issues are usually more important than material selection.

CHAPTER 9

Creating a Safe
Indoor Environment

A GREEN HOME should not only minimize risk to the outdoor environment — the air and water and ecosystems we all depend on — but it should also minimize risk to the indoor environment. If you build a superinsulated, passive solar house made entirely from recycled products — but your family gets sick living in it — you haven't succeeded.

Americans spend 85 to 95% of their time indoors, yet some of their indoor spaces have air quality as bad as the outdoor air in the most polluted cities. High moisture levels in many houses result in mold growth or create environments where dust mites and other microorganisms can thrive, causing or exacerbating asthma and other health problems. Combustion gasses, including deadly carbon monoxide, can leak from furnaces, water heaters, and other combustion appliances. Many of the thousands of materials and products that go into houses both during and after construction offgas VOCs. Radon and various toxins, including pesticide residues and hydrocarbons from past spills, can enter houses through the soil, putting families at risk for years. Even electrical wiring is generating magnetic fields that, according to some studies, may be harmful.

ELIMINATE, ISOLATE, AND VENTILATE

The oft-repeated mantra for creating a safe indoor environment is to *eliminate, isolate,* and *ventilate.* You should first try to eliminate materials that are likely to cause *indoor air quality* *(IAQ)* problems. When you can't eliminate a hazardous material or pollution source, you should isolate it from the living space. And, finally, most building science experts now agree that you need to mechanically ventilate a house — replace stale, contaminated air with fresh outdoor air — to ensure a healthy indoor environment. These three components of healthy design

Chemical Sensitivity

According to some estimates, 10% of Americans are chemically sensitive. This means that they can't tolerate even modest exposure to certain chemicals. Medical professionals don't fully understand what creates this extreme sensitivity to chemicals, but most experts seem to agree that the immune system is compromised in these people.

In some cases, this damage to the immune system is caused by a particular event, such as a one-time exposure to high levels of a particular pesticide. In other cases, it appears that such chemical sensitivity can build up over time as we become exposed to a wide range of chemicals, from perfumes to cleaning fluids to chemicals emitted from paints and building products. Some occupational health experts use the analogy of a bucket, representing the capacity of an individual's immune system at birth. Over time, the bucket is filled up until it can absorb no more exposure, at which point the individual becomes chemically sensitive.

Once a person becomes acutely chemically sensitive, very special measures may be required to build a house that he or she can tolerate. One individual, for example, may not be able to tolerate the small amount of terpenes that are emitted over time from softwood lumber, so that individual will need a house with virtually no softwood in it. Another person might do fine with lumber but be unable to tolerate certain VOCs emitted from carpeting or *particleboard*. To complicate matters, these sensitivities can change over time.

For individuals with acute chemical sensitivity, the process of selecting materials for a house can be very difficult and time-consuming. Essentially, every product being considered for the house will have to be tested by exposing the individual to it, and only those products that do not cause a reaction can be used.

This chapter does not attempt to address house design for people with acute chemical sensitivity. (For specialized information on the needs of people with chemical sensitivity, see the references in the accompanying web site.) Rather, this chapter seeks to show how a house can be built that will pose little risk of sickening someone who is not chemically sensitive (i.e., not adding to the bucket in the earlier analogy), and that will be unlikely to worsen the sensitivity of someone with moderate chemical sensitivity.

recur throughout this chapter in relation to general house design strategies, product and material selection, and ventilation systems.

HOUSE DESIGN FOR A HEALTHY INDOOR ENVIRONMENT

There are a number of strategies for keeping your indoor environment healthy that relate to the overall house design and construction detailing. Discuss these with your architect, designer, or builder.

Construction Detailing to Avoid Moisture Problems

Among the most severe indoor air quality problems in homes are those caused by moisture. If surfaces remain wet or very humid for extended periods of time, mold can grow. There are many types of molds, including mildew and dry rot (not really dry at all), and many people are allergic to them.

While it is the mold spores that cause most IAQ problems, a more dangerous problem may be the toxic chemicals that are given off by certain molds to ward off other organisms that compete for the same food sources. A type of black mold, known by the Latin name *Staccybotrys*

FIGURE 9.1—*For chemically sensitive people, even shopping at the grocery store might not be possible, due to the offgassing of chemicals from cleaning fluids, scented soaps, and packaging.*

chartarum (or *Staccybotrys atra*), can be highly toxic, especially to children. Certain illnesses, such as organic toxic dust syndrome (OTDS) and pulmonary hemorrhage and hemosiderosis (PH/H), result from exposure to this type of mold toxin. In severe cases, infants have died from PH/H, including — according to some experts — a widely publicized cluster of infant deaths in Cleveland, Ohio, in the 1990s.

Moisture-related problems are not limited to mold. High moisture levels in homes also can lead to growth of other biological contaminants and allergy-causing dust mites, particularly in carpeting. And in addition to causing IAQ problems, rotting wood can cause structural problems in houses. Rot often shortens building life; in extreme cases, houses can collapse from moisture-induced decay.

Strategies for avoiding moisture problems in houses are numerous and well beyond the scope of this book. A few include:

- Eliminate moisture sources in houses. For example, never dry firewood indoors, and avoid having too many houseplants in living areas.
- Install quiet bathroom fans and use them whenever showering. If the fan is too noisy, you and your family are unlikely to use it.
- Install a kitchen range hood fan that exhausts to the outdoors. Look for a variable-speed model that is quiet enough to be used regularly; at a low setting, the SONE rating should be less than 3.0.
- Ensure proper flashing and roofing details to keep rainwater out of houses.
- Provide roof overhangs to keep most rain off walls and keep roof runoff away from foundation walls.
- Slope the ground away from house walls so that rainwater will be less likely to run into the basement or reach foundation walls.
- Provide a moisture barrier under concrete floor slabs to prevent moisture from wicking up from the ground.
- Provide a dampproofing coating and proper drainage on the outside of foundation walls.
- Provide a continuous air barrier in the building envelope to minimize air leakage and keep moisture out of wall and ceiling (or roof) cavities. (Most moisture that gets into wall cavities is carried there by air leakage, rather than by diffusing through permeable surfaces in the wall system.)
- Provide a vapor diffusion retarder on the warm side of the insulated envelope. In cold climates, this will typically be on the inside of

walls; in warm climates where air conditioning is widely used, it is more likely to be on the exterior side.

🏠 Use a rainscreen on the outside of walls so that there is an air space between the exterior wall sheathing and siding. This detail allows the siding to dry out between rainstorms, and it prevents heat or wind from driving moisture into the wall cavity.

🏠 In relatively humid climates (most of the eastern US, Pacific Northwest, etc.), insulate cold-water pipes to prevent condensation, which can drip onto wood surfaces. Toilet tanks can also be insulated (on the inside using special kits) to prevent condensation on the outside surface.

🏠 Keep plantings a few feet away from house walls to allow air circulation and drying.

Design to Control Radon and Other Soil Gasses

Radon is a colorless, odorless, radioactive gas that occurs naturally in certain types of bedrock. The US Environmental Protection Agency considers radon to be the number-two cause of lung cancer in the United States (after smoking), responsible for about 20,000 deaths per year. Radon is widely occurring, so we should almost always assume that it *could* be a problem. Other soil gasses, such as volatile hydrocarbons, can also be a problem in some areas, as can pesticides and water vapor, particularly

FIGURE 9.2—*Radon is a natural soil gas that is found in many parts of the country. As radon decays, it releases radioactive particles that can cause lung cancer.*

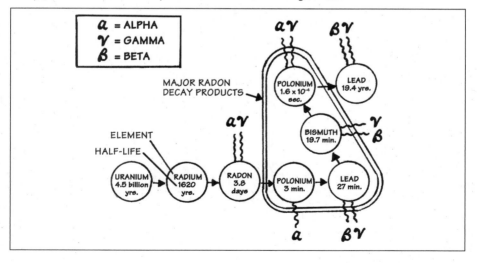

on building sites that have been contaminated by past industrial uses or chemical spills (*brownfields*) and farmland.

Houses should be designed to: a) reduce the likelihood that radon and other soil gasses will enter; and b) enable easy mitigation of soil gasses should high levels ever be found. A few of the most important recommended strategies include:

1. Make sure your foundation contractor installs an impermeable moisture barrier under the floor slab. With a crawl space, install a moisture barrier on top of the ground, holding the barrier in place with a thin layer of sand or earth.

2. Provide a drainage layer under any concrete floor slab and on the outside of foundation walls. Under the slab, provide at least 4 inches of crushed stone. Along the walls, backfill with crushed stone and/or

FIGURE 9.3—*Designing and building a house for radon control involves planning ahead so that a radon-mitigation system can be added if radon testing later shows that mitigation is necessary.*

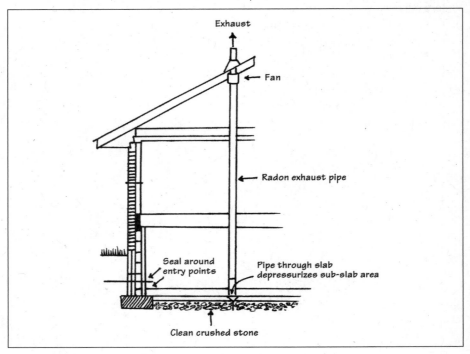

a specialized drainage material (such as stiff woven polypropylene matting sold for this purpose), after coating the outside of the wall with a dampproofing layer to keep moisture from seeping through.

3. Seal all penetrations, cracks, and gaps in the basement floor slab and walls with a high-quality caulk that works well with concrete. Sealing basement sumps is especially important; airtight lids are available from specialty suppliers of radon-mitigation equipment.

4. In areas where radon problems are common or on sites where there may once have been oil, gasoline, or chemical spills or significant pesticide use, install a vent pipe through the basement floor slab that extends into the sub-slab crushed stone, and cap this vent pipe. Should high radon levels or other soil gas problems ever be found, this will allow easy installation of an exhaust fan. The idea of such a system is to depressurize the area immediately under the slab and outside the foundation walls to keep radon and other soil gasses from leaking into the house.

Design to Eliminate the Need for Pesticide Treatments

In some areas of the US regular pesticide treatments are widely used to control termites or other insects. Even though the highly toxic and long-lasting pesticide chlordane has now been banned, modern pesticide treatments can still be very hazardous. It makes sense to do what you can in designing the house to reduce the need for such treatments. For example:

- In areas of very heavy termite infestations, consider framing the house out of steel instead of wood, or use borate-treated or sodium-silicate-treated lumber.
- If local building officials allow, use recycled plastic lumber or wood-plastic composite lumber for sill plates.
- Consider a stone patio instead of a wooden deck.
- Keep vegetation at least a few feet away from the house.
- Don't bury wood scraps or other cellulose-based material (which termites eat) when backfilling around the house.

Keep the Garage Separate from the House

Attached garages or (worse) garages beneath living space allow exhaust fumes and other hazardous gasses from the garage to enter the house.

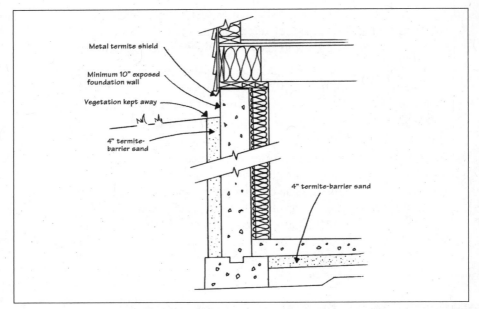

FIGURE 9.4— *In areas with subterranean or Formosan termites, special measures can be taken to prevent infestation. Strategies include termite-barrier sand (a uniform-sized aggregate that termites can't tunnel through), a metal termite shield, and inedible wood framing.*

Even with fairly tight construction and a well-sealed door between the garage and house, leakage of hazardous gasses into the house is still very common. Much better is to keep the garage totally separate from the house.

Design to Minimize Exposure to Electromagnetic Fields

While there is still no scientific consensus on whether *electromagnetic fields* (*EMFs*) cause cancer, some studies have indicated that they may, or that they may cause other health problems. EMFs are generated whenever electrical current flows, especially when there is separation between the positive and negative conductors. It makes sense to practice what experts call *prudent avoidance* in minimizing EMF exposure in houses. These are easy measures that cost little if anything during construction. Here are a few recommendations:

🏠 Avoid building sites along high-voltage power lines or near utility substations.

- Keep the electrical supply conduit and electrical panel(s) away from the most heavily occupied spaces. For example, the electrical supply can be located on the outside wall of a closet instead of in a bedroom.

- Ask your electrician to avoid creating *current loops,* in which the hot and neutral conductors are separated. These may be created, for example, if certain shortcuts are taken in wiring three-way light switches.

- Consider running most wiring in the basement with wires extending up for outlet receptacles, instead of running all the wires through the perimeter walls.

- Keep large electrical loads, such as *air handlers* for heating systems and air conditioners, away from the most heavily occupied spaces.

- Minimize electrical use. The less current flowing through a house, the lower the potential EMF exposure.

CHOOSING PRODUCTS AND MATERIALS FOR THE HOUSE

Keeping unhealthy materials out of your house is an extremely important strategy in healthy house design. The more successful you are at keeping toxins out of your house, the less critical are ventilation strategies to remove contaminated air. A number of strategies are described below.

FIGURE 9.5—*To eliminate the risk of car exhaust entering the house, keep the garage separate, connected by a breezeway.*

Avoid Combustion Appliances that are Not Sealed-Combustion

Avoid equipment or appliances that use household air for combustion or rely on natural draft to carry flue gasses up the chimney. Of highest priority, *never* install an *unvented (vent-free) gas heater*. These increasingly popular and heavily advertised heaters are designed to look like wood stoves with visible flames. Although they operate with very high combustion efficiency, unvented gas heaters can still introduce trace amounts of nitrogen oxides and carbon monoxide, as well as significant quantities of water vapor and carbon dioxide (the two primary products of combustion), directly into the home.

Gas cooking ranges introduce similar combustion products, but the burners are much smaller, and they can often be vented with a range hood fan. Electric ranges are preferable from an IAQ standpoint.

Gas-fired water heaters and oil- or gas-fired furnaces and boilers should be sealed-combustion, meaning that outside air is supplied directly into the combustion chamber and flue gasses are exhausted directly outdoors, never interacting with household air. If a true sealed-combustion model is not available or too expensive, a power-vented

FIGURE 9.6—*Sealed-combustion water heaters, furnaces, and boilers eliminate the risk of backdrafting; outside combustion air is supplied directly to the combustion chamber, and flue gasses are exhausted directly outdoors.*

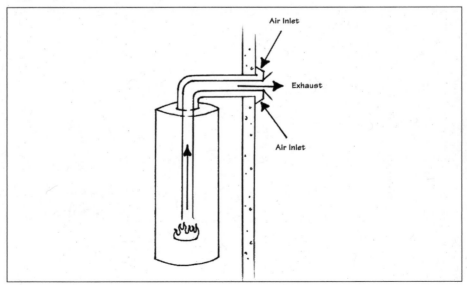

model (with a fan to push flue gasses up the chimney or out through a wall vent) should be installed. Water heaters and heating systems that rely on natural draft are undesirable, because they are prone to *back-drafting,* a not-uncommon situation in which some of the flue gasses spill into the house instead of going up the chimney.

Minimize Use of Wall-to-Wall Carpeting

Wall-to-wall carpeting has improved significantly in recent years, but it can still be a significant source of indoor air pollutants. There are three categories of pollutants associated with carpeting: 1) offgassing of VOCs from the carpet itself, from the carpet pad (or cushion), and from the adhesives used to glue it to the subfloor; 2) biological contaminants that can live in carpeting; and 3) pollutants tracked in from outdoors that may become trapped in carpet and later affect occupants.

Offgassing of VOCs from carpeting has dropped significantly since the 1980s and early '90s, when carpeting was implicated in several highly publicized "sick building syndrome" problems, including at the US Environmental Protection Agency headquarters in Washington, D.C.

In 1992, the Carpet and Rug Institute (CRI) established a testing and labeling program setting limits on VOC and formaldehyde emissions from carpeting. This Green Label standard was strengthened in 1994, and in 2004 the Green Label Plus program was launched, offering yet a higher standard of indoor air quality. Most carpeting today carries at least the CRI Green Label. Green Label and Green Label Plus designations are also available for carpet pads and carpet adhesives. You should always look for these labels, but realize that not all carpet manufacturers are members of CRI and that only member companies can use the CRI label.

Natural-fiber carpets made from wool, cotton, and other textile fibers have low offgassing and have long been available, but tend to be significantly more expensive than synthetic carpets. Also, many natural-fiber carpets contain chemicals to kill moths or other organisms for which the carpeting could be a food source.

Generally of greater concern than the VOC emissions from carpeting is the risk of biological contaminants and toxins tracked in from outdoors. Under high-humidity conditions or where spills occur, carpeting may support mold growth or dust mites. At a minimum, avoid carpeting in a basement that may be damp or prone to spills, and in kitchens and bathrooms.

FIGURE 9.7—*Instead of wall-to-wall carpeting, consider a hard-surface floor with area rugs that can be removed for cleaning or drying if they get wet.*

Pollutants from outdoors can also be trapped in carpeting, including pesticides, heavy metals (e.g. lead from paint that has chipped off the outside of houses over the years), hydrocarbon residues, and so forth. At entryways, install *track-off mats* that capture moisture and a wide range of contaminants that would otherwise be tracked into the house; mats should be removable for easy cleaning.

From an indoor air quality standpoint, it makes sense to minimize the use of wall-to-wall carpeting in houses and avoid it altogether in entranceways (where tracked-in contaminants and moisture are most problematic). In place of carpeting, use solid-surface flooring (hardwood, tile, polished concrete, etc.) with area rugs (throw rugs) where a softer surface is needed. If wall-to-wall carpeting cannot be avoided, look for carpeting that carries the CRI Green Label Plus. With products not manufactured by CRI member companies or not carrying the Green Label Plus, ask the manufacturer for test data on VOC emissions from the carpeting.

Avoid Standard Particleboard and MDF

Most kitchen and bath cabinets and some types of subflooring are made from particleboard or *medium-density fiberboard* (*MDF*) containing *urea-formaldehyde* (*UF*) *binders*. These products can offgas significant quantities of formaldehyde, which is a human carcinogen. (Some cabinets are sealed to prevent offgassing.)

Avoid products containing urea-formaldehyde when possible; instead, choose those produced using polyurethane or *MDI* (*methyl diisocyanate*) *binders*. A soy-based binder introduced in 2005 is not only formaldehyde-free, but also derived from a renewable resource. For cabinets, exterior-grade plywood, which is made with *phenol-formaldehyde binder,* offgasses less formaldehyde than interior-grade plywood made with urea-formaldehyde binder.

Choose Zero-VOC or Low-VOC Paints, Finishes, Caulks, and Adhesives

Zero-VOC and low-VOC paints, finishes, caulks, and adhesives result in better indoor air quality, and also contribute less to outdoor air pollution. There have been tremendous advances with these products in recent years, and most major manufacturers have products on the market that offgas far lower quantities of VOCs than the norm. In the 1980s and early '90s, water-based acrylic (latex) paints tended to be less durable than solvent-based paints, but they have improved dramatically, largely due to the extensive research manufacturers have invested in them.

Pay Attention to New Concerns about Hazardous Chemicals

In recent years, there have been growing concerns about a number of classes of chemicals that are commonly used in building materials and

FIGURE 9.8—*Use zero-VOC paints to keep offgassing to a bare minimum.*

consumer products. These chemicals include brominated flame retardants, including PBDEs; phthalates, which are used as plasticizers in PVC as well as in such consumer products as cosmetics; fluoropolymers, such as Teflon®, Stainmaster®, and the perfluorooctanoic acid (PFOA) used in producing these chemicals; and bisphenol-A, a chemical used in producing epoxies and polycarbonate plastics. Concerns with these chemicals range from persistence in the environment and in our bodies, to developmental impacts from exposure before birth, to disruption of endocrine (hormone) function (see Chapter 8).

Roughly 80,000 chemicals are used to produce everything from caulk to shampoo, and the vast majority of these chemicals have never been tested for toxicity. Especially now that new regulations in Europe require testing of many chemicals that have been in use for decades, we will be learning more about health effects, and new concerns are sure to come to light. As you make purchases for your home, it pays to be an informed consumer by keeping up with the latest information. See the resources listed in the companion web site.

Seal Products to Trap Harmful Chemicals

In some situations, it's impossible to avoid using building products that contain harmful chemicals. This is where the "isolate" part of the eliminate, isolate, ventilate strategy for good IAQ comes in.

For example, it's hard to find cabinets made with material other than standard particleboard or MDF, and any you find are likely to be more expensive. Instead, you can buy cabinets that are pre-sealed at the factory to keep the formaldehyde from being released, or you can buy standard cabinets and seal the particleboard surfaces yourself.

In sealing manufactured wood products, use a low-VOC sealer. If you will be painting on top of the coating, make sure the sealant can be painted; do some testing on a block of particleboard or wood first.

VENTILATION STRATEGIES

Ventilating is the final part of the eliminate, isolate, ventilate approach to ensuring good indoor air quality. Once upon a time, it may have been fine to rely on the natural leakiness of a house to get rid of indoor air pollutants and to introduce adequate fresh air. Most building scientists today, however, argue that this strategy is no longer adequate.

Even in a very loose house, there will only be good airflow through the building envelope if there is a pressure difference between the inside and outside. That pressure difference occurs only when it's windy or when there's a big temperature difference between indoors and out. There will be many times when those conditions will not exist, particularly during the spring and fall, and very little fresh air will find its way into the house — or there may be places in the house that get very little fresh air.

To promote good airflow, providing either continuous or intermittent *mechanical ventilation* is strongly recommended. In a tight house, which a green home should be, mechanical ventilation is even more important. Three different options are described and illustrated below.

Exhaust-Only Ventilation

The simplest type of mechanical ventilation system, *exhaust-only ventilation* uses one or more exhaust fans to pull air out of the house, and passive air inlet ports to introduce fresh outside air — providing *make-up air*. The exhaust fans should be located in areas of the house where

Dealing with Trade-Offs in Material Selection

In selecting building materials, you may need to weigh and balance trade-offs. Product A might be a lot better than product B in terms of overall environmental performance (embodied energy, raw materials, pollution from manufacturing), but not as good in terms of indoor air quality. In some cases, a product that is safer in our homes may be more toxic to manufacture.

Consider manufactured wood products, for example. The most common binder for particleboard is urea-formaldehyde, which offgasses significant quantities of formaldehyde. The alternative, used in a few products, is MDI, a type of polyurethane. MDI doesn't contain any formaldehyde and is very inert in the finished product, but during manufacture the chemical is highly toxic. Emissions have to be very carefully controlled in the factory. In selecting this material, we are trading off potential risk to workers in the factory to reduce the risk to ourselves in our homes.

Or consider natural linoleum. This is an environmentally attractive alternative to sheet vinyl (PVC) flooring in bathrooms and kitchens, but some people are sensitive to the odor of newly installed linoleum. The fatty acids released from the linseed oil in linoleum have a strong odor, even at very low concentrations. For this reason, some IAQ experts recommend avoiding natural linoleum.

A good designer who is familiar with green building will be able to help you work through trade-offs like these as you plan what products you will use in your house. You can also learn about these trade-offs in publications such as *Environmental Building News* or other references listed in the companion web site.

moisture or pollutants are generated, usually bathrooms and the kitchen, but sometimes hobby rooms as well. Individual fans can be used in these locations, or a central exhaust fan can be used with ducts to these locations. The passive air inlet ports (essentially, intentional holes through the wall that are designed to keep out insects and minimize drafts) should be located in bedrooms, the living room, and other places where you spend the most time.

For exhaust-only ventilation to be safe and effective, there are several requirements:

1. The exhaust fans should be durable (designed for continuous use), quiet, and energy-efficient. If the fans are too noisy, you and your family will be less likely to use them as often, or as long, as needed.

2. The house has to be very tight. If the house has a lot of leaks in the envelope, the replacement air from outside will enter the house close to the exhaust fans instead of through the intentionally placed inlet ports in your bedrooms or living room, and so the fresh air won't circulate throughout the house.

3. Exhaust-only ventilation should not be used with forced-warm-air heating, and it is not particularly effective in houses that use furnaces or heat pumps with ducts for heat delivery. It is most effective with baseboard hot-water heat, radiant-electric heat, individual space heaters, and passive solar systems that don't use supplemental heating.

FIGURE 9.9—*With exhaust-only ventilation, kitchen and bath fans exhaust stale air, and replacement air enters through passive air inlets.*

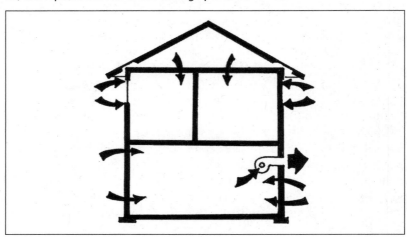

4. All combustion equipment in the house should be sealed-combustion. This means that outside air is supplied directly to the combustion chamber, and flue gasses are exhausted directly to the outdoors. With fireplaces and wood stoves, combustion air should be ducted directly to the firebox, and there should be tight-sealing doors.

5. Air should be able to circulate easily from room to room in the house. This may require providing grilles through walls and/or providing air gaps under doors.

Balanced Ventilation

In a *balanced ventilation* strategy, a central exhaust fan pulls stale air from various locations in the house, typically the kitchen, bathrooms, and locations where pollutants are generated. Fresh air is supplied using a separate fan and ducting. Most commonly, the two fans (exhaust and supply) are located in the same housing.

This system is called "balanced" ventilation because about as much fresh air is supplied as is removed. By contrast, the exhaust-only ventilation system depressurizes the house.

Balanced ventilation is the most reliable and effective type of ventilation system; it is also the most expensive. Not only is the central ventilator unit expensive (because it has two fans and, usually, a heat exchanger), but this system also requires separate ducting for both the exhaust air and the supply air.

In cold climates, it makes sense to use a *heat-recovery ventilator* (*HRV*) or *energy-recovery ventilator* (*ERV*) as the ventilation unit. With an HRV or ERV, most of the heat in the exhaust airstream is transferred to the incoming fresh air, so there is less of an energy penalty associated with ventilation. An HRV transfers only heat, while an ERV also transfers water vapor (humidity) to the incoming air stream; in cold climates, the ERV results in less drying of the house air when bringing in very dry outside air.

Central Exhaust Fan with Make-Up
Air through the Heating System

In houses with forced-warm-air heating and/or central air conditioning, it often makes sense to integrate the ventilation system with the distribution system used for heating and/or air conditioning. This approach uses a central exhaust fan and ducts to remove stale air from various locations in the house (kitchen, bathrooms, etc.), but instead of using a separate set of ducts to distribute fresh air, the heating/air

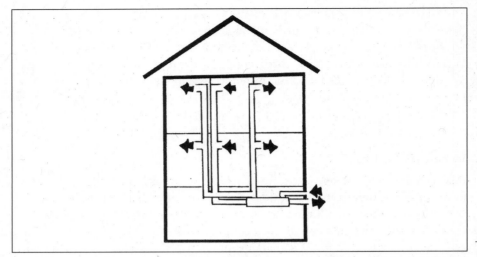

FIGURE 9.10—*In a balanced ventilation system, incoming and outgoing airstreams balance one another. Heat in the outgoing airstream can be captured with an HRV or ERV.*

conditioning ducts are used for that purpose. A fresh-air inlet duct providing *make-up air* is connected to the return side of the air handler (the part of your furnace, air conditioner, or heat pump that blows the warmed or cooled air throughout your house).

This ventilation strategy only works in houses with forced-warm-air heating or central air conditioning, and it can be quite complicated. Sophisticated controls are required to integrate the operation of the ventilation system with the heating and/or air conditioning system. In the winter when the heating system is on a lot, or in the summer when the air conditioner is operating, you can save energy because the air handler would be operating anyway (i.e., you don't need to be operating a second fan just for ventilation). But when you only need ventilation and not heat or air conditioning, there is the risk of too much airflow and wasted energy. For this reason, variable-speed controls on the air handler are recommended; *electronically commutated motors* (*ECMs*) are best, because they operate efficiently at a range of speeds.

While integrating a ventilation system with a heating and/or air conditioning system can be quite complicated, there are some combination systems coming onto the market that carry out all of these functions. As the need for ventilation becomes more accepted, more of these fully integrated systems should become available.

Determining Ventilation Requirements

How much fresh air is required in your house? The total ventilation requirements depend on the house's size and how many people live there. ASHRAE Standard 62.2 (2003) from the American Society of Heating, Refrigeration and Air Conditioning Engineers calls for a continuously operating, whole-house ventilation system in most homes that delivers at least 7.5 cubic feet per minute (cfm) per occupant, plus one cfm for every 100 square feet of occupied floor area. For a typical home, this standard results in a total continuous ventilation rate of about 50 cfm. Exceptions to this recommendation include houses without air conditioning in hot climates, vacation houses and cabins that are occupied only a small portion of the year, and houses in hot, dry climates where residents typically ventilate by opening windows.

In addition to the continuous, whole-house ventilation, ASHRAE Standard 62.2 requires that a local exhaust system be installed in the kitchen and in each bathroom. The kitchen range hood fan must be rated at a minimum of 100 cfm; bath fans must be rated at a minimum of 50 cfm.

While Standard 62.2 has not yet been adopted into many building codes, it remains a good voluntary standard to follow in achieving effective ventilation.

FIGURE 9.11 — *In homes with forced-air heating or air conditioning, the most cost-effective whole-house ventilation system utilizes the home's forced-air distribution system.*

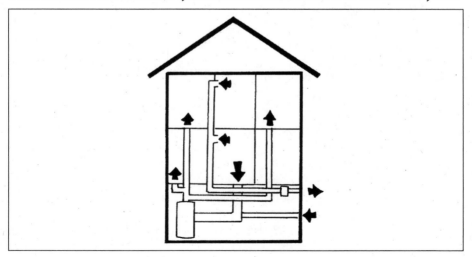

KEEPING A HEALTHY HOUSE HEALTHY

Ensuring a healthy indoor environment is not only a function of how you build that house and the type of ventilation system it has. You also need to pay attention to how you operate the house, what stuff you put in it, and how you maintain it.

Most modern furniture, for example, is made predominantly from particleboard, which offgasses formaldehyde. Some upholstery fabrics and curtains also contain formaldehyde that is released over time. Upholstery padding and carpet pads often contain high levels of brominated flame retardants. Many cleaning products release VOCs. Tobacco smoking in homes introduces very significant levels of pollutants, dwarfing virtually all others in terms of health risk, hurting even people who aren't themselves smoking. Vacuuming, unless done with a high-efficiency (HEPA) vacuum cleaner or an outside-venting central vacuum system, can redistribute harmful dust around a house. Pesticides, including flea powders, introduce harmful toxins. Cooking can introduce smoke, VOCs, and (with gas ranges) combustion products into the air; although an exhaust fan can remove most of these pollutants, electric ranges are recommended over gas ranges from an indoor-air-quality standpoint. People can track in toxins from outdoors. Houseplants can provide environments for mold and fungi, especially if they are overwatered. And there are lots of sources of excess moisture in a home that have little or nothing to do with how it was designed and built — for example, drying firewood, showering, and cooking.

Even if you follow all the recommendations for designing and building a healthy house, it is crucial that you operate the house in a health-conscious way. Protect the investments you made during design and construction of a "healthy home" by operating it in an intentional — and healthy — manner. References in this book's companion web site provide guidance for healthy operation of your home.

Paying attention to the indoor environment should be a high priority for any home that is to be called "green." A home that makes its occupants sick cannot be considered green. A big part of healthy design and construction is simply common sense and good construction practices: keeping water out; avoiding products and materials that will introduce pollutants into the house; choosing heating and water heating equipment that won't release combustion products into the home; and keeping the garage isolated from the house. But some other strategies are not so obvious — and even counter-intuitive. For example, you

FIGURE 9.12—*Even if your house is built from healthy materials, if you use conventional cleaning fluids that are full of perfumes and other chemicals, you could still be putting yourself and your family at risk.*

might think that keeping the house leaky is the best way to ensure adequate fresh air, but experts argue that it's better to make the house envelope very tight and provide mechanical ventilation. Other recommendations will be hard for many people to accept, such as avoiding gas ranges in a home. But taken together, the strategies laid out in this chapter should ensure you of the healthiest house possible for you and your family.

CHAPTER 10

Respecting and
Conserving Water

W ATER, OF COURSE, is an integral part of our lives. Without water to drink, we can survive no more than a few days. Without clean water for washing, diseases can flourish. Without rainfall, forests and non-irrigated crops die.

Water sustains us, yet we waste it and abuse it with abandon. We send millions of gallons of water down the drain needlessly. We overload sewage treatment plants. We prevent rainwater from soaking into the ground, causing runoff to erode our land and carry pollutants and silt into surface waters. We channel rainwater into pipes and carry it off-site and directly into our rivers without giving it an opportunity to seep back into the ground, creating a need for ever-larger levees and dikes along rivers to protect us from ever-more-severe flooding.

Some experts say that water will be a far greater challenge to humanity in the 21st century than energy. Evidence suggests that the recent droughts in the American West may be the norm rather than the exception, that the relatively high rainfall of the past 150 years, during the time the West was settled, may have been an anomaly. Perhaps more significantly, global climate change may alter rainfall patterns, producing frequent droughts in areas that have not experienced such conditions historically.

For many reasons, we may be forced in the not-too-distant future to adapt to water scarcity, not only in the West, but elsewhere as well. In some areas aquifers are already dropping. North America's most

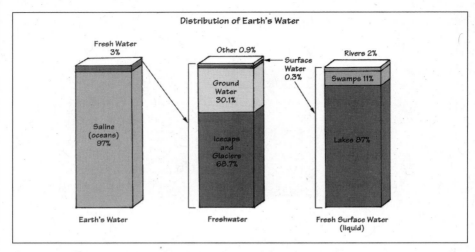

FIGURE 10.1—*There is a finite amount of water on Earth, the vast majority of which is salt-water in the oceans. Most fresh water is locked up in ice caps or in underground aquifers; just a small amount of total fresh water is available in surface waters.*

significant source of underground water, the Ogalalla Aquifer that stretches from South Dakota to Texas and accounts for 30% of farm-land irrigation in the US, is being depleted faster than it is being recharged in many areas. And many aquifers, while not being depleted, are being contaminated by toxic chemicals and nutrients from indus-try and wastewater disposal; 85% of Superfund sites in the US involve groundwater contamination. Saltwater intrusion into fresh-water aquifers is also wreaking havoc in some areas, and this problem is like-ly to increase as global warming raises ocean levels.

A green home is frugal in its use of water. Reduced water consumption not only helps stretch a limited resource, but it also reduces the burdens on sewage treatment plants or local aquifers when that water goes down the drain. By collecting rainwater off your roof and putting it to use in your garden or home, you further reduce water use. By designing your home's landscape to absorb and infiltrate rainwater, you reduce runoff and recharge aquifers. This chapter offers strategies for using water more responsibly and managing its movement through the landscape.

WATER CONSERVATION IN THE HOME

Conserving water in the home reduces burdens on fresh-water supplies and on wastewater treatment systems. Conserving hot water also reduces energy consumption, as water heating is typically the third largest use of energy in a home; in an energy-efficient home, water heating can actually be the number-one energy consumer.

The easiest way to conserve water in your home is to install only water-efficient plumbing fixtures and appliances. Federal regulations are helping to conserve water in the US; since 1994, federal standards have required that new toilets can use no more than 1.6 gallons per flush (gpf), far below the 3.5 to 7 gallons used by most older toilets. Showerheads and faucets can use no more than 2.5 gallons per minute. Consider these to be the minimum water conservation levels for plumbing fixtures; it's possible to do significantly better. Always check the water consumption ratings on these products; if you can't find that information, ask for it.

As you seek out plumbing fixtures that minimize water use, pay attention to performance. It has been widely reported that not all 1.6-gpf toilets work effectively; some of these toilets have problems with clogging or require flushing twice. The problem is that when the federal standards went into effect, some companies simply modified their standard toilets with water-saving flush mechanisms and retained bowls that weren't designed to function with less than 3 gallons per flush. Most toilets now

FIGURE 10.2 —*All new toilets, showerheads, and faucets have to meet federal water conservation standards in the U.S., but some new fixtures use significantly less than the federal limit.*

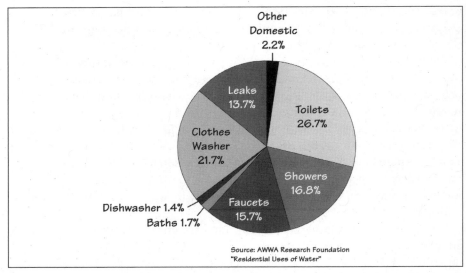

Other Domestic 2.2%

Leaks 13.7%

Toilets 26.7%

Clothes Washer 21.7%

Showers 16.8%

Dishwasher 1.4%

Faucets 15.7%

Baths 1.7%

Source: AWWA Research Foundation "Residential Uses of Water"

FIGURE 10.3—*This chart shows the average water uses in a new home; in an older home, a larger fraction of water use would be for toilet flushing.*

on the market incorporate totally redesigned bowls and flush mechanisms that are optimized to function with just 1.6 gallons per flush.

In the quest for water savings, some people want to go beyond conventional toilets. Some *gravity-flush* models work very well with as little as 1.28 gpf. Toilets with water consumption at least 20% less than the federal standard (1.28 gpf or less) are designated as *high-efficiency toilets (HETs)*. In this book's companion volume, *Green Building Products,* only HETs are included in the toilet category, and all must achieve excellent flush performance based on independent testing. A number of *pressure-assist* toilets are on the market that use as little as 1.0 gpf and provide highly satisfactory performance, although most pressure-assist toilets make a little more noise flushing. A new class of toilets called *dual-flush* models offer two different flush volumes: one for solid wastes and another, lower-volume flush for liquid wastes and paper. Dual-flush toilets have become the norm in Australia and parts of Europe, and are beginning to gain popularity in North America. For the ultimate in water savings, consider *composting toilets,* which don't use any water at all (see discussion under "Dealing with Wastewater" below).

In older homes, showers typically use the next largest amount of water, after toilets. New showerheads use significantly less water than older ones, but, as with toilets, some are far better than others. Many low-flow showerheads produce such a fine spray or weak flow that users find them unsatisfactory. The best models have sophisticated designs resulting in forceful showers that feel like 3 or 4 gallons per minute, while using as little as 1.5 gpm. Several of the particularly effective products on the market use a *Venturi design* that mixes air with the water, increasing the force of the water flow; others incorporate sophisticated engineering to optimize droplet size and spray pattern for highly satisfactory performance.

To conserve water at sinks, you can add simple screw-on aerators to faucets. Depending on the aerator installed, these can turn a standard faucet using 2.5 gpm (or more with an older model) into a highly conserving one using as little as 0.5 gpm. This half-gallon per minute is often adequate at a bathroom sink for brushing teeth, face washing, and shaving, but it won't be enough for a kitchen faucet that you're using to fill cooking pots. (Note also that with a 0.5-gpm bathroom faucet, your wait for hot water can be fairly long — see sidebar.)

In a kitchen, rather than reducing the flow rate of the faucet, it usually makes more sense to install a standard, 2.5-gpm faucet, so that pots can be filled quickly, but provide a means of conveniently turning the water off between uses, such as when washing or rinsing dishes. Foot and knee controls for kitchen faucets are a significant water-saving feature and a great convenience, allowing you to operate the faucet hands-free.

Along with choosing water-efficient toilets, showerheads, and faucets (and, if necessary, dealing with hot-water distribution), you can also select water-conserving clothes washers and dishwashers. New horizontal-axis (front-loading) clothes washers use just one-third to one-half as much water as the conventional vertical-axis (top-loading) machines. According to most studies, they also do a better job of getting clothes clean. If you must have a top-loader, at least choose a water-efficient model that meets the EPA ENERGY STAR standards.

Although dishwashers use a lot less water than clothes washers, their water consumption is still significant, and there are big differences in water consumption among available models. Because water consumption is fairly proportional to energy consumption, look for energy-efficient dishwashers that meet ENERGY STAR standards, or that have *Energy Factor* ratings of 0.60 or higher.

Check with your local utility company or state energy office to find out if rebates might be available for buying energy- and water-efficient dishwashers and clothes washers.

Dealing with the Wait for Hot Water

In the typical American home, up to 10,000 gallons of water per year are wasted waiting for hot water to reach the tap; in some homes, it's a lot more. How long it takes hot water to reach a bathroom or kitchen fixture depends on a) how far that point of use is from the water heater; b) how quickly the water is flowing through the hot-water pipes (the flow rate of the fixture drawing water); and c) the diameter of the hot-water pipes.

With large-diameter pipes (3/4-inch is now standard in much of the country), low-flow faucets and showerheads, and a sprawling house, the wait for hot water can easily be three minutes or longer. The waste can be even greater if a homeowner turns on the water and then leaves the room to do something else while waiting for hot water; if he or she gets distracted and hot water runs for a few minutes, significant quantities of both water and energy are wasted.

To solve the water waste problem, continuous-circulation systems are being installed in many homes. These systems, commonly used in hotels, circulate hot water around the building continuously, so that hot water is always a few seconds away; you don't waste water waiting for hot water to reach your sink or shower. The problem with this solution is that the hot-water pipes end up acting like round-the-clock radiators that waste water-heating energy year-round and contribute to a home's air conditioning load in the summer months.

Much better is an on-demand hot-water circulation system. At least two manufacturers produce a user-activated pump that very quickly brings hot water to the point-of-use and returns the cooled-off water that had been sitting in the hot-water pipes back to the water heater. The pump can be activated manually with a button or wired to an occupancy sensor to turn on automatically when someone enters the room; the pump turns off when hot water reaches a sensor at the point-of-use. These systems are very different from continuous-circulation systems in that the hot water is only brought to the bathroom or kitchen when needed; you have to wait a little longer, but no water is wasted. In new houses, a separate return line back to the water heater is installed; with existing houses, the cold water supply line is used as the return.

Another solution to the problem of wasting water while waiting for hot water is to install small-diameter tubing for the hot water lines. In some regions, these *home-run plumbing systems* have become quite popular; they use small-diameter cross-linked polyethylene (PEX) tubing, with each fixture being served by its own supply tubing that is sized to the fixture's flow rate, typically 3/8 or 1/2 inch, but larger for a bathtub. The individual tubes extend off a central manifold near the water heater. Much less water is wasted because less water is held in the tubing, and hot water reaches the point of use quickly.

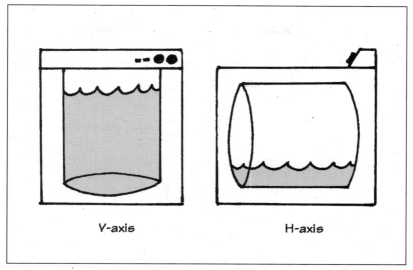

V-axis   H-axis

FIGURE 10.4 — *Front-loading (horizontal-axis) washers use significantly less water than conventional top-loading models.*

WATER CONSERVATION OUTDOORS

In many parts of North America, especially in the West, a typical home-owner uses more water outdoors than indoors. Unfortunately (but not surprisingly), the places where outside irrigation is most common are usually the places where water is in shortest supply. The new subdivisions in Las Vegas have lawns that are just as sparkling green as those in suburban Atlanta, even though the annual precipitation in Las Vegas is less than five inches per year. Even in regions with higher annual precipitation, drought can be a problem. And many experts on global climate change predict that droughts will become more and more common in parts of North America as the climate changes in the 21st century.

In arid and drought-prone regions it makes sense to design out-door landscapes that are appropriate to those climates and don't require irrigating. Xeriscaping — dry-adapted landscaping — not only requires less water, but also generally has lower maintenance requirements and saves money. In the American Southwest, xeriscaping may involve planting cactus and other plants that can exist for months with no rain and survive on just a few inches of rain per year. In the Plains states, xeriscaping might utilize native prairie plants that evolved very deep root systems to survive on limited rainfall (although more than ten

FIGURE 10.5—*Xeriscaping is the practice of water-efficient landscaping. Locally adapted native plants do not require irrigation and are tolerant of local drought conditions.*

inches per year typically) and intermittent drought. Environmentally responsible xeriscaping should include only locally adapted native plants, so as not to risk ecological problems caused by release of non-native, invasive species into local ecosystems.

By contrast, the Kentucky bluegrass lawns most of us are used to are both non-native and water-intensive. Most lawn grasses came from the British Isles, where they evolved on about 40 inches of rainfall per year. In regions that receive less than 40 inches per year, or that experience periodic droughts, these lawn grasses require irrigation.

While it makes good environmental sense to get away from lawns in favor of ecologically diverse plantings, there are some grasses that are drought-tolerant and native. Buffalo grass (*Buchloe dactyloides*) is gaining popularity in sunny locations throughout the drier Plains states, and native mixes of fescues can work very well in shadier and somewhat wetter locations. In addition to these grasses not requiring irrigation, they may not need mowing either; lawn mowers belch out huge amounts of air pollution, far more than most cars.

When shiny green lawn is simply a must-have or when vegetable or flower gardens are planned, irrigating may be unavoidable. In this case, make it water-efficient irrigation. A local home center will probably have the needed supplies, including timers, soil-moisture meters for controlling irrigation, and drip irrigation equipment. Be aware that studies in the southwestern US have shown that improperly installed or poorly "tuned" drip irrigation equipment does not achieve significant water savings. These systems are fairly sophisticated and must be properly installed and maintained. Other options for irrigating lawns and flower beds are to use collected rainwater or, where permitted by codes, to collect and use graywater from the house (see discussion of these options later in this chapter).

DEALING WITH WASTEWATER

Responsibly dealing with wastewater is one of the biggest challenges with a green home. Conventional wastewater systems generally are not environmentally responsible. Standard practice is to mix our nutrient-rich waste with clean potable water and flush it down the toilet, using 1.6 gallons for every flush (with an older toilet, often a lot more). After being flushed down the toilet, these highly diluted wastes flow through a network of sewer pipes to an energy-intensive sewage treatment plant, where action by aerobic bacteria metabolize some of the waste and separate the solids out as sludge. The sludge is hauled off to a landfill or for surface application to land somewhere, and the water is further treated with chemicals (especially chlorine) and then dumped into a nearby river, lake, or ocean.

FIGURE 10.6—*Drip irrigation puts the water only where it's needed and eliminates the evaporation that occurs with spray irrigation.*

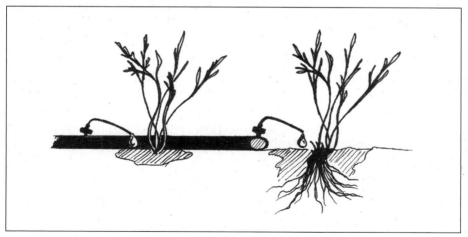

If the house is in a rural area and not hooked up to a municipal sewage treatment plant, the diluted wastes flow down to an on-site *septic tank* where bacteria go to work metabolizing some of the organic matter and settling out solids; then, the still-nutrient-laden water seeps into the ground through a *leach field* or drainage field.

A standard o*n-site wastewater system* is designed to kill potentially harmful bacteria, but it is not designed to remove nutrients. Even when properly designed and functioning, such a system will usually deliver unwanted nutrients (nitrates and phosphorus) into the groundwater. Not only can the excess nitrate levels cause health problems for those who drink well water, but the unwanted nutrients can result in excessive algae growth where springs feed surface waters. In many areas with on-site wastewater disposal, the groundwater now has unacceptably high levels of nitrate.

From an environmental standpoint, there are better alternatives. On the municipal scale, ecological wastewater treatment systems (often referred to as *Living Machines* or *Solar Aquatic*™ *systems*) are being used in a few places. In these systems, the wastewater flows through a series of tanks that support a balanced ecosystem of microorganisms, plants, and animals that purify the water. In some other locations, *constructed wetlands* are doing pretty much the same thing in a more naturalized, outdoor ecosystem.

But most homeowners do not have environmentally attractive municipal treatment options such as these. If your home will be on a municipal sewer system, there is usually little you can do to achieve greener wastewater treatment, other than reducing your wastewater volume by using less water. If you're in a rural area with an on-site wastewater system, you have several greening options, below.

Composting Toilets

According to many green building experts, the best solution for wastewater treatment is to not create it in the first place. Composting toilets don't mix potable water with human waste; instead, they use biological decomposition to convert human waste primarily into carbon dioxide and water vapor over time. Composting toilets destroy pathogens, dramatically reduce the volume of the solids, and produce nutrient-rich fertilizer that can be used on non-food plants. Most household-sized composting toilets produce just a few pails of composted humus annually, because the vast majority of the solid waste has been converted to carbon dioxide and water vapor and exhausted up the vent stack.

There are many different brands of composting toilets on the market. In general, the larger, more expensive composting toilets are more dependable and have higher user satisfaction in primary residences than smaller models, which are more appropriate for vacation cabins. The most recognized brand of composting toilet is the Clivus Multrum, which was developed in Sweden. This has a large sloping fiberglass tank in which the waste gradually slumps downhill. Some other brands use this same approach; some offer other features such as tines for mixing and aerating the waste to speed decomposition.

Be aware that a composting toilet can be quite expensive, especially if combined with a graywater system for handling wastewater from showers, sinks, clothes washer, and other wastewater sources in the house (see discussion below). Good composting toilets often cost $3,000 to $5,000; a graywater separation, storage, and in-ground disposal system can cost at least that much again. This might still be less expensive than an in-ground septic system if soil conditions on your property

FIGURE 10.7—*Composting toilets eliminate toilet flushing, dramatically reducing water use in a home, but they do require occasional removal of composted humus.*

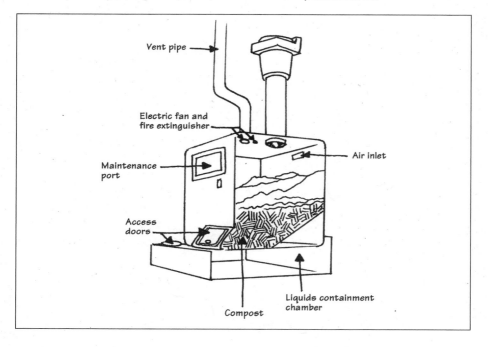

require an engineered raised mound system, which is often needed if the natural soil does not allow water to soak in (percolate) quickly enough. Further adding to the costs, in some areas, code officials or mortgage bankers may require that you install a full in-ground septic tank and disposal field even if you don't plan to use them because you're installing a composting toilet.

Recirculating Sand Filter

Another option for on-site wastewater treatment and disposal is a *recirculating sand filter*. This is a good option for sites that cannot support a conventional septic system due to shallow depth to groundwater, non-percolating soils, or other limitations. In this system, a septic tank is used as in a normal on-site wastewater system, and then the effluent from the septic tank passes into another tank filled with sand. The effluent filters through this tank, where both aerobic and anaerobic bacteria go to work on it. These bacteria remove nitrogen from the wastewater by converting it, through several steps, into atmospheric nitrogen (N_2) and releasing it into the air. A pump may be used to ensure more complete breakdown of the waste and removal of the nitrogen. Water coming out of the sand filter is usually pretty clean, and it is generally discharged into the ground through an absorption field.

Constructed Wetland

Yet another option for environmentally responsible wastewater treatment is to build an artificial, constructed wetland. While these systems are more typically quite large and designed for municipal sewage treatment, considerable success is being found in some parts of the country with small-scale constructed wetland systems designed for individual houses or to be shared by a few houses.

In a typical, subsurface-flow constructed wetland, the effluent from a septic tank flows through the root zone of wetland plants, and bacteria living in the soil around the plant roots break down the wastes and purify the water. Generally, a long shallow bed is created with an impermeable base and sides and a very slight pitch. This is filled with crushed stone, and wetland species are planted. The nutrient-rich effluent from the septic tank flows downhill through the crushed stone. The wastewater is always below the ground surface. As with a sand filter, the water emerging at the other end of the constructed wetland is highly purified and usually discharged into the ground.

GRAYWATER SEPARATION AND TREATMENT

Collecting and using graywater for below-ground irrigation can be a great idea, particularly in regions that are arid or prone to droughts. Graywater is usually used to mean wastewater generated from showers, bathroom sinks, and clothes washers — not including wastewater from toilets, kitchen sinks, or dishwashers. Sometimes, though, "graywater" refers to all the wastewater generated except that from toilets; for instance, in homes that have composting toilets, all the wastewater generated in the house is often considered graywater and treated in the same way.

To use graywater, you must collect it separately from the house's other wastewater. If conventional flush toilets are used, dual wastewater plumbing is needed. The graywater generally flows through a filter of some sort to a central surge tank, from which it flows or is pumped to a subsurface irrigation system. You don't want to hold the graywater for any length of time, because the organic matter in it will start to break down and, lacking oxygen, that decomposition will be anaerobic, and smelly. But holding the graywater briefly in the surge tank enables distribution to the irrigation system in surges, which spreads the water further than if it simply trickles out into the irrigation field as it is generated in the house.

Due to risk that graywater might be contaminated with coliform bacteria and pathogens, its use above ground or on vegetable gardens is generally not permitted by code. The state of California now has state-wide graywater regulations that its local municipalities can adopt; an appendix was added to the California Plumbing Code in 1994 so that homeowners could use graywater for irrigating lawns during times of drought. The regulations were inspired by extensive periods of drought

FIGURE 10.8 —*With a constructed wetland, organisms living in and around the root systems of wetland plants purify wastewater passing through.*

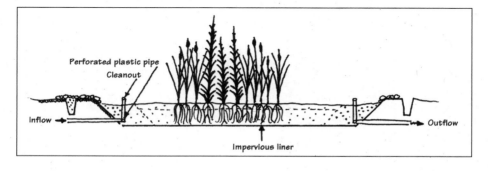

during the 1980s and '90s that resulted in many California municipalities banning irrigation of lawns, while millions of gallons of water that could be used for irrigation were going down the drain.

So if you're in California you're in luck. In most states, unfortunately, permitting a graywater system can be difficult and is often impossible. Even so, it might still make sense to put in dual wastewater plumbing, with a set of drain pipes for graywater that feeds back into the main waste line in a central location. Then if graywater separation becomes legal at some point, you can easily add a surge tank and distribution system.

If you put in a graywater system, you should carefully examine what you put down the drain. Some soaps and detergents are better for plants than others, and some intense cleaning agents can be very detrimental. Avoid *phosphates* in your detergent, for example, and never use intense caustics like chemical drain cleaners. Companies that supply graywater system equipment often sell, or at least recommend, appropriate household cleaning compounds. The publications on graywater listed in this book's accompanying web site also provide recommendations.

FIGURE 10.9—*Much of the wastewater generated in a home is safe enough to use outdoors for subsurface irrigation, but doing so requires collection, storage, and delivery of that water. Unfortunately, building codes prevent the use of graywater systems in most areas.*

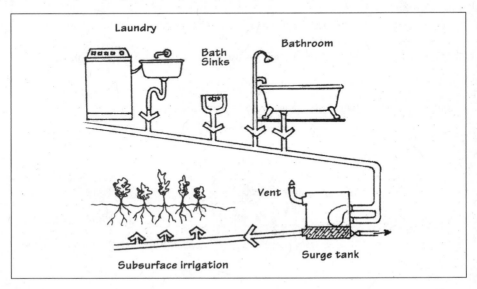

RAINWATER HARVESTING

Rainwater collected off roofs is another under-utilized source of water for landscape irrigation — and for other uses, including drinking water. Rainwater harvesting has been done for centuries. Pueblo Indians in the American Southwest depended on rainwater collected on their roofs and cliff dwellings. More recently, homeowners in the Appalachian Mountains have made extensive use of rainwater harvesting, and it remains commonplace on many island communities, including Hawaii, and St. John in the US Virgin Islands. Around Austin, Texas, where officials are trying to protect the threatened Edwards Aquifer and the endangered species it supports, developers are allowed to build houses at a higher density if rainwater harvesting is used instead of pumping water out of deep wells.

In addition to reducing pressures on water supply, rainwater harvesting reduces problems relating to stormwater runoff. Erosion and downstream flooding are reduced, since much of the rainfall in a storm event is collected and stored. Plus, rainwater is usually quite pure with very little of the hardness that plagues well water in many areas.

Harvesting and using rainwater can be as simple as putting a large barrel at the corner of your house beneath the downspout, then dipping into this with a bucket to water plants. At least a dozen manufacturers produce more sophisticated rain barrels that include covers to keep mosquitoes and sunlight out and hose fittings for using the water (see the companion book, *Green Building Products*).

If the rainwater will be used as a potable water supply, a much more sophisticated collection, storage, and treatment system is generally used. The components are:

- **Collection.** The roofing should be carefully selected to minimize risk that anything harmful will be leached from it and introduced to the water. In general, a factory-coated metal roof is best.

- **First flush.** Roofs collect dust, heavy metals, pollen, and other particulates. To keep these contaminants out of the collected rainwater, a system is often employed to get rid of the first rainwater coming off the roof during a rainstorm. This is usually a very simple pipe that fills up with the first runoff; once the pipe is full, additional rainwater flows into the storage tank. Simple screens should also be incorporated into the collection system to eliminate leaves and other large detritus.

FIGURE 10.10 —*A rain barrel situated beneath a downspout provides a very simple way to use rainwater for watering gardens.*

🏠 Storage. The storage tank or cistern should be large enough to carry the house through reasonably expected periods of drought. It must be covered to keep out sunlight (which would result in algae growth), insects, rodents, and children. Common materials for tanks include galvanized steel, concrete, ferrocement, fiberglass, polyethylene, and wood (typically cypress, redwood, or another durable species). Salvaged wooden wine storage vats, whiskey barrels, and even pickle barrels have been used very successfully as cisterns.

🏠 Treatment. For potable water use, most health experts recommend treatment of rainwater prior to use in order to eliminate bacteria and other biological contaminants. Options include fine filtration, ozonation, and UV light treatment. It may not be necessary to treat all the collected water to bring it up to potable standards; some people save money by carrying out the full treatment only on water that will be used for drinking and cooking (often the water going to the kitchen sink), while other water used in the house is not treated.

For rainwater harvesting to satisfy all of a family's needs, particularly in a more arid climate, the house must be as water-efficient as possible.

It might incorporate, for example, water-conserving plumbing fixtures and appliances, natural (non-irrigated) landscaping, and, for greatest savings, composting toilets.

MANAGING STORMWATER

In our increasingly urbanized landscapes, rainwater has less and less opportunity to filter into the ground to replenish our underground aquifers. Our rooftops, driveways, parking lots, and roadways are *impervious surfaces*. Instead of infiltrating the ground as happens in nature, much of our rainwater (or stormwater, as it is often called) is collected and transported through pipes (storm sewers) directly to rivers, streams, lakes, or other surface waters. By carrying away that stormwater, not only do we fail to replenish our underground aquifers, but we also often contribute to downstream flooding and erosion.

In creating a green home, do whatever you can to encourage stormwater infiltration on your site. The following checklist provides a few recommendations; some of these relate to development patterns, while others apply to individual houses and landscaping.

Stormwater Management Checklist

🏠 Cluster houses. By clustering houses in a development, the amount of pavement can be minimized.

🏠 Minimize driveway width and parking lot dimensions. The less impervious surface created, the less stormwater runoff will be generated.

🏠 Avoid directly connected impervious areas. For example, leave a gap between a driveway and sidewalk and fill it with crushed stone. If a lot of runoff is expected, you can dig a trench and fill it with large stones or rubble to store the runoff and allow it to soak slowly into the ground.

🏠 Avoid standard gutters and downspouts unless rooftop rainwater is being harvested for use. Instead, build gravel-filled *Dutch drains* at the base of the wall or use special louvered gutters to disperse the water outward away from the wall. Especially when eliminating gutters, be sure to provide adequate drainage along the foundation, dampproof the foundation wall, and slope the ground to allow surface water to flow away from the foundation.

🏠 Install porous pavement instead of a conventional asphalt driveway or concrete sidewalk. Porous mixes are available with both asphalt and concrete, and a wide range of *porous grid-pavers* are available.

FIGURE 10.11—*Porous pavement systems allow stormwater to soak into the ground and replenish aquifers instead of being collected in storm sewers and carried off-site.*

These surfaces allow stormwater to filter through the pavement instead of running off over the surface.

- Avoid curbs. Instead of installing a curb along your driveway, allow surface water to flow off into a vegetated *swale* where water can soak into the ground.
- Avoid steep slopes. In planning for your house, avoid creating steep slopes where runoff and erosion may be a problem.
- Avoid soil compaction. Compacting soil during construction can significantly reduce the ability of rainwater to infiltrate.
- Consider rainwater harvesting. See discussion above.

In the green building field, water is rarely given the attention it deserves. We don't pay a lot for potable water, and most of us don't think much about it. But conserving water in the home, limiting or optimizing irrigation water use outdoors, and responsibly managing the flow of rainwater during storms should be high priorities in creating a green home.

CHAPTER 11

Dealing with Construction Waste

B UILDING A GREEN HOME involves not only careful design of the house
— making it energy-efficient, resource-efficient, and healthy —
but also the process of building it. One of the issues to consider
when planning your green home is what to do with the construction waste
that will be generated. This chapter takes a look at strategies to minimize
and properly manage construction waste on the job site. Such strategies will enable you to haul less waste off to the landfill, which not only
helps the environment, but saves money as well. The 3 "R"s of waste
management — Reduce, Reuse, Recycle — apply very well to construction waste and will serve as the organizing principle for this chapter.

REDUCING JOB-SITE WASTE

Many of the strategies to reduce construction waste should be addressed
primarily during house design. Those strategies are covered elsewhere
in this book, but we offer a quick review of them below, followed by various other suggestions.

Design Strategies for Reducing Job-Site Waste

Minimize house size. In general, the smaller the house, the less waste
will be generated during construction. Minimizing house size also
reduces resource use for materials and energy use by the finished house.

FIGURE 11.1—*"Reduce, Reuse, and Recycle" should be the driver of a construction waste management plan.*

Design the house dimensions on 2-foot or 4-foot modules. If the length and width of house walls are standard dimensions, there will be far less cut-off waste of framing lumber, panel sheathing, drywall, and so forth. These materials will be used more efficiently, and less waste will be generated.

Design the house with standard ceiling heights. Wood and steel studs are sold in standard lengths, and panel products, such as drywall and sheathing, are sold in standard widths and lengths. If wall heights match these standard dimensions, there will be less waste, and construction may be more rapid as well, since less cutting is required.

Use resource-efficient construction details and building systems. Advanced framing, two-stud corners (with drywall clips), *engineered headers* above windows, and structural insulated panels are examples of construction details and building systems that can reduce the amount of material used in construction — and the amount of waste generated.

Buy Building Materials with Minimal Packaging

Packaging waste — cardboard, pressboard, paper, and plastic — can account for a very significant percentage of the total job-site waste generated when building a house. Look for products, or ask your contractor to look for products, that have minimal packaging, and try to buy from manufacturers that will take back the product packaging. Don't buy nails and drywall screws in plastic throwaway blister packs, for example, if they can be purchased in bulk. If minimally packaged materials aren't available at your building supply center, ask for them. Consider e-mailing manufacturers. Just a few people complaining about over-packaged materials can make a big difference.

Buy Building Materials Made from Recycled Waste

When you buy building materials made from recycled polyethylene or cardboard or newspaper, you're boosting demand for recycling. The greater the demand for recycled materials, the more successful municipal or private recycling programs will be, and the easier it will become to recycle waste. This cyclical system builds on itself. So, when you buy wall sheathing made out of recycled cardboard, you're indirectly making it easier to recycle cardboard on your job site. (See Chapter 8 for more on choosing recycled-content building materials.)

REUSING JOB-SITE WASTE

The second part of the "3 Rs" waste management mantra is to reuse materials that would otherwise be thrown away. When remodeling your house, consider what products can be salvaged for reuse. If you can't use the medicine cabinet that's being removed, donate it to a local nonprofit

FIGURE 11.2—*Buy building materials in bulk to minimize packaging waste.*

housing agency, or sell it at a tag sale, or just put it out by the street with a sign saying, "Free." (You'll be amazed at what people will take!)

During construction, keep a pile of shorter lumber cut-offs; they can be used for blocking or headers above windows. The same strategy may work for drywall, although if specialized drywall subcontractors

FIGURE 11.3—*Materials that can't be salvaged for reuse can sometimes be given away, saving you the expense of hauling them away.*

A Role for You on the Job Site — Managing the Construction Waste Plan

If a builder or general contractor will be building your house and you'd like to play a role, offer to manage the waste management plan. These tasks can be a hassle for builders; they may jump at the idea of you taking charge of the effort. Ask your builder how you could be most helpful, but here are some ideas:

To aid in reusing materials, you could collect and sort reusable materials after the construction crew has left at the end of each work day. Separate usable scraps of lumber by dimension (2x4, 2x6, etc.) and length, and organize piles so that the contractors can quickly find what they need. With materials that can't be reused, collect them into bins for recycling according to the waste management plan.

are brought in to hang the drywall, they may work so quickly that segregating usable scraps isn't practical.

RECYCLING JOB-SITE WASTE

Despite your best efforts, and the best efforts of your contractor, to produce less waste and reuse as much of it as possible, it is inevitable that construction waste will be generated in building a new house. This is where recycling comes in — the last of the "3 Rs."

A responsible builder should develop a *waste management plan* addressing the recycling of job-site waste. If he or she doesn't seem inclined to develop such a plan, offer to help. The waste management plan should identify types of job-site waste that are expected to be generated, where such materials can be recycled, and how to segregate (if needed) and store them on the site to facilitate easy recycling. Your local municipal waste management agency can be a big help in researching these options. Many such offices publish directories of places that accept recyclable materials.

In some areas, separation of construction waste isn't actually needed. Large construction companies may rely on waste disposal services, where the recyclable materials are separated at a central *materials*

FIGURE 11.4—*Sorting waste materials into different bins will make delivery of those materials to the recycling facility (or facilities) easier and also keep the job site tidier.*

Recycling Options

Material	Recycling Options
Lumber and plywood	Untreated, unpainted lumber scraps that can't be reused can be separated for use as kindling. If your contractor doesn't want to bother with short pieces of wood and plywood, your children might want to keep a pile for various projects—from tree houses to stables for the toy horses. (Be aware of nails and other hazards.) If your municipality has a chipper for yard waste, they may also accept clean scrap wood for chipping. Preservative-treated wood should not be recycled.
Clean sawdust	Sawdust from new, unpainted and untreated lumber can be com posted. Never add sawdust from preservative-treated wood.
Drywall	A few drywall manufacturers will take back clean drywall scraps for recycling into new drywall. Ask at your building supply yard if that's an option. Where this option exists, manufacturers back-haul drywall for recycling on the trucks used to deliver new drywall. In some other areas, clean, unpainted drywall is recycled by the municipality or area farms into a soil amendment—or this can be done right at the job site using a brush chipper.
Masonry	Broken chunks of concrete, masonry block, and brick can be used as drainage around a building or as clean fill under a driveway. For larger demolition projects, a local construction and demolition (C&D) waste facility may accept these materials for crushing and processing into clean fill.
Metals and appliances	Metal waste products (for example, rebar scraps, old radiators, old appliances, piping, and aluminum siding) are generally recyclable at municipal solid waste centers. Copper pipe and flashing scraps are readily recyclable; facilities may even pay for these materials.
Cardboard and paper packaging	Corrugated cardboard and most paper is readily recyclable at munici-pal facilities. Markets for recycled cardboard and paper are highly volatile. When prices are up, companies may pick up such materials for free; when prices are down, you may have to pay for pick-up.
Insulation materials	Most insulation materials are not recyclable today, but these mate-rials can often be put to use quite effectively. For example, extra fiberglass batt insulation can be used to insulate interior walls—providing sound control in the process. Polystyrene insulation is accepted for recycling in some areas.
Asphalt shingles	In some parts of the country, asphalt shingles removed during re-roofing (and new shingle cut-offs) are recycled into road-patch material. You will still have to pay to drop off shingles for recycling, but this should cost less than landfill disposal.

(continued)

Recycling Options *(continued)*

Material	Recycling Options
Plastic and vinyl	Plastic packaging and scrap vinyl (PVC) can be recycled in some areas. Plastic shrink-wrap and the plastic used to wrap fiberglass batts is generally polyethylene, which is one of the easiest types of plastic to recycle. Look for the recycling symbol designating the type of plastic on drywall buckets and other containers. Check with your local solid waste office to find out which materials are recyclable in your area.
Paints	Leftover paint can often be donated to local theater groups or low-income housing agencies. Some municipalities collect leftover latex paint for reprocessing into a low-cost primer.
Miscellaneous	Branches, stumps, and other waste from land clearing can often be taken to a municipal facility for chipping. Worn-out nickel-cadmium (NiCad) batteries used in power tools should be disposed of through a municipal facility, the place of purchase, or the manufacturer. (If landfilled or incinerated, NiCad batteries pose serious pollution risk.) Fluorescent lamps and older ballasts should also be dropped off at a municipal facility for safe disposal or recycling to avoid risk of pollution.

FIGURE 11.5

recovery facility (*MRF*). But in most situations, job-site separation of waste will make the most sense.

When taking recyclable materials to recycling facilities, try to combine trips so as to reduce fuel use and environmental impacts of driving. One large load is more efficient than several smaller loads.

Some examples of what can be done with common construction waste materials are shown in Figure 11.5.

PROPER DISPOSAL OF WASTES THAT CANNOT BE RECYCLED

Some scrap materials — such as wood treated with chemical preservatives, painted products, and some composite products made from more than one material — won't be accepted by any recycling facility. Be sure your contractor disposes of these materials properly. Construction waste should never be burned on-site because of the risk that plastics, treated wood scraps, paints, and other potentially hazardous materials may end up in the burn pile. Uncontrolled burning of waste in open piles or barrels results in significant release of air pollutants, including such toxins as dioxin.

FIGURE 11.6—*In some areas, with enough care, the waste generated from building a new house can be nearly eliminated.*

Clean, unpainted lumber scraps can be saved as kindling for use in wood stoves, fireplaces, or masonry heaters. The best disposal option for preservative-treated wood is landfilling. This is especially true with older CCA-treated wood (which is no longer used in most residential construction). Even though municipal incinerators fitted with state-of-the-art pollution-control equipment do a good job at controlling air emissions, the heavy metals in CCA-treated wood will end up in the incinerator ash, which will then have to be landfilled. These heavy metals are highly leachable from the ash and can pollute groundwater if the landfill liner fails.

Depending on how good a job you and your contractor do with the 3 "R"s of waste management — Reduce, Reuse, and Recycle — remarkably little waste may be left over for disposal. A builder in Seattle has succeeded in reducing the total waste from an average house he builds down to a single trash barrel. Not only does this make the builder feel proud for helping the environment, but it also saves hundreds of dollars that are normally spent disposing of the wastes produced in building a new house.

CHAPTER 12

Landscaping and Plantings

MANY OF THE LANDSCAPING DETAILS around a new home will already be determined by the time construction begins — exactly where the house is, how it relates to existing vegetation, how steep the slopes are around the house, and so forth. These issues were touched upon in Chapter 3, Where to Build. We have also addressed water use for landscaping in Chapter 10. In this chapter, we address how to protect your site during construction and some of the ways you can landscape and manage your site after the house is completed.

PROTECTION OF SOILS AND VEGETATION DURING SITE WORK

The process of building a house can be very damaging to the immediate environment. Typically, a large swath of land is cleared of all trees and shrubs, and the land is leveled. This makes the process of excavation easier, but you lose the potential for nearby trees to shade the house from summer sun, and topsoil that took hundreds of years to produce may be bulldozed under sterile subsoil. The land is prone to erosion, and the stripped soils are prone to revegetation by non-native, invasive plants.

There is a better way. By carefully controlling the house excavation and site work, it is possible not only to minimize damage to the

FIGURE 12.1—*Standard practice for home construction involves clearing and leveling the lot and later starting over with the ubiquitous lawn and shrubs that look the same whether in Portland, Maine, or Phoenix, Arizona. You can do better.*

immediate environment, but also to ensure that your property will be capable of supporting a rich, healthy natural ecosystem.

Pay special attention to trees: Saving trees is not only good for the environment; it's worth a lot of money! Studies show that a single large tree can add as much as $10,000 to the value of a new home, and planting new trees can easily run into thousands of dollars. Be aware, however, that construction activities may destabilize trees close to the house. You certainly don't want a tree to fall on your home, so it may be necessary to remove *some* nearby trees.

If there are existing shade trees on the east, west, or south sides of the site, protect them, as they can help lower air conditioning bills by shading the house from the summer sun. On the west and north (where the prevailing winter winds typically come from), trees can help maintain a buffer to shield your house from winds, helping keep energy bills down.

The checklist below will help you and your contractors protect trees and topsoil on your site during construction.

LANDSCAPING FOR ENERGY CONSERVATION

How you landscape around a house can affect energy use in a number of ways. Shading is generally the most important consideration, since solar heat gain through windows is usually the largest contributor to unwanted

Checklist

Strategy	Discussion
Inventory the site	Before beginning site work for a house, survey what's on the site (trees, shrubs, wetland areas, etc.) and decide how to protect it. If possible, hire an arborist or landscape designer to help determine which trees to protect. If clearing a large area but saving only a few trees, choosing which trees to keep is especially important—the biggest, tallest trees may not be the ones that will be most likely to survive the thinning. In deciding which trees to keep and which to cut, be sure to consider solar access and shading (see Chapter 3).
Site buildings, driveway, utilities, and septic to minimize site impacts	In determining the exact location of your house, outbuildings, driveway, buried utility lines, and (if relevant) on-site wastewater system, keep away from trees you want to save. Trenching, paving, and even soil compaction can all kill trees. A good rule-of-thumb is to avoid any impact to the area under the drip line of trees you want to save (the area beneath the trees' outermost branches). Fence off this area to keep vehicles, equipment, building materials, and people from compacting the ground.
Select excavation contractor carefully	Make it clear to your builder that protection of the site is a high priority and that an excavation contractor should be hired who is willing to go out of his or her way to minimize the impact area. Consider an incentive clause in the excavator's contract that rewards protection of existing trees.
Minimize grade changes	Try to minimize changes to the grade on a site—grade changes will damage the soil and trees whose roots occupy the upper layers of that soil. If grade must be altered, use terracing, retaining walls, and large tree wells to maintain existing grade around important trees (out to the drip line).
Leave the soil around a house as undisturbed as possible	Minimize grading and stump removal to avoid damage to trees being retained and to the soil ecosystem.
Save topsoil from areas to be excavated	Where excavation will occur for the house or driveway, have the topsoil scraped off and stockpiled. Limit topsoil removal to only those areas where absolutely necessary. Topsoil should be stockpiled in a flat area away from trees (so as not to suffocate tree roots). Cover the topsoil with erosion-control matting or seed it with grass to prevent erosion. If you are planning to landscape with native plants, be careful about what to seed the topsoil with; turf grasses may be difficult to get rid of!
Control erosion	Use natural or biodegradable, erosion-control matting (geotextiles) on steep sites where excavation or grading is done.
Reduce shock to trees	When clearing a house site from a heavily wooded area, the trees being kept may experience stress from sunlight exposure and drying. Consult an arborist for recommendations on how to minimize injury and increase chances of survival.

FIGURE 12.2

FIGURE 12.3—*The key to providing a healthy landscape around your house is to protect what's already there during construction.*

heat in houses, either increasing discomfort or raising air conditioning bills. This unwanted solar heat gain is generally greatest on the west side of a house, followed by the east. Deciduous trees, tall annuals, and vines on trellises are all effective vegetation for shading, because they don't block as much sunlight in the winter, when light and solar heat are desirable.

In houses relying on passive solar heating to a significant extent, it's best to avoid trees altogether on the south side — even deciduous trees, whose trunks and branches still block as much as 50% of the light after the leaves are gone. If you plant trees on the south, choose deciduous trees that will grow tall with few lower branches. If the branches are mostly above the roof plane, there will be relatively little wintertime shading, yet the house will be shaded from the summer sun, which rises high overhead.

In warm climates, the need for air conditioning can also sometimes be reduced by channeling summer breezes through a house. To aid in this, it may be possible to plant hedgerows that funnel breezes from the west, the direction the prevailing winds are from in most of North America.

In cold climates, you may be able to achieve some energy savings by planting evergreens and densely growing shrubs on the north and west to *block* winds. As we've learned to build houses that are more airtight, though, this benefit is not as great as it was in our grandparents' day, when shielding from cold winter winds was a very important design priority.

LANDSCAPING FOR BIODIVERSITY

As our countryside becomes ever more developed and as ecosystems become ever more degraded, providing diverse ecosystems and wildlife habitat in our backyards becomes more and more important. In many cities and suburbs today, small patches of native ecosystem provide vital habitat for songbirds, butterflies, and wildflowers. If carefully planned, our backyards can serve this function. Even more importantly, if we string together patches of native habitat, we can provide corridors through which wildlife can pass to help maintain biodiversity.

Lawns

The first priority in boosting your backyard biodiversity is to consider alternatives to conventional lawns. Conventional lawns are biologically barren monocultures of grass species native to Europe (usually "Kentucky" bluegrass, even though the origin of this grass has nothing to do with the state of Kentucky).

Conventional lawns carry several other significant environmental burdens. They require heavy fertilizer applications; they may be treated with herbicides to get rid of broad-leaved plants such as dandelions, or with pesticides to eliminate insects; and they often require watering.

FIGURE 12.4—*Even though deciduous trees lose their leaves in the winter, the branches still block a lot of sunlight. On the south side of a passive solar house, the better option is to maintain a clearing.*

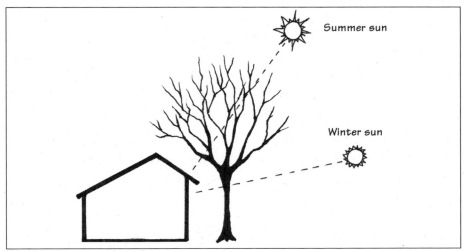

FIGURE 12.5—*Well-planned landscaping can help to funnel summer breezes toward the house — allowing you to get by more of the time without air conditioning.*

They also require frequent mowing, and typical gasoline mowers generate large amounts of air pollution. Lawn mowers have not been regulated until recently, and using an older two-cycle mower (the kind that runs on a mixture of gasoline and oil) for a couple of hours can produce as much non-carbon-dioxide air pollution as driving a modern car halfway across the country. For a green home, it makes sense to minimize lawn area.

If a lawn is a must, try to restrict the size of the lawn, and/or plant native grasses. Buffalo grass is a good choice for dry, sunny areas; it is drought-tolerant, and will only grow about six inches tall if left unmowed. For wetter regions and shady areas, native fescues can be planted. Buffalo grass and native fescues are available from specialty suppliers of native plants.

In place of a conventional lawn, consider planting regionally appropriate, native vegetation. For relatively open, sunny areas, especially in drier regions, prairie vegetation can be established. Tall-grass prairies are native to most of the US Midwest and as far east as Ohio; short-grass prairies are native to drier areas further west. In cooler, shadier areas, native fescues, ferns, mosses, and wildflowers can be established.

Establishing a Prairie

Establishing a prairie may involve removing the non-native grasses, a labor-intensive process of hand-digging the sod. Selective use of herbicides can help in the removal of non-native vegetation, although herbicide use is best kept to a minimum. Prairie plants can be established by broadcast seeding of regionally appropriate prairie seed mixes (available from native plant nurseries or mail-order suppliers) or by planting seedling plugs. Often a mix of broadcast seeding and individual plant-ings makes the most sense. It will take several years for a prairie to become established, during which time some weeding of invasive plants (dandelions, thistles, etc.) is needed.

Once established, prairie plantings do not require fertilizers, watering, herbicide applications, or frequent mowing. To keep shrubs and trees from gradually taking over, however, annual mowing or burning may be required.

Annual controlled burning is the best way to maintain an area of prairie, even though it is potentially dangerous. Prior to European set-tlement in North America, periodic fires kept millions of square miles of land open prairie. Fires were started either by lightning or Native Americans. Burning will kill many non-native invasive species, while not harming — and actually benefiting — prairie-adapted plants. Controlled burns do generate air pollution, but if burns are done in the late summer or fall, when the vegetation is dry, these fires burn hot and fast, creating relatively little air pollution. Before carrying out any con-trolled burn, check with your local municipality to find out about burning restrictions and permits.

FIGURE 12.6—*Providing a patch of naturalized tall-grass prairie in place of lawn can support wildlife while cutting down on the costs and environmental burdens of lawn maintenance.*

FIGURE 12.7—*For large properties, controlled burns of natural landscapes can be an impor-tant strategy to maintain healthy ecosystems. Great care is needed in carrying out these burns, however.*

Woodland Plantings

Woodlands provide an alternative to lawns in much of North America, particularly the eastern third of the country and the West Coast. There are so many beautiful native trees and shrubs to choose from that exot-ic species usually aren't needed.

In selecting trees and shrubs, consider those that provide food and shelter for songbirds and other wildlife (although near your front and back doors, you should avoid plantings that will drop berries or other fruit that could be tracked into the house). By planting vegetation that supports wildlife, you will be rewarded not only by the plantings them-selves, but also by the wildlife that will be attracted. From an ecological standpoint, these pockets of wildlife forage are very important, especial-ly in our more built-up areas. There are many excellent books on native landscaping and plantings for birds and other wildlife; the companion web site to this book lists a few.

If there are already woodlands around your house site, they may be degraded. If possible, have a landscape designer or arborist with knowl-edge of native plantings walk your land with you. Look into how you can restore these areas to the healthier, more diverse ecosystems that once existed there. This may involve removing invasive vines and shrubs, opening up some areas (e.g. cutting down trees to provide clearings), and planting of native vegetation.

Native trees, shrubs, and wildflowers can be found in nurseries specializing in native plants. When buying these plants, make sure that they were not dug from the wild; some areas (even National Parks) are being denuded of rare wildflowers by irresponsible nurseries. Ask the nursery to provide proof that the plants you are considering were nursery-propagated and not taken from the wild. If the nursery is unable or unwilling to do this, take your business elsewhere.

The only exception to the rule of not digging plants from the wild is the practice of salvaging native plants from areas being developed. You can certainly dig up wildflowers, shrubs, and young trees from areas of your own property that will be excavated for the house or cleared for a driveway. You may also find salvage opportunities in nearby developments or road construction projects. Always ask permission before digging in such areas, but you are likely to find little resistance if you explain your interests. A few native plant nurseries even specialize in salvage.

WATER-CONSERVING LANDSCAPING

A green home should use water very efficiently, both inside and out. In drier parts of the country, in areas where droughts are common, and

FIGURE 12.8—*In cooler, cloudier regions, such as the US Northeast and Northwest, a naturalized woodland with wildflowers and woodland paths can provide a great landscape.*

in municipalities where water supply is limited, water-conserving land-scaping is particularly important (see Chapter 10).

EDIBLE LANDSCAPING

As you think about various landscaping strategies around your house, consider how you might use your landscape for food production. Most of our fruits and vegetables are produced hundreds, or even thousands, of miles from where we live. They are grown using huge quantities of fertilizers and pesticides, then shipped across the country by truck. Or even worse, they are grown in other countries (often developing countries with few safeguards on pesticide use), and then flown to our markets. Any food we can grow ourselves, especially if we grow it organically, will help to reduce the environmental impacts of our food industry.

In designing the landscape around your home, try to provide space for a home vegetable garden. In choosing trees and shrubs, consider those that will produce food for your family. Permanent plantings for food production are aspects of a practice known as *permaculture*. Ask at local nurseries about appropriate plantings. Depending on where you live,

FIGURE 12.9 —*While digging plants from the wild is generally taboo, the exception is when land is to be cleared for development or a road; ask the owner if you can salvage wild plants before the clearing occurs.*

FIGURE 12.10—*By dedicating part of your landscape to vegetable gardens and fruit trees, you can reduce your dependency on produce being trucked in from far away, and you can control which chemicals are used on the crops.*

consider apple, peach, plum, cherry, citrus, avocado, raspberry, blueberry, kiwi, and a wide range of nuts (walnut, chestnut, pecan, filbert, etc.). While some of these are not native plants, most will not become invasive (taking over natural vegetation), and their benefits in food production justify their use.

The landscape around your house is the first thing visitors will see; it's also what will greet you when you arrive home from work or look out your window on a Saturday morning. The perfect complement to a green home is a landscape that supports the region's natural biodiversity, that requires little, if any, irrigation or fertilizing, that requires a minimum of mowing, that keeps rainwater on the site and able to soak into the ground, that helps reduce energy use in your home, and that even provides for some locally grown fruits and vegetables. All this can be achieved with a little planning and care. And once established, an environmentally responsible landscape should cost less to maintain than a conventional landscape of lawn and shrubs.

CHAPTER 13

Costs of Building Green

HERE IS A COMMON PERCEPTION that building a green home costs a lot more than building a conventional home. It is true that many green features and products are more costly — from photovoltaic panels for electricity to natural-fiber area rugs and FSC-certified hardwood cabinets. Indeed, most of the widely publicized green homes built over the past decade have been quite expensive, high-end homes.

But a green home need not cost any more than a conventional home. There are many green building strategies that cost no more than standard construction and some that actually reduce building costs. And if your designer carries out careful integration during the design of your home, some of the more expensive green features can often be paid for through savings elsewhere.

This chapter reviews strategies for building green at little or no additional cost, then takes a look at the concept of *life-cycle cost*— which explains why it often makes sense to invest more upfront in building a house in order to reduce the costs of operating it. We'll also take a look at some innovative ways of paying for a green home.

CONTROLLING CONSTRUCTION COSTS

As noted above, many green building strategies increase construction costs, but by no means do all green building strategies increase costs. The

Strategy Explanation

Strategy	Discussion	Background
Build a smaller house	An obvious way to reduce construction cost is to build smaller. By downsizing from 3,000 to 2,000 square feet, you could spend a third-again as much money per square foot on better materials and higher quality construction and still save money. Along with costing less to build, a more compact house will carry lower environmental burdens in its construction and cost less to operate.	Chapter 4
Build close to utilities	By building a house close to existing infrastructure (roads, electric utilities, sewer, and water), significant savings in construction costs can be realized: less asphalt for pavement, fewer utility poles, shorter runs of buried utilities, and so forth. Eliminating one utility pole can save several thousand dollars, and each foot of reduced length of buried water and sewer line can save $30 or more.	Chapter 3
Orient house to benefit from solar energy	This strategy won't *reduce* construction costs, but it shouldn't significantly *increase* cost either. By shifting the orientation so that more of the windows face south (even without a full-blown passive solar design), you'll benefit from *suntempering* — potentially reducing your heating costs by up to 10 percent and cutting air conditioning costs even more.	Chapter 7
Optimize building dimensions	Material waste can be reduced by keeping the overall building dimensions in multiples of two or four feet and using standard ceiling heights. You'll save money both in the purchase of materials and in the disposal of waste.	Chapters 8 and 11
Use advanced framing	Advanced framing optimizes lumber use — for example, studs 24 inches on-center, two-stud corners, a single top plate, and rafters or roof trusses aligned with wall studs. These techniques can reduce wood use by as much as 25% and reduce costs by up to $0.29 per square foot of wall area, according to Built Green, a green building rating program in Washington State.	Chapters 5 and 8
Use integrated energy design	By spending more money on the building envelope (more insulation, better windows, etc.), it's often possible to spend a lot less on heating and cooling equipment. This is *integrated design*, where the mechanical system design is directly informed by the building envelope design, and vice versa. For example, with an extremely well-insulated envelope, it may be possible to eliminate a distributed heating system, getting by with just one or two through-the-wall-vented gas space heaters — saving nearly as much money as you spent on the better envelope. And you'll save money (and reduce pollution) year after year through lower energy use.	Chapter 6

(continued)

Strategy Explanation (continued)

Strategy	Discussion	Background
Reduce waste during construction	When we can reduce waste during construction, we save money through reduced disposal cost. Until the 1990s, the cost of disposal was rarely considered, but in many parts of North America, it has become a significant expense associated with building — 1 to 2% of construction costs in some places.	Chapter 11
Protect trees	Trees cost a lot to plant and maintain while they get established. By protecting existing trees on a construction site — which necessitates maintaining the existing grade as much as possible and avoiding soil compaction — you can save a great deal when it comes to landscaping. Plus, large established trees add considerable value to a home, which can be a benefit with appraisal for refinancing or eventual resale.	Chapter 12
Use native landscaping	It often (though not always) costs less to establish native, regionally adapted vegetation than it does to establish a large lawn, which often requires a buried irrigation system. Maintaining a natural landscape is nearly always less expensive — and better for the environment — than maintaining lawn.	Chapter 12
Use salvaged building materials	With a tight budget, buying salvaged building materials from a local salvage yard can make your dollars go further — although you will have to spend more of your time. Examples of salvaged materials you can use include lumber, slate or granite countertops, sinks, brick, hardwood flooring, and period millwork.	Chapter 8

FIGURE 13.1

checklist above reviews a few examples in which green building strategies cost no more, or even *reduce* construction costs. This is not a comprehensive list, but serves to illustrate just how broad these possibilities are.

CONSTRUCTION COSTS VS. OPERATING COSTS

While you don't *have* to spend more money to build green, it often makes good economic sense to do so. Investments in energy efficiency, renewable energy systems, and highly durable or low-maintenance materials will pay for themselves over time through reduced *operating costs* and avoided replacement costs. Some of these investments can be offset from the start with savings elsewhere, but many such investments do increase construction costs.

FIGURE 13.2—*Protecting large trees on a building site can save a lot of money on landscaping, and mature trees will significantly boost the value of a new house.*

The process of examining the cost or savings of something over time is referred to as *life-cycle cost* analysis. You can think of it as the cost of ownership. The idea is illustrated in Figure 13.3, which compares various water heater options. For each of the water heaters, the *first cost* (installed cost), annual energy cost, and expected life of the equipment are given. With this information, the total costs of providing hot water using each water heating system can be compared over a certain period of time — in this case, 13 years, the expected lifetime of most of the equipment. A more sophisticated analysis would factor in the discount rate and inflation, but this simple approach gets the idea across.

As you can see from the table, the least expensive water heater to buy, an electric storage-type unit, actually costs the most over 13 years. The least expensive options over 13 years are demand gas and an indirect-fired water heater that operates off a boiler used for space heating. Solar water heating may do even better, depending on the type of backup heating used.

Another very good example of life-cycle cost analysis is to compare a conventional electric light bulb with a compact fluorescent lamp (CFL) that has comparable light output. From a first-cost standpoint, the incandescent light bulb is a much better deal: about 75¢ vs. $7 for the CFL. But because the incandescent light bulb only lasts 750 to 1000 hours and uses three times as much electricity, the CFL is a better deal from a life-cycle cost standpoint (see Figure 13.4).

Another way to express life-cycle cost savings is through the *payback period*. This is the number of years (months in some cases) that it will take for energy savings to pay back the added cost of the more energy-efficient device or the cost of replacing a standard product with a more efficient product. As you can see from the table, for a light that is on 5 hours per day, the payback for putting in a CFL instead of an incandescent lamp is less than one year; in other words, the one-year life-cycle cost of the 75-watt incandescent lamp is greater than the one-year life-cycle cost of the 23-watt CFL.

As you can see, it often makes good economic sense to invest more upfront in equipment or products that will save money over time. The same argument can be applied to products that last longer or require less maintenance, although the economic benefits are often harder to measure.

FIGURE 13.3

Life-cycle Costs of Various Water Heaters

Water Heater Type	Annual Efficiency	Approx. Installed Cost[1]	Annual Energy Cost[2]	Expected Life (Years)	Cost Over 13 Years[3]
Conventional gas storage	57%	$380	$271	13	$3,903
High-efficiency gas storage	65%	$525	$237	13	$3,606
Conventional electric storage	90%	$350	$410	13	$5,680
High-effic electric storage	95%	$440	$380	13	$5,380
Demand gas	70%	$650	$242	20	$3,796
High-effic demand gas (no pilot)	84%	$1,200	$136	20	$2,968
Electric heat pump	220%	$1,200	$140	13	$3,220
Indirect water heater with gas- or oil-fired boiler	79%	$600	$151	30	$2,563

Notes:
1. *Average costs—considerable variation is possible.*
2. *Assumes average hot water use by a family of four; energy costs as follows: electricity 10¢/kWh; natural gas $1.04/therm (2004 U.S. average).*
3. *Future operation costs are neither discounted nor adjusted for inflation.*

Source: Consumer Guide to Home Energy Savings, 8th Edition *(2003), American Council for an Energy Efficient Economy; data adjusted with more recent energy costs.*

Life-Cycle Costs of Incandescent and Compact Fluorescent Lamps

					Life-cycle cost[2]		
Light Source	Purch. Cost	Lamp life (hours)	Hours on per day	Annual energy cost[1]	1 Year	3 Yrs.	5 Yrs.
75-watt incandescent	$.75	750	2	$5.48	$6	$19	$31
			5	$13.69	$16	$47	$78
			10	$27.38	$31	$93	$156
23-watt CFL	$7.00	10,000	2	$1.68	$9	$12	$15
			5	$4.20	$11	$20	$28
			10	$8.40	$15	$39	$56

Notes:
1. Assumes electricity cost of 10¢/kWh.
2. Includes lamp replacement based on rated life; values neither discounted nor adjusted for inflation.

FIGURE 13.4

THE COST OF GOOD DESIGN

The one area in which a green home almost always costs more than a conventional home is the design work. It takes more time to design a compact, energy-efficient home that sits lightly on the land. Integrated energy design takes time and skill and often involves sophisticated computer modeling. You should expect to pay for that additional design time.

Indirectly at least, you should also expect to pay a little more for the education required of a green designer or builder. To keep up to date on green building materials and practices, that building professional has to buy books, read key periodicals, attend conferences or workshops, and perhaps spend time surfing the Web. The knowledge acquired through such efforts will enable the builder or designer to do a better job with your green home. But because of that investment of time, his or her hourly rates may be a little higher than the competition's. That's all right. You are likely to get a lot more in the long run. Avoid the temptation simply to go with the low bid when it comes to having your house designed and built.

PAYING FOR A GREEN HOME

While a green home should be pretty much like a conventional home when it comes to paying for it, there are a few differences that can make the financing process more difficult. There can also be some benefits when it comes to financing.

On the downside, lenders may not be familiar with some aspects of a green home. If you've been able to eliminate a central heating system or air conditioning system through top-notch integrated energy design, your lender may not be comfortable providing the mortgage — because all the other homes in your area have both central heating and air conditioning. If you've used an innovative construction system for your home, especially an oddball material like strawbale, your lender may not be able to find any comparable houses in the area to base an appraisal on — and appraisals are a key part of obtaining a mortgage.

To make the mortgage process go as smoothly as possible, offer to explain the features of your house design to the banker. Show him or her the computer modeling results that demonstrate energy savings and passive solar heating. If you want to build with something like strawbale or rammed-earth construction, provide some articles that explain how these systems work, and find some examples in your area, if possible. Be willing to educate lenders, and don't get defensive if they are at first negative about the idea. Remember, you are not only seeking your own mortgage, but you are also paving the way for others in

FIGURE 13.5—*Good design comes at a price. Plan to spend more upfront to get a top-quality, energy-efficient, green home.*

FIGURE 13.6—*Mortgage lenders may not be familiar with new building systems or characteristics of green homes; plan to spend some time educating them before they approve your loan.*

the future who will be going through the same process. If you do a really good job, then with the next customer, the banker may actually be the one suggesting some of the green building elements that can be used.

On the positive side, more and more lenders are beginning to offer something called an *energy-efficient mortgage* (*EEM*) that may make you eligible for a larger mortgage. Here's the idea behind an EEM: If you live in an energy-efficient house, you will spend less money each month for energy; as a result, you can afford to spend more on the mortgage payment. Lending institutions that provide EEMs will factor the expected savings in operating costs into their analysis of how much debt you can carry, and they will let you carry a larger debt-to-earnings ratio with your mortgage.

If, based on your household income, you would be eligible to buy a conventional house worth $140,000, a lending institution that offers EEMs might let you spend $150,000 on the house. Even though your mortgage payments will be higher, your total monthly bills will be lower (due to the energy savings) than if you paid $140,000 for a home without the efficiency upgrades. So you get a better house *and* more money in your pocket (if the reduction in monthly energy expenses is greater than the increase in the mortgage payments). Some EEM providers also offer slightly reduced interest rates or reduce some upfront costs of closing the loan.

Fannie Mae, the largest lending company in the US, recognizes EEMs and is working on other innovative lending programs for green homes. The company is piloting *green mortgages* that consider not only energy efficiency, but also water and transportation cost savings, in their EEM calculation. Homes with lower water bills due to xeriscaping and horizontal-axis clothes washers, for example, will have lower operating costs, so the buyers could qualify for higher mortgage payments. Homes located close to public transportation allow households to get by with fewer vehicles, reducing living expenses significantly. These sorts of benefits can be built into green mortgages, allowing you to buy a more expensive — but higher value — green home.

BENEFITING WHEN YOU SELL A GREEN HOME

Experience is showing that energy-efficient green homes appreciate in value faster than conventional homes. The landmark Village Homes community in Davis, California, completed in 1982, consists of 240 houses laid out in small clusters on 60 acres, with protected farmland and access to a network of bicycle pathways. Houses here have increased in value far faster than those in neighboring, conventional subdivisions. Fifteen years after completion, these homes were selling at $10 to $25 per square foot more than standard homes in the area.

The same experience has been found with the more recently built EcoVillage at Ithaca cohousing community in Upstate New York, located on 176 acres with 90% of the land protected as wildlife habitat and organic farmland. There is a waiting list for any of the 60 homes that might come onto the market, and there is strong demand for building a third neighborhood. Those that bought into this cohousing community made an excellent investment.

With energy prices rising dramatically during the first decade of the 21st century, the home value differential between green homes and conventional homes is likely to grow. Any home that costs one-half or one-quarter as much to heat and cool as others in the area will be a hot item in the real estate market if natural gas and heating oil prices continue to rise. Building an energy-efficient green home is a very good investment.

Construction cost is something you will most likely be thinking about throughout the planning, design, and construction of your new home — starting at the very earliest stages. While green homes have a reputation for being more expensive than standard homes, that certainly doesn't have to be the case. As you have seen in this chapter, there are many opportunities to achieve green features at little or no additional cost — some, in fact, that can actually reduce costs. In thinking about costs, however, keep in mind that the cost of building your home is only one part of what you will spend on it over the years or decades you live there; operating costs are also an important consideration. One of the greatest features of a green home will be its low operating costs — due to energy-conserving design, solar heating, water-conserving plumbing fixtures, and whatever other features you've managed to incorporate into your home. Saving money is one of the many features your green home will provide.

CHAPTER 14

Living in Your
Green Home

HE ENVIRONMENTAL IMPACTS of houses don't stop when the final coat
of paint goes on or when the owners move in. In fact, even though
there are significant impacts associated with the building materials, site work, and construction of your house, most of a home's
environmental burden occurs *after* you've moved in.

As you have learned throughout this book, you can minimize a lot
of the operating impacts of a home through diligent efforts during
design and construction — an energy-efficient building envelope, water-
efficient fixtures, cabinets that don't offgas VOCs, and so forth. But how
a house is *operated* will still be a major determinant of how green it is.
That's the subject of this chapter.

UNDERSTANDING HOW YOUR HOUSE
WORKS — THE HOMEOWNER'S MANUAL

An increasing number of progressive homebuilders provide homeowners with some sort of owner's manual. This is an excellent idea; if your
builder does not normally provide such a manual, ask for one. The manual should include the owner's manuals for the various pieces of
equipment in the house, all in one convenient binder for safekeeping.
It should list key subcontractors who worked on the house (plumber,
electrician, etc.) and how to reach them. It should explain how your

195

FIGURE 14.1—*Ask for a homeowner's manual for your new house; this is where appliance owner's manuals, as well as special instructions for maintenance and upkeep of the house, should be kept.*

house works, especially if the house includes such features as passive solar heating or natural ventilation.

Some builders include a set of construction photos that can be referred to down the road if changes are being made to the house. Photos of walls before insulating and drywalling, for example, will show the location of wiring; this can prove useful if you later need to modify the wiring, or cut into a wall for some reason. By showing the location of framing, these photos will help you figure out how to hang new cabinets. By showing plumbing runs, they can help you or a plumber track down and fix a leak. You'll be surprised at how invaluable these photos will be.

Like an automobile manual, a homeowner's manual should suggest how frequently maintenance of various systems and components should be done. Approximate maintenance schedules might be included for exterior painting, pointing of brick chimneys or siding, tune-ups of heating and air conditioning equipment, chimney cleaning, and so forth. Maintenance is discussed in greater detail later in this chapter.

ENERGY EFFICIENCY

If you've followed the advice in this book, your home will be designed and built to minimize the use of energy. To function as efficiently as it was designed and built to, however, your house and the various pieces of equipment in it have to be operated properly. Ideally, your homeowner's manual will explain such maintenance and adjustment. If not, ask your builder what's needed and take careful notes. Examples of the sort of maintenance that may be required include seasonal adjustment of special overhangs for solar shading, cleaning of glass on solar collectors and passive solar glazing, installation of storm windows or storm panels if the windows are so configured, replacement of filters in the furnace or air conditioner, and tune-up of mechanical equipment by service technicians.

To keep your energy use low, whenever you are buying or replacing a piece of equipment, look for energy-efficient products. This applies not only to furnaces, air conditioners, and refrigerators, but also to more common purchases like light bulbs. When light bulbs burn out, buy compact fluorescent lamp (CFL) replacements. Replacing a single incandescent bulb with a CFL will save the equivalent of 1,000 pounds of coal through energy savings over the CFL's life. Energy-saving products can be found in this book's companion volume, *Green Building Products,* and other information resources are listed in this book's companion web site at <www.BuildingGreen.com/YourGreenHome>.

FIGURE 14.2—*Keeping energy consumption as low as possible may necessitate some regular maintenance.*

The same arguments for energy efficiency and green design also apply to any remodeling projects or additions that you may decide on down the road. Make sure top-quality energy-conserving details are used. If you're replacing windows or adding new ones, make sure that they have energy-conserving glazing that is appropriate for your climate and the windows' orientations.

How you operate your house will also have a huge impact on its energy use. With two identical houses, it is not unusual for one house to use twice as much energy as the other one, based on different lifestyles, different comfort thresholds, and different living habits. Examples of a few energy-saving strategies that relate specifically to a home's operation are listed in Figure 14.4.

This list is by no means comprehensive, but it offers some strategies for more efficient operation of your house. You can no doubt come up with lots of others.

It's also a good idea to examine your energy bills carefully; keep track of monthly gas and electric bills and periodic heating oil or propane deliveries. By paying attention to your standard level of energy consumption, you'll be more likely to notice a jump in consumption that could indicate that something's wrong — such as a water pump that isn't turning off or a faulty zone control that's heating part of your house even during the summer months. (If you find a big jump in electricity consumption, your utility company may be able to lend you a

FIGURE 14.3—*If you have light fixtures with incandescent light bulbs that are used more than an hour per day, replace burned-out bulbs with compact fluorescent lamps to save energy.*

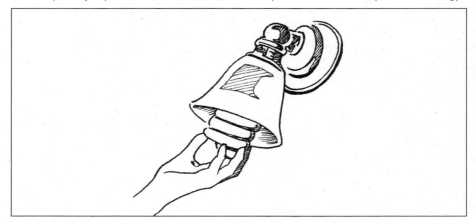

**Saving Energy through Better Operation of Your Household:
A Sampling of Strategies**

Turn off lights when leaving a room

Set back thermostats as night

Keep unused rooms cooler in the winter and warmer in the summer by controlling registers or zones

Close windows and doors during the cooler months when the outside temperature drops below the indoor temperature

Open windows in the summer for natural ventilation

Close blinds during summer days to limit heat gain

Avoid long showers or frequent baths

Don't leave the hot water running when washing dishes or shaving

Turn down the thermostat setting on your water heater to 120°F

Add extra insulation to a storage-type water heater

Use energy-saving cycles on dishwashers, clothes washers, dryers, and refrigerators

---

FIGURE 14.4

meter that you can use to try to pinpoint the problem by plugging various appliances into it and measuring electricity usage.) And simply the *process* of regularly looking at your energy consumption is likely to make you more aware of how you use energy and how to conserve.

WATER EFFICIENCY

As described in Chapter 10, there are many ways to conserve water in and around your home. The toilets, showerheads, and faucets you install should be water-conserving models that meet federal water efficiency standards. Unfortunately, some of these products do not perform as well as they should. Hopefully, you and your builder or designer will research toilets carefully and purchase models that perform very well. You may not look into showerheads as carefully, though; most people just order what comes with the shower control mechanism. If this showerhead doesn't perform well, replace it with a top-quality model that will deliver the performance you want—perhaps even with consumption below the 2.5 gallon-per-minute maximum allowed by law. There are some very well-designed water-conserving showerheads available, but expect to pay more for the best.

Outdoors, follow the suggestions in Chapter 10 for water-conserving, native landscaping. If you do need to water gardens, *mulch* to retain

FIGURE 14.5—*Not all low-flow showerheads are created equal. If yours isn't delivering a strong, satisfying stream of water, replace it with a better product.*

that water and use drip irrigation systems with a timer and/or soil-moisture-sensing controls to minimize waste. Better yet, build a simple rainwater collection system to capture water off your roof for irrigation. Consider gradually replacing a large lawn with less water-intensive and less chemical-intensive landscaping alternatives.

MAINTENANCE

Regular maintenance is essential to ensure longevity of your house and the components in it. A well-built house should last more than 200 years, but not without periodic maintenance. Mechanical equipment in the house won't last anywhere near 200 years, but if well-maintained, most furnaces, water heaters, and ventilation equipment should last 20 years or more.

Exactly what maintenance is needed will depend on specifics of your house and equipment. Any painted or stained windows, exterior walls, and trim will require recoating every 5 to 15 years, depending on the material and the detailing used during installation. (Paint should last much longer on siding if a rainscreen detail is used — see Chapter 6.) Bathroom and kitchen tile may require re-grouting or sealing of grout periodically. Wood floors may require refinishing or waxing. Stone countertops in the kitchen may need to be resealed. The *cathodic protection rod* in the water heater (a sacrificial metal rod that protects against corrosion) should be checked periodically and replaced if necessary to increase your water heater's life. If you have an in-ground septic system and reasonably water-efficient fixtures, the septic tank will need to be inspected and pumped every 5 to 10 years.

When you need to repaint a bedroom or refinish a wood floor later on down the road, be sure to use the same considerations that you used in the original selection. You probably won't have the benefit of an environmentally conscious builder or architect to guide you in product selection, so this may entail some additional research. The companion book, *Green Building Products,* should be useful.

SELECTION OF FURNISHINGS

From an indoor air quality standpoint, furnishings, curtains, shower curtains, bedding, and the like can be as significant a source of VOCs (including formaldehyde) as your kitchen cabinets. Look for furniture made with non-formaldehyde particleboard or MDF, or use solid wood. Some furniture is now being made with straw-based particleboard that contains no formaldehyde. As with wood products in new construction (see Chapter 8), look for FSC-certified wood or salvaged wood when you select furniture.

Many experts on indoor air quality recommend avoiding wall-to-wall carpeting, both because of chemicals that may be emitted from the carpet,

FIGURE 14.6—*Regular maintenance of a house can take a lot of time and expense, and can cause significant environmental impacts.*

carpet pad, or adhesive, and because the carpeting can provide an environment where allergy-causing dust mites, mold, and other biological contaminants may live. Natural-fiber area rugs are generally preferred. Area rugs are available made from cotton, wool, sisal, ramie, and other natural fibers. If possible, buy products that haven't been treated with pesticides; products from developing countries may include residues from pesticides that are banned in North America. A big advantage of area rugs, as opposed to fixed wall-to-wall carpeting, is that the area rugs can be removed for washing and dust removal. Hanging a rug on an outside line and beating it — just as your grandmother probably did — is still usually the best way to clean dust out of a rug.

With bedding and towels, if your budget allows, consider unbleached, organic cotton. Even though cotton is a natural product, conventional cotton farming in the United States uses tremendous quantities of fertilizer and pesticide. Fabric dyeing also carries significant environmental burdens. Buying sheets, bedspreads, and towels made from organically grown, unbleached, or naturally dyed cotton is an excellent way to minimize your total environmental footprint.

Avoid vinyl (PVC) products such as inflatable plastic chairs and most shower curtains. A typical vinyl shower curtain may lose a third

FIGURE 14.7—*Area rugs on a hardwood floor are generally preferred over wall-to-wall carpeting.*

of its weight over a period of years as the plasticizers leach out into the air — into the air you and your family are breathing! That's what you smell with a new vinyl shower curtain: plasticizers — usually phthalates, a class of chemicals recently implicated in various health and environmental problems (see Chapter 8).

CLEANING PRODUCTS

Cleaning products are introduced into your home's indoor air or wastewater every time you clean your house, or wash clothes or dishes. Select cleaning products carefully. Look for products that won't add a lot of VOCs to your indoor air. These may be easiest to find from catalog retailers that specialize in "green living" products. You might also be able to use some common, environmentally safe household products such as vinegar and baking soda in place of products whose ingredients you need a degree in organic chemistry to understand. Some excellent references on natural cleaning products are included in this book's companion web site.

Also look for laundry and dishwashing detergents that won't introduce phosphates into your wastewater. Phosphates cause problems in streams and other surface waters by supporting excessive algae growth. Even if your wastewater goes into the ground through an on-site wastewater system, most of the phosphates will end up in the groundwater and will eventually flow into streams or lakes.

DEALING WITH WASTE

Americans generate more waste per capita than just about anyone else. According to the US Environmental Protection Agency, in 2003 each of us produced over 1,600 pounds of municipal solid waste (household and office waste) — that's 4.5 pounds per day. Of the 236 million tons of municipal solid waste produced in the US in 2003, a total of approximately 72 millions tons, or 31%, was recycled or composted. For a few materials, the recovery rate is higher — 48% for paper and cardboard, 56% for yard trimmings. But there is clearly plenty of room for improvement. The easier and more convenient we can make recycling in our homes, the faster our national recycling rate can grow.

In thinking about how to manage waste in your home, consider first how to reduce the amount of waste your family produces. Look at your buying habits. Are there opportunities to buy food and other goods in bulk to minimize packaging? Try to select products with minimal packaging waste; let store owners know why you are choosing the less-packaged products; encourage them to shift their buying habits and relay feedback to manufacturers and distributors.

In addition to reducing waste generation through more careful purchasing, you have huge opportunities to reduce the amount of waste that actually ends up going to a landfill. A reasonable goal for a green household is to reduce outgoing trash by 80%. A family that used to generate five bags of trash per week should be able to get that down to one bag.

How you manage recycling in your home depends to a large extent on how recycling is handled at the municipal level. In some towns and cities, curbside recycling is available for a wide range of materials: newspaper, office paper, cardboard, glass, various types of plastics, and metal cans. In other locales, all these materials can be recycled, but homeowners have to bring the materials to centralized locations where the recyclables are put in separate bins. In some places very few types of materials can be recycled. Contact your municipal solid waste department to find out what your recycling options are.

It is usually necessary to carry out some level of separation of recyclables in the home. If you have weekly curbside pickup of recyclables, your storage areas for these materials can be quite modest. In municipalities where you need to drive to recycling locations, it makes good

FIGURE 14.8—*Be aware that many cleaning products release VOCs into the indoor air or pose other risks to you and the environment. Look for greener cleaning compounds.*

FIGURE 14.9 —*Store recyclables in clearly marked bins that are readily accessible, yet out of the way. How the materials should be sorted depends on what is recyclable in your area.*

environmental sense to plan for fairly long-term storage of recyclables so that your auto trips to the recycling center are minimized. If we have to use up a gallon of gasoline to recycle a bag of old newspapers or soda bottles, we'll be no further ahead for the recycling.

The key to success with recycling is convenience. If recycling ends up being inconvenient, it may lose favor in your home.

COMPOSTING ORGANIC WASTE

Along with recycling all waste that can be recycled, consider setting up a *composting system* to deal with organic waste. A well-managed composting system will both dramatically reduce the volume of organic matter (because most of it is converted into carbon dioxide and water vapor) and produce a very good soil amendment. You should be able to get much useful information on composting from a county agricultural extension agent or your local library.

Buy durable outdoor composting bins with latchable lids to keep animals out. Keep a closable composting container in the kitchen so that you can collect a few days' worth of compost before dumping it in an outside bin. It is usually beneficial to have two outdoor composting bins: one that you are adding material to and a second bin that is able to sit for a while after being filled until you spread the compost on the garden.

FIGURE 14.10 —*Organic waste, including kitchen scraps and weeds from the garden, can be composted in an outdoor compost bin; having two bins is handy.*

Most kitchen scraps and leftover food scraps can be composted, although experts usually recommend against composting of meat scraps.

Many people assume that composting simply means throwing organic waste into a compost bin and leaving it alone; these people are often disappointed with the results. To be most successful, composting involves a layering of different types of organic matter and periodic aeration or mixing of the pile. If most of the compost is food scraps, it may be too high in nitrogen and need more carbon for optimal breakdown; yard waste, such as grass clippings and weeds from the garden, can be added to achieve a better mix. Also, oxygen is needed to break down the waste; without enough oxygen, the compost may begin to decompose anaerobically, resulting in odor problems. Special implements are available for aerating the pile.

If outdoor composting won't work because of raccoons or other animals getting into your bin, you might want to consider a *worm bin* in your basement. This may sound gross, but the process is actually quite clean and fairly easy. Worms eat the organic waste, producing a clean fertilizer ideal for adding to your garden. You will need a special worm bin and an out-of-the-way, dark location where the temperature stays above 60°F. You may also have to chop up waste to some extent so that the worms can consume it more easily.

INVOLVE THE WHOLE FAMILY IN WASTE MANAGEMENT

Recycling and composting should involve the whole family. Children who grow up in households that recycle and compost waste will probably grow up being better environmentalists. Provide incentives for your kids to play a part in your recycling efforts — or put your kids in charge! You may be surprised at the creative approaches they come up with and their sense of ownership of the program's success.

TRANSPORTATION

Your household environmental impacts aren't limited to your home. How you get around also has a big impact on your overall environmental footprint. If you're lucky enough to have easy access to light rail, that's a great way to commute, but relatively few of us have that option. If taking the train or subway isn't possible, consider riding a bicycle, walking, taking a bus, or carpooling instead of driving a single-occupancy automobile.

For these alternatives to be used, they should be as convenient as possible. Make sure bicycles are conveniently stored, for example, so that family members can easily get a bike out and easily put it away. If you want to jog or bicycle to work, try to convince your employer to provide showers and a changing area. Covered, secure bicycle parking is also a big help.

FIGURE 14.11—*Storing and retrieving bicycles should be convenient so as to encourage bicycling instead of driving whenever practical.*

FIGURE 14.12—*Create spaces in your home or outside it where you and your family will be able to enjoy views of nature; appreciating the outdoors will inspire you to protect it.*

Or consider working from home. Telecommuting can save hundreds of gallons of gasoline a year, and it can be a whole lot less stressful. With today's e-mail, high-speed Internet connections, and high-tech telephone switching options, telecommuting is easier than ever. The fact that you are working in your slippers and bathrobe out of a home office can be totally hidden from your business associate on the other end of the phone. The company receptionist patches the call to you, and the caller assumes that you're in a conventional cubicle surrounded by filing cabinets and fellow office workers. Unless your dog starts barking, there need be no clue that you're in your home.

ENJOY THE OUTDOORS

Spending time outdoors is good for you (as long as you don't get too much direct sun on unprotected skin). An important part of living in a green home is appreciating why you went to all that effort to create a home that would sit lightly on the land. Whether weeding your garden, enjoying an outdoor meal with your family, reading a book on the front porch, or working on your laptop under a tree out back, being outdoors will put you in closer touch with nature. It may help remind you and your family why it's important to keep the air clean and the nearby woodlands or prairies healthy and diverse.

Afterword

A S I PUT THE FINISHING TOUCHES on this book, working outside on my deck on a glorious, blue-skied, September afternoon, the urgency for greening our housing stock seems ever more clear. Gasoline at our local gas station has hit an all-time record high, while we're paying 75% more for heating oil than we were last year, and natural gas prices nationwide are nearly double what they were just three years ago. The devastation wrought by Hurricane Katrina on New Orleans and throughout the Gulf Coast has caused the largest dislocation of American people since the Dust Bowl of the 1930s, when drought and loss of topsoil turned hundreds of thousands of Americans into refugees.

Global climate change is warming our oceans, which, scientists tell us, will increase the magnitude of storms like Katrina. The same climate change will continue to increase the incidence of drought in some regions, while significantly causing flooding elsewhere.

Meanwhile, toxicologists are gaining new understanding of widely used chemicals that mimic our natural hormones and may be causing birth defects, developmental problems, and behavioral changes in our children. Most of these chemicals are still being manufactured, and some 1,800 new chemicals are still being introduced in North America each year with little or no toxicity testing. We are the testing laboratory for these chemicals, and most of us have little opportunity for opting out of this experiment.

Building your own home provides an opportunity to take charge of your future. You can protect yourself from the future's higher energy prices — increases that may come when you are on a fixed income during retirement. You can reduce your need for long automobile commutes or hopping in a car for every errand. You can design passively heated, naturally cooled, and even PV-powered houses that will keep you comfortable and illuminated even in the event of prolonged power outages or fuel shortages. You can design landscapes that will survive periodic droughts. You can choose materials for your home that will not poison your children.

Moving into your own green home won't solve all of the world's problems, but it is a step — an important step. It not only offers you direct benefits, but it will serve as a model for others. By creating a home that sits lightly on the land, that is frugal in its use of resources, and that is healthy for its occupants, you will be showing others the potential of what is possible. You will be paving the way for a better future for us all.

It may feel overwhelming to consider so many green building issues on so many different levels — where you build and how that affects your commuting options; the overall configuration of your house and how that will influence energy consumption; the selection of materials used in building the house; strategies for ensuring that the indoor environment will be healthy; how to design the landscaping around your house to minimize environmental impacts. Indeed, the issues are many, and balancing — or even thinking about — all of them can be both complex and challenging.

The intent of this book has not been to overwhelm, but rather to help you think about issues that can help you and your family live healthier lives with lighter impact on the environment. Don't look at the ideas presented in this book as being things you have to do. To be sure, nothing would make me happier than to hear about hundreds or thousands of homes that embody the full-blown ideas presented here — homes carrying the deepest shade of green. But even modest changes in how houses are built, if implemented broadly, will have a huge effect on improving the Earth we leave to our children and grandchildren.

Implement what you can of the ideas presented in this book and celebrate those successes. If you build another house 10 years or 20 years down the road, try to take these greening ideas further. Little by little, progress will be made. Your grandchildren and great-grandchildren will thank you for making a difference.

— Alex Wilson
Dummerston, Vermont

Glossary

Active closed-loop solar water heater: Solar water heater in which an electric pump circulates a freeze-protected heat-transfer fluid through the *collector* and *heat exchanger* within a storage tank.

Active drainback solar water heater: Solar water heater in which water or another heat-transfer fluid is pumped through the *collector* and drains back to a tank in the house when the pump turns off.

Advanced framing: House-framing technique in which lumber use is optimized, improving both the material efficiency of the house and the energy performance of the *building envelope.*

Air barrier: Layer in the *building envelope* that effectively blocks air movement, which also blocks the flow of most water vapor.

Air handler: Fan that a furnace, *whole-house (central) air conditioner,* or *heat pump* uses to distribute heated or cooled air throughout the house.

Air-source heat pump: *Heat pump* that relies on the outside air as the heat source and *heat sink;* not as effective in cold climates as *ground-source heat pumps.*

Airtight drywall: Use of drywall with carefully sealed edges and joints to serve as the *air barrier* in a wall or ceiling system.

Annual Fuel Utilization Efficiency (AFUE): Energy efficiency of a heating system that accounts for start-up, cool-down, and other operating losses that occur during real-life operation; AFUE is always lower than *combustion efficiency.*

Autoclaved aerated concrete (AAC): Masonry building material used throughout much of the world for more than 70 years; made of *portland cement,* sand, and water; an autoclaving process (heating under pressure) during the setting results in the production of air pockets in the material, making it less dense and better insulating.

Backdrafting: *Indoor air quality* problem in which potentially dangerous combustion gasses escape into the house instead of going up the chimney.

Balanced ventilation: Mechanical ventilation system in which separate, balanced fans exhaust stale indoor air and bring in fresh outdoor air; often includes heat recovery or heat and moisture recovery (see also *heat-recovery ventilator* and *energy-recovery ventilator*).

Batch solar water heater: See *integral collector storage (ICS) solar water heater.*

Binder: Glue used in manufacturing wood products, such as *medium-density fiberboard (MDF), particleboard,* and *engineered lumber.* Most binders are made with *formaldehyde.* See *ureaformaldehyde binder* and *methyl diisocyanate (MDI) binder.*

Bioaccumulate: Process by which toxins can build up in the food chain; small organisms often store toxins in their fatty tissues, and when larger organisms eat them, those toxins become more concentrated. At the top of the food chain (polar bears and humans, for example), the levels of toxins can become very high.

Blowing agent: Compound used in producing foam insulation; mixed as a liquid with the foam ingredients under pressure, the blowing agent evaporates, creating gas bubbles that provide the insulation. Until recently, most blowing agents (*HCFCs* and *CFCs*) depleted the Earth's protective ozone layer; except for *extruded polystyrene,* industry has now switched to ozone-safe blowing agents.

Boiler: System used to heat water for *hydronic heating.* Most boilers are gas-fired or oil-fired, although some are electric or wood-fired; a boiler can also heat water through a *tankless coil* or an *indirect water heater.*

Borate: Chemical containing the element boron that provides fire resistance to materials such as cellulose insulation and decay resistance to wood products.

Brominated flame retardant (BFR): Chemicals added to various plastics and foam materials to provide fire resistance; there is growing concern that BFRs are harmful to humans.

Brownfield: Land that has been contaminated from past (usually industrial) uses.

Btu: British thermal unit, the amount of heat required to raise one pound of water (about a pint) one degree Fahrenheit in temperature; about the heat content of one wooden kitchen match.

Building envelope: Exterior layer of a house that provides protection from colder (and warmer) outdoor temperatures and precipitation; includes the house foundation, framed exterior walls, roof or ceiling, and insulation.

Capillary forces: Forces that lift water or pull it through porous materials, such as concrete.

Carbon-neutral: House that, on an annual basis, does not result in a net release of carbon dioxide (a greenhouse gas that contributes to global warming) into the atmosphere.

Catalytic combuster: Specialized component in a combustion device, such as a wood stove, that results in more complete combustion, thus improving efficiency and reducing pollution.

Cathodic protection rod: Metal rod in a storage-type water heater that protects the tank from corrosion; the sacrificial cathodic protection rod is eaten away over time and can be replaced.

Cavity-fill insulation: Insulation installed in the space created by wall, ceiling, roof, or floor framing; most commonly fiberglass-batt, spray-applied or dense-pack cellulose, or spray polyurethane.

Chromated copper arsenate (CCA): Type of wood preservative that has now been eliminated from most wood products due to concerns about leaching and toxicity; huge quantities of CCA-treated wood remain in use, especially in residential decks.

Cistern: Vessel for storing water, such as that collected with a rainwater harvesting system.

Clerestory windows: Vertical, or close-to-vertical, windows in a flat-roof house that bring sunlight deeply into the building.

Cohousing: Development pattern in which multiple (typically 8 to 30) privately owned houses or housing units are clustered together with some commonly owned spaces, such as common house, workshop, greenhouse, etc.; automobiles are typically kept to the outside perimeter of the community, resulting in a protected area where children can play.

Combustion air: Air used for burning fuel in heating and water-heating systems; outdoor air may be delivered directly to the *combustion chamber* in a *sealed-combustion* system.

Combustion chamber: Portion of a *furnace, boiler,* or other combustion appliance where fuel is burned to produce useful heat.

Combustion efficiency: Efficiency at which a fuel is burned in a combustion appliance when operating at its rated output; the combustion efficiency is always higher than the *annual fuel utilization efficiency (AFUE).*

Compact fluorescent lamp (CFL): *Fluorescent* light bulb in which the tube is folded or twisted into a spiral to concentrate the light output; CFLs are typically 3 to 4 times as efficient as incandescent light bulbs, and they last 8 to 10 times as long.

Composting system: Outdoor bin or group of bins for converting vegetable scraps, weeds from the garden, and other plant matter into a rich, high-organic-content *soil amendment.*

Composting toilet: Toilet that does not flush human waste down the drain using *potable water;* instead, the wastes are stored in a composting chamber that decomposes the waste. Most of the waste

is converted into water vapor and carbon dioxide and vented into the outside air; a small amount of rich, organic humus is removed annually and can be spread around non-food plants.

Concrete masonry unit (CMU): Block made of concrete used for wall construction; hollow cores can be filled with concrete to reinforce walls.

Conduction: Movement of heat through a material as kinetic energy is transferred from molecule to molecule; the handle of an iron skillet on the stove gets hot due to heat conduction. *R-value* is a measure of resistance to conductive heat flow.

Constructed wetland: Specialized artificial wetland that relies on microorganisms living around plant roots to purify *wastewater.*

Convection: Movement of heat from one place to another by physically transferring heated fluid molecules, usually air or water. Natural convection is the movement of that heat naturally; forced convection relies on fans or pumps.

Cost-plus basis: System of payment for services in which a builder charges an hourly rate for construction labor, the direct cost of materials, and a pre-established profit level.

Cripple studs: Studs in a wall system that support headers above windows or doors; these additional studs result in extra heat loss because they do not insulate as well as the insulation in the wall cavity.

Cross-linked polyethylene (PEX): Specialized type of polyethylene plastic that is strengthened by cross-linking (chemical bonds formed in addition to the usual bonds in the polymerization process). PEX is used primarily as tubing for hot- and cold-water distribution and *radiant-floor heating.*

Current loop: In electrical wiring, a situation in which separation of hot and neutral leads results in higher-than-normal *electromagnetic fields (EMF)*.

Curtain truss: Known also as a Larson truss, a non-structural truss that extends out from a structural wall system for the purpose of holding *cavity-fill insulation*. Often used on timber-frame houses, curtain trusses may be as much as 12 inches deep, providing an insulating value greater than R-40. Since they aren't structural, curtain trusses are often constructed from 2x2s with plywood reinforcement flanges to minimize wood use.

Daylighting: The use of sunlight for daytime lighting needs.

Deep-cycle battery: Specialized battery for storing electricity that can be deeply discharged and recharged many times; used for homes with *stand-alone power systems* (non-grid-connected) that rely on *photovoltaic* or *wind power*.

Degree day: Measure of heating or cooling requirements based on the average outdoor temperature. To calculate the number of heating degree days for a given day, find the average of the maximum and minimum outdoor temperatures and subtract that from 65°F. The annual number of heating degree days is a measure of the severity of the climate and is used to determine expected fuel use for heating. Cooling degree days, which measure air conditioning requirements, are calculated much the same way, but based on the difference between the average outdoor temperature and an indoor base temperature, usually 75°F.

Demand water heater: Water heater that heats water only as needed; there is no storage tank and, thus, no standby heat loss. While electric demand water heaters may make sense for a remote sink in a house, demand water heaters fired by natural gas or propane are generally more practical for whole-house use, given the hot water loads of showering and clothes washing.

Design temperature: Reasonably expected minimum (or maximum) temperature for a particular area; used in sizing heating and cooling equipment.

Design-build firm: Company that handles both house design and construction; since both services are provided by the same firm, integrated design can easily be achieved.

Diffuser: With forced-warm-air heating system, a register or grille attached to ducting through which heated or air conditioned air is delivered to the living space; with *tubular skylight* and electric light fixture, a cover plate through which diffused light is delivered.

Direct-gain system: Type of *passive solar heating* system in which south-facing windows provide heat gain during the daytime and high-mass thermal-storage materials absorb and store that heat to keep the space warm at night. This is the simplest type of passive solar heating system, but careful design is required to prevent overheating.

Double wall: Construction system in which two layers of studs are used to provide a thicker-than-normal wall system so that a lot of insulation can be installed; the two walls are often separated by several inches to reduce *thermal bridging* through the studs and to provide additional space for insulation.

Drywall clips: Simple metal or plastic clips that are used to tie sheets of drywall together, especially at inside corners; use of a few clips can eliminate one or two wall studs, thus leaving more room for insulation. Because such a corner can float, cracking of the drywall joint is less common.

Dual-flush toilet: Toilet that provides two flush levels: a full-volume flush for use with solid wastes, and a reduced-volume flush (often half the volume) when only liquid waste and paper need to be flushed.

Dutch drain: Open drain at the bottom of a house wall to carry *stormwater* (rainwater runoff) away from the house.

Earth-bermed: Earth built up around the walls of a house to reduce heat loss, protect against wind, and reduce noise; superb moisture management and drainage are critically important with earth-bermed and underground houses.

Ecological footprint: Measure of the amount of land and water required to support a person or population of people; includes both resource extraction and waste disposal.

Effective R-value: See *mass-enhanced R-value.*

Electric-resistance heat: Heat provided by electricity in which high-resistance wires convert electric current directly into heat. See also *heat pump.*

Electromagnetic field (EMF): Field given off by electric current flow. Some health experts are concerned that the magnetic field component of EMFs may be harmful or even cancer-causing. Magnetic fields are stronger near current in which there is separation between the positive and neutral leads.

Electronically commutated motor (ECM): Specialized, energy-efficient electric motor whose output can be reduced to save energy; most commonly used with fans and pumps.

Embodied energy: Energy that goes into making a product; typically includes energy for transporting both the raw materials and the finished product.

Endocrine disruptor: Chemical that mimics natural hormones, such as estrogen, and may interfere with reproductive development or alter behavior in offspring. Includes such commonly used chemicals as *phthalate plasticizers* used in PVC plastic and bisphenol-A used in epoxies and polycarbonate plastic.

Energy efficiency rating (EER): As most commonly used, EER is the operating efficiency of a room air conditioner, measured in *Btus* of cooling output, divided by the power consumption in watt-hours; the higher the number the greater the efficiency.

Energy factor: Efficiency measure for rating the energy performance of dishwashers, clothes washers, water heaters, and certain other appliances; the higher the number the greater the efficiency.

Energy-efficient mortgage (EEM): Special type of mortgage in which the lending institution raises the allowable mortgage amount for a given earnings level, since energy-saving features in the house will reduce the monthly operating costs, thus leaving more money available to pay the mortgage.

EnergyGuide: Label from the Federal Trade Commission that lists the expected energy consumption of an appliance, heating system, or cooling system, and how that consumption compares with other products in that category; the energy performance is based on specified operating conditions and average energy costs — your actual performance may vary.

Energy-recovery ventilator (ERV): Type of *heat-recovery ventilator (HRV)* that captures water vapor as well as heat from the outgoing airstream in a *balanced ventilation system.* In winter months, this can reduce the drying that occurs when outdoor air is brought indoors and warmed.

ENERGY STAR: Labeling system sponsored by the US Environmental Protection Agency and the US Department of Energy for labeling the most energy-efficient products on the market; applies to a wide range of products, from computers and office equipment to refrigerators and air conditioners.

Engineered header: A framing member made of *engineered lumber*, used to carry a wall or roof load above a window or door.

Engineered lumber: Lumber made by gluing together veneers or strands of wood to create very strong framing members; stronger and less prone to warping than standard framing lumber and can be made from smaller-diameter trees.

Environmental footprint: Measure of one's overall burdens or impacts on the environment. See also *ecological footprint.*

Evaporative cooler: Energy-efficient cooling system in which a fine mist of water is evaporated, lowering the air temperature; most appropriate in dry climates, as they add humidity to a house. Also known as a *swamp cooler.*

Exhaust-only ventilation: Mechanical ventilation system in which one or more fans are used to exhaust air from a house, with *make-up air* supplied passively. See also *balanced ventilation.*

Expanded polystyrene (EPS): Type of rigid foam insulation; unlike *extruded polystyrene (XPS)*, EPS does not contain ozone-depleting *HCFCs.*

Extruded polystyrene (XPS): Type of rigid foam insulation that is widely used below-grade, such as underneath concrete floor slabs; in North America XPS is currently made with ozone-depleting HCFC-142b.

Fan-coil: Electric or hydronic heating or cooling element installed in a duct; lets ventilation air also warm or cool the living space.

Ferrocement: Mix of *portland cement,* sand, and water that is sprayed on a steel mesh, creating a thin, strong material; often used for cisterns.

Fiber-cement siding: Siding material made from wood fiber and *portland cement* that is highly durable, moisture-resistant, and fire-proof; developed in New Zealand, is becoming common as a siding material in North America.

First cost: Initial cost of buying or building something, as distinguished from the *operating cost.*

Flashing: Material, usually sheet metal, rubber, or plastic, installed to keep rain from entering a building; when properly installed in a wall or roof assembly, flashing sheds rain to the exterior.

Fluorescent lighting: Type of energy-efficient lighting introduced in the 1930s in which electric discharge within a sealed glass tube energizes mercury vapor, producing ultraviolet (UV) light; this UV light is absorbed by a phosphor coating on the inside surface of the glass tube, which in turn fluoresces, generating visible light. See also *compact fluorescent lamp.*

Fluoropolymer: Polymer (compound made up of many identical molecules linked by chemical bonds) containing the element fluorine; the most recognized fluoropolymer is DuPont's Teflon®, or polytetrafluoroethylene (PTFE). A key constituent in making fluoropolymers, perfluorooctanoic acid (PFOA), has come under fire as a "likely carcinogen."

Forced-air heating: Heat distribution system in which heat is delivered by forcing warm air through a network of ducts. A *furnace* or *heat pump* typically generates the warm air.

Formaldehyde: Chemical found in many building products; most binders used for manufactured wood products are formaldehyde compounds. Reclassified in 2004 as a "known human carcinogen." See also *phenol-formaldehyde binder* and *urea-formaldehyde binder.*

Fuel cell: Electrochemical device similar to a battery in which electricity is generated by chemically reacting hydrogen with oxygen; electricity, water vapor, and heat are the only products.

Furnace: System used to heat air for a *forced-air heating* system. Furnaces can be gas-fired, oil-fired, wood-fired, or electric.

Galvanized coating: Protective zinc coating added to steel to reduce corrosion.

Glazing: When referring to windows or doors, the transparent or translucent layer that transmits light; high-performance glazings may include multiple layers of glass or plastic, *low-e coatings,* and *low-conductivity gas fill.*

Gravity-flush toilet: Toilet whose flush is powered solely by the force of falling water. See also *pressure-assist toilet.*

Graywater: *Wastewater* from a building that does not include flush-water from toilets and (as most commonly defined) water from kitchen sinks or dishwashers.

Green building: Design and construction of buildings that minimize impacts on the environment while helping to keep occupants healthy.

Green electricity: Electricity generated from *renewable energy* sources, such as *photovoltaics* (solar power), *wind power,* biomass, and small-scale *hydropower.* (Large, conventional hydropower sources usually are not included in definitions of green electricity.)

Green mortgage: Mortgage that acknowledges a green home's lower monthly operating costs due to reduced energy use or reduced need for automobiles. Because of these lower monthly operating costs, the amount of allowable mortgage is increased.

Green power: See *green electricity.*

Greenfield: Site that has not previously had a building on it. See also *brownfield.*

Grid-connected power system: Electricity generation system, usually relying on *photovoltaics* or *wind power,* that is hooked up to the utility company's electric grid through a *net-metering* arrangement so that electricity can be obtained when the locally generated power is not sufficient. See also *stand-alone power system.*

Ground-source heat pump: *Heat pump* that relies on the relatively constant temperatures underground as the heat source and *heat sink.* The energy performance of ground-source heat pumps is usually better than that of *air-source heat pumps.*

Gut-rehab: Building renovation in which the walls are gutted (reduced to the wall framing and sometimes *sheathing*).

Hard-coat (pyrolytic) low-e: Type of *low-e coating* in which a heat-reflective metal coating is formed into the surface of the glass during manufacturing (pyrolytic refers to heat), rather than being applied after the glass is made — as is the case with *soft-coat low-e coatings.*

Heat distribution: System for delivering heat throughout a house. See *forced-air heating* and *hydronic heating.*

Heat exchanger: Device that allows for transfer of heat from one material to another. An air-to-air heat exchanger, or *heat-recovery ventilator,* transfers heat from an outgoing airstream to an incoming airstream. A copper-pipe heat exchanger in a solar water heater tank transfers heat from the heat-transfer fluid circulating through a *solar collector* into the *potable water* in the storage tank.

Heat pump: Heating and cooling system in which specialized refrigerant fluid in a sealed system is alternately evaporated and condensed, changing its state from liquid to vapor, by altering its pressure; this phase change allows heat to be transferred into or out of the house. See *air-source heat pump* and *ground-source heat pump.*

Heating Season Performance Factor (HSPF): Energy performance of an *air-source heat pump* operating in heating mode; it is the ratio of the estimated seasonal heat output divided by the seasonal power consumption. See also *seasonal energy efficiency ratio (SEER)*.

Heat-recovery ventilator (HRV): *Balanced ventilation system* in which most of the heat from outgoing exhaust air is transferred to incoming fresh air via an air-to-air *heat exchanger*. See also *energy-recovery ventilator*.

Heat sink: Where heat is dumped by an air conditioner or heat pump used in cooling mode; usually into the outdoor air or ground. See *air-source heat pump* and *ground-source heat pump*.

High-efficiency toilet (HET): Toilet that provides at least 20% water savings over the federal standard of 1.6 gallons per flush and still meets rigorous standards for flush performance.

Home-run plumbing system: Water-distribution piping system in which individual plumbing lines extend from a central manifold to each plumbing fixture or water-using appliance; piping is typically *cross-linked polyethylene* (PEX). Because diameter of the tubing can be matched to the flow of the fixture or appliance, hot water can be delivered more quickly.

Horizontal-axis clothes washer: Washing machine (typically front-loading) in which the laundry drum is configured horizontally; this allows significant water savings, because the laundry is dipped into and out of the wash water as the drum rotates. See also *vertical-axis clothes washer*.

Hydrochlorofluorocarbon (HCFC): Compound commonly used as a refrigerant in compression-cycle mechanical equipment (refrigerators, air conditioners, and heat pumps) or as a *blowing agent* in producing foam insulation. HCFCs are damaging to the Earth's protective ozone layer.

Hydronic heating: Heat distribution system in which hot water produced by a *boiler* is circulated through pipes and baseboard radiators or tubing in a radiant floor. Also called baseboard hot-water heating.

Hydropower: Generation of electricity from falling or flowing water.

Impervious surface: Surface that does not permit *stormwater* runoff to infiltrate the ground. See also *porous paving*.

Incandescent light: Light produced by a standard light bulb when electric current heats a tiny coiled filament to glowing; converts about 90% of the electricity into heat and only 10% into light. See also *fluorescent lighting*.

Indirect water heater: Water heater that draws heat from a *boiler* used for space heating; a separate zone from the boiler heats water in a separate, insulated tank via a water-to-water *heat exchanger*. See also *tankless coil*.

Indoor air quality (IAQ): Healthfulness of an interior environment; IAQ is affected by such factors as moisture and mold, emissions of volatile organic compounds from paints and finishes, *formaldehyde* emissions from cabinets, and ventilation effectiveness.

Infill site: Building site sandwiched between existing buildings in a fairly developed area; by developing infill sites, there is less pressure on *greenfield* sites and residents often have better access to public transportation.

Instantaneous water heater: See *demand water heater*.

Insulated concrete form (ICF): Hollow insulated forms, usually made from *expand- ed polystyrene (EPS)*, used for building walls (foundation and aboveground); after stacking and stabilizing the forms, the aligned cores are filled with concrete, which provides the wall structure.

Integral collector storage (ICS) solar water heater: A simple solar water heater in which *potable water* is heated where it is stored.

Integrated design: Building design in which different components of design, such as the building envelope, window placement and glazings, and mechanical systems are considered together. High-performance buildings can be created cost-effectively using integrated design, since higher costs in one place can often be paid for through savings elsewhere — e.g. by improving the performance of the building envelope, the heating and cooling systems can be downsized, or even eliminated.

Inverter: Device for converting direct-current (DC) electricity into the alternating-current (AC) form required for most home uses — necessary if home-generated electricity is to be fed into the electric grid through *net metering* arrangements.

Kilowatt-hour (kWh): A measure of electricity consumption; a 100-watt light bulb burning for 10 hours consumes 1 kWh.

Leach field: An area of permeable soil into which effluent from a septic tank is able to infiltrate the ground; a component of an on-site *wastewater* disposal system.

Leaching: Relative to materials, this is the process by which chemicals can escape in the environment; for example, arsenic can leach out of older *pressure-treated wood.*

Life cycle: Entire life of a product or material, from raw material acquisition through disposal.

Life-cycle assessment (LCA): Examination of environmental and health impacts of a product or material over its *life cycle;* provides a mechanism for comparing different products and materials for green building.

Life-cycle cost: Economic cost of a product or building over its expected life, including both *first cost* (purchase cost) and *operating cost.*

Living Machine: Ecological wastewater treatment system that relies on biological systems (microorganisms, plants, and animals) to purify *wastewater,* usually used for municipal-scale treatment systems.

Low-conductivity gas fill: Transparent gas installed between two or more panes of glass in a sealed, insulated window that resists the conduction of heat more effectively than air; boosts a window's *R-value* and reduces its *U-factor.*

Low-e coating: Very thin metallic coating on glass or plastic window glazing that reduces heat loss through the window; the coating emits less *radiant energy* (heat *radiation*), which makes it, in effect, reflective to that heat; boosts a window's *R-value* and reduces its *U-factor.*

Make-up air: Outside air supplied to replace household air that was used in a combustion appliance or exhausted through a ventilation system.

Manifold: With a *home-run plumbing system,* the manifold is the component that distributes the water; it has one inlet and many outlets to feed different fixtures and appliances.

Masonry heater: Specialized, high-mass, wood-burning fireplace in which a small fire is burned very efficiently at very high temperature; the fire heats up the thermal mass of the masonry heater, which then radiates heat to the living space. In a well-insulated home, it often only has to be burned once or twice per day.

Mass-enhanced R-value: The higher *R-value* performance of a high-mass wall material; it takes into account the fact that such a material absorbs and stores heat during the daytime and, thus, results in lower overall heat loss. Mass-enhanced R-values are climate-specific; in sunny climates with high daily temperature swings, such as Rocky Mountain states, the boost will be more significant. Also called *effective R-value,* and commonly exaggerated by manufacturers of masonry building systems.

Materials recovery facility (MRF): Solid waste processing facility, often operated by a municipality, in which waste materials are separated for recycling or separate disposal streams.

Mechanical ventilation: Ventilation system using a fan or several fans to exhaust stale indoor air from a home as a way to ensure adequate *indoor air quality*. See *exhaust-only ventilation* and *balanced ventilation*.

Medium-density fiberboard (MDF): Panel product used in cabinets and furniture; generally made from wood fiber glued together with binder; similar to *particleboard*, but with finer texture, offering more precise finishing. Most MDF is made with *formaldehyde*-emitting *urea-formaldehyde binders*.

Methyl diisocyanate (MDI) binder: Non-*formaldehyde* binder used in some *medium-density fiberboard* and *particleboard* products, including straw-based particleboard.

Mixed-use development: Development pattern in which such building types as residential, retail, and commercial office are located in the same area; beneficial because it can reduce dependence on automobiles.

Mulch: Organic material, such as leaves, straw, or chipped wood waste, spread on the ground and around plantings to reduce the need for irrigation and weeding.

Net metering: Arrangement through which a homeowner who produces electricity using *photovoltaics* or *wind power* can sell excess electricity back to the utility company, running the electric meter backwards. The utility effectively buys the power at the retail price, but the amount of electricity the utility company will "buy" in a given month is limited to the amount that the homeowner buys; any excess electricity is purchased at a much lower, wholesale price. See *grid-connected power system*.

Offgassing: Release of volatile chemicals from a material or product. See also *volatile organic compounds*.

On-center: As used in house construction, the distance from the center of one framing member to the center of another; in wood-frame construction, studs are typically 16 or 24 inches on-center.

On-demand hot water circulation: System to quickly deliver hot water to a bathroom or kitchen when needed, without wasting the water that has been sitting in the hot-water pipes, which circulates back to the water heater.

On-site wastewater system: Treatment and disposal of *wastewater* (sewage) from a house that is not connected to a municipal sewer system; most on-site systems include a septic tank and *leach field*.

Operating cost: Cost of operating a device or building; includes energy, maintenance, repairs, etc.

Operating energy: Energy required to operate something, such as a house.

Oriented strand board (OSB): Wood *sheathing* or subfloor panel made from strands of wood glued together in layers oriented for strength; most OSB is made using *phenol-formaldehyde binder* or *methyl diisocyanate (MDI) binder*.

Owner-builder: Homeowner who builds his or her own home.

Particleboard: Panel product used in cabinets and furniture; generally made from wood fiber glued together with binder. Similar to *medium-density fiberboard (MDF)*, but with a coarser texture. Most particleboard is made with *formaldehyde*-emitting *urea-formaldehyde binder*, although some wood particleboard and all straw particleboard uses a non-*formaldehyde methyl diisocyanate (MDI)* binder.

Passive solar heating: Building design in which solar energy provides a significant portion of the heating without the use of fans or pumps; the building itself serves as the solar *collector* and heat storage system. See also *direct-gain system* and *thermal storage wall.*

Payback period: Length of time it takes to pay back the cost of the investment. For example, water and energy savings from replacing an old showerhead with a new, water-saving model can often pay back the investment in a few months; the payback period for a *photovoltaic* power system will be much longer.

Peak watt: Unit of rated power output, for example from a *photovoltaic (PV)* module in full sunlight, as distinct from its output at any given moment, which may be lower.

Pellet stove: Wood stove designed to burn pellets made from compressed sawdust; screw-auger feeds pellets into the firebox at a metered rate; electric fan provides combustion air.

Permaculture: Term coined by Bill Mollison for the practice of designing sustainable human habitats; intended to mean both "permanent agriculture" and "permanent culture."

Phenol-formaldehyde binder: *Formaldehyde*-based binder used for wood products, especially those made for exterior applications; lower formaldehyde emissions than *urea-formaldehyde binder.*

Phosphate: Nutrient contained in some detergents that results in excessive vegetative growth in water bodies.

Photovoltaic (PV) cell: Device that generates electricity from sunlight; multiple PV cells are combined into a *PV module.*

Photovoltaics (PV): Generation of electricity directly from sunlight. A *photovoltaic (PV) cell* has no moving parts; electrons are energized by sunlight and result in current flow. See also *PV module* and *PV array.*

Phthalate plasticizer: Chemical added to *polyvinyl chloride (PVC)* and some other plastics to make them more flexible; phthalates are *endocrine disruptors.*

Pier foundation: Building foundation consisting of piers instead of continuous walls; resource-efficient because it avoids the need for continuous foundation walls.

Plasticizer: Chemical compound added to a material to make it more flexible or softer. See *phthalate plasticizer.*

Platform framing: The most common house framing system in North America; a platform, or deck, is constructed at each floor level, and on top of this the house walls are erected.

Polychlorinated biphenyl (PCB): Highly toxic chemical that was long used as a fire-resistant coolant in electrical ballasts and other products; PCBs were banned in the 1970s, but remain a very significant problem today.

Polyisocyanurate (polyiso): Type of rigid foam insulation used in above-grade walls and roofs; typically has a foil facing on both sides; was made with ozone-depleting HCFC-141b *blowing agent*, but manufacturers have switched to ozone-safe hydrocarbons.

Polyurethane foam: Insulation material made from polyol and isocyanate and a *blowing agent* that causes it to expand; typically sprayed into wall cavities or sprayed on roofs.

Polyvinyl chloride (PVC): Most common plastic in building construction; widely used in such applications as drainage piping, flooring, exterior siding, window construction, and electrical wire. Also known as *vinyl.*

Porous grid paver: Concrete or stone *porous paving* material designed to allow *stormwater* to infiltrate the ground.

Porous paving: A paving material that allows rainfall to percolate through and infiltrate the ground, rather than contributing to stormwater runoff; can be asphalt, concrete, or *porous grid paver.*

Portland cement: The most common building material in the world; a fine gray powder made from limestone, gypsum, and shale or clay; when mixed with water, cement binds sand and gravel into concrete. Portland cement was invented in 1824 by Joseph Aspdin, a British stone mason, who named it after a natural stone quarried on the Isle of Portland off the British coast.

Post-and-beam construction: Construction system using a relatively small number of structural timber, steel, or concrete framing members, with non-structural infill walls or insulated panels. See also *timber framing.*

Post-consumer recycled material: Material recovered from a waste product that has been in use by a consumer before being discarded. See also *post-industrial recycled material.*

Post-industrial (pre-consumer) recycled material: Material recovered from the waste stream of an industrial process that has not been placed in use. See also *post-consumer recycled material.*

Potable water: Water considered safe for drinking and cooking.

Pressure-assist toilet: Toilet that uses air pressure, generated as the toilet tank refills, to produce a more forceful flush; some of the highest-performance, *high-efficiency toilets (HETs)* rely on pressure-assist technology.

Pressure-treated wood: Wood that has been chemically treated to extend its life, especially when outdoors or in ground contact. The most common pressure-treated wood until a few years ago, chromated copper arsenate (CCA), has now been phased out for most applications, due to health and environmental concerns.

Prudent avoidance: Strategy using relatively easy and low-cost tactics to avoid exposure to something that may prove to be harmful, such as *electromagnetic fields (EMFs).*

PV array: Group of *PV modules* wired together to increase total power output.

PV module: Panel made up of *photovoltaic cells*; generates electricity directly from sunlight.

R-value: Measure of resistance to heat flow; the higher the R-value, the lower the heat loss. The inverse of *U-factor.*

Radiant energy: Energy transmitted by electromagnetic waves.

Radiant-floor heating: Heat distribution system in which a floor serves as a low-temperature radiator. When used with *hydronic heating,* hot water is usually circulated through tubing embedded in a concrete slab; alternately, the tubing can be installed on the underside of wood subflooring, although the benefit of thermal mass is lost.

Radiation: Movement of energy via electromagnetic waves.

Radon: Colorless, odorless, short-lived radioactive gas that can seep into homes and result in lung cancer risk. Radon and its decay products emit cancer-causing alpha, beta, and gamma particles.

Rainscreen: Construction detail appropriate for all but the driest climates to prevent moisture entry and to extend the life of siding and *sheathing* materials; most commonly produced by installing thin strapping to hold the siding away from the sheathing by a quarter-inch to three-quarters of an inch.

Recirculating sand filter: Treatment system in which *wastewater* is circulated through a bed of sand or specialized media, where both aerobic and anaerobic conditions support bacteria that break down organic matter and convert nitrates into atmospheric nitrogen.

Reflective roofing: Roofing material that reflects most of the sunlight striking it to help reduce cooling loads; the ENERGY STAR Cool Roof program certifies roofing materials that meet specified standards for reflectivity.

Refrigerant: Compound used in refrigerators, air conditioners, and heat pumps to transfer heat from one place to another, thus cooling or heating a space. Most refrigerants today are *hydrochlorofluorocarbons (HCFCs)*, which deplete the ozone layer.

Renewable Energy: Energy produced using solar, wind, hydropower, or biomass energy sources; can be thermal or electric energy.

Room air conditioner: Air conditioner installed in a window or through a wall; usually used to cool a relatively small area — although with a very energy-efficient, tight house, a single room air conditioner may be able to cool the entire space. See also *whole-house (central) air conditioner.*

Salt-box: Style of house, commonly built in Colonial New England, in which most of the windows are on the taller south-facing wall, and the roof slopes down to a relatively short north wall to help deflect wind.

Sealed combustion: Combustion system for space heating or water heating in which outside *combustion air* is fed directly into the *combustion chamber* and flue gasses are exhausted directly outside.

Seasonal energy efficiency ratio (SEER): Energy performance rating of a *whole-house (central) air conditioner* or *heat pump* operating in the cooling mode; it is the ratio of the estimated seasonal cooling output divided by the seasonal power consumption in an average climate.

Semiconductor: Material, such as silicon, whose electrical properties can be altered to make it either electrically conductive or insulating; used in electronic devices such as computer chips and in *photovoltaics.*

Septic tank: Tank into which raw *wastewater* (sewage) from a house with an on-site wastewater disposal system flows. Anaerobic (oxygen-deprived) bacteria in the tank destroy pathogens in the wastewater and decompose the organic waste; effluent from the tank flows through pipes and drains into the ground in a *leach field.*

Sheathing: Material, usually plywood or *oriented strand board (OSB),* installed on the exterior of wall studs, rafters, or roof trusses; siding or roofing installed on sheathing.

Soft-coat low-e: Very thin metallic coating that is sputtered onto glass to improve its performance in reducing heat loss; because they are delicate, soft-coat *low-e coatings* must be protected within sealed insulated-glass units. See also *hard-coat (pyrolytic) low-e.*

Soil amendment: Material added to soil to make it more fertile or improve its moisture-holding capacity; chopped, recycled drywall can be used as such.

Solar Aquatic™ system: See *Living Machine.*

Solar collector: Device for capturing solar energy and transferring heat to water or air that circulates through.

Solar gain: Sunlight entering a building; for example, a passive solar *direct-gain system.*

Solar heat gain coefficient (SHGC): The fraction of solar gain admitted through a window, expressed as a number between 0 and 1.

Spec house: House built on speculation — in other words without a buyer already identified.

Spline: With *structural insulated panel (SIP)* construction, refers to connectors used to join panels; plywood splines are often installed in routed grooves in the foam insulation next to the interior and exterior *oriented strand board (OSB)* skins.

Stand-alone power system: Self-contained electricity generation and storage system, usually powered by *photovoltaics* or *wind power,* that is not connected to the electric grid. See also *grid-connected power system.*

Stormwater: Runoff from rain that is either carried offsite in storm sewers or allowed to infiltrate the ground; stormwater can be reduced through the use of porous paving and other infiltration strategies.

Straw: Stems left after harvesting cereal grains. Baled straw is used for *strawbale construction*; chopped straw can be manufactured into *particleboard.*

Strawbale construction: Construction system in which walls are built out of stacked baled *straw* and plastered on the interior and exterior surfaces. strawbale walls can be load-bearing (carrying the roof load) or non-load-bearing (in which a *post-and-beam* structural frame carries the roof load).

Stress-skin panel: Non-structural, insulated panels used for enclosing and insulating a *timber-frame* house; the interior skin is typically drywall and the exterior skin is *oriented strand board (OSB).*

Structural insulated panel (SIP): Building panel usually made of *oriented strand board (OSB)* skins surrounding a core of *expanded polystyrene (EPS)* foam insulation. SIPs can be erected very quickly with a crane to create an energy-efficient, sturdy home.

Sump: Reservoir or pit in the basement of a house into which water can drain, especially during flooding; a sump pump is used to pump collected water out of this reservoir.

Sunspace: Passive solar extension on the south side of a house used as a sunny daytime living space and as a heat source for the house; a key design feature is the ability to close the connections between the sunspace and house (typically windows and doors) at night. Can also be used for growing plants.

Suntempering: Practice of using a modest area of south-facing windows to provide limited *passive solar heating* to a house.

Superinsulate: To insulate extremely well; a house with very efficient windows and tight construction results in very low heating and cooling costs.

Swale: Low area of ground used for drainage and, often, the infiltration of *stormwater.*

Swamp cooler: See *evaporative cooler.*

Tankless coil: *Heat exchanger* integrated into a *boiler* used for heating water. Effective in the winter months when the boiler is operating for space heating, but tankless coils waste energy in warmer months, since they require the boiler to fire up every time hot water is drawn.

Therm: Unit of heat equal to 100,000 British thermal units *(Btus)*; commonly used for natural gas.

Thermal bridging: Heat flow that occurs across more conductive components in an otherwise well-insulated material, resulting in disproportionately significant heat loss. For example, steel studs in an insulated wall dramatically reduce the overall energy performance of the wall, because of thermal bridging through the steel.

Thermal mass: Heavy, high-heat-capacity material that can absorb and store a significant amount of heat; used in *passive solar heating* to keep the house warm at night.

Thermal storage wall: Type of *passive solar heating* system in which sunlight shines through south-facing glass or plastic glazing and is absorbed by the outer surface of a high-mass wall; the wall surface heats up and that heat is stored in and conducts through the wall to warm the living space. Also called a *Trombe wall.*

Thermosiphon solar water heater: Solar water heater that operates passively (through natural *convection*) to circulate water through a *solar collector* and into an insulated storage tank situated above the collector; pumps and controls are not required.

Timber frame: Type of *post-and-beam construction* relying on large structural timbers.

Top plate: In wood-frame construction, the framing member that forms the top of a wall. In *advanced framing*, a single top plate is often used in place of the more typical double top plate.

Track-off mat: Mat at a house entrance across which people scuff their feet to remove moisture, dirt, and other particulates; important for keeping contaminants out and reducing cleaning requirements.

Trombe wall: Pronounced "Trome." See *thermal storage wall.*

Tubular skylight: Round skylight that transmits sunlight down through a tube with internally reflective walls, even through an attic space; it delivers *daylighting* through a ceiling light *diffuser.* Most tubular skylights are 12 to 16 inches in diameter and deliver light comparable to several 100-watt incandescent light bulbs.

U-factor: Measure of the heat conducted through a given product or material — the number of British thermal units (*Btus*) of heat that move through a square foot of the material in one hour for every 1 degree Fahrenheit difference in temperature across the material (Btu/ft² °Fhr). U-factor is the inverse of *R-value.*

Universal design: Design that makes a building accessible to as many individuals as possible, including older people and those with physical handicaps.

Unvented (or vent-free) gas heater: Gas-burning space heater that is not vented to the outdoors. While unvented gas heaters burn very efficiently, *indoor air quality* experts strongly recommend against their use because combustion gasses, including high levels of water vapor, are released into the house.

Urea-formaldehyde binder: Interior-grade *formaldehyde*-based binder used for *particleboard, medium-density fiberboard (MDF),* and hardwood plywood; higher formaldehyde emissions than *phenol-formaldehyde binder.*

UV light treatment: Water treatment system in which water passes through a column where it is exposed to ultraviolet light to kill any pathogens.

Vapor diffusion: Movement of water vapor through a material; water vapor can diffuse through even solid materials if the permeability is high enough.

Vapor retarder: Layer that inhibits *vapor diffusion* through a *building envelope*; examples include polyethylene sheeting, foil facing, and low-permeability paints.

Ventilation: Replacement of stale indoor air with fresh outdoor air — usually with fans, but sometimes naturally through building design elements. See also *heat recovery ventilator.*

Venturi effect: Increase in fluid velocity as flow is constricted; also, the principle by which air is drawn into a stream of water to increase the force of the flow. Used to enhance performance of some low-flow showerheads.

Vernacular: The architectural style that is specific to a certain region and that typically evolved in response to local climatic conditions.

Vertical-axis clothes washer: Top-loading washing machine with a tub that rotates back and forth and spins on a vertical axis, i.e., the center of rotation is a line extending up from the center of the tub. See also *horizontal-axis clothes washer.*

Vinyl: Common term for *polyvinyl chloride (PVC).* In chemistry, vinyl refers to a carbon-and-hydrogen group (H₂C=CH–) that attaches to another functional group, such as chlorine (vinyl chloride) or acetate (vinyl acetate).

Volatile organic compound (VOC): An organic compound that evaporates readily into the atmosphere; as defined by the US Environmental Protection Agency, VOCs are organic compounds that volatize and then become involved in photochemical smog production.

Waste management plan: Plan that addresses the collection and disposal of waste generated during construction, usually including the collection and storage of recyclable materials.

Wastewater: Used water from toilets, showers, sinks, dishwashers, clothes washers, and other sources in the home, including all contaminants; can either flow into a municipal sewer system or be treated with an *onsite wastewater disposal system*.

Waterborne finish: Finish for wood or other materials that uses water as the carrier, instead of an organic solvent; waterborne finishes generally have much lower *volatile organic compound (VOC)* levels.

Whole-house (central) air conditioner: Air conditioning system that serves an entire house; cooled air is delivered through a system of ducts. See also *room air conditioner.*

Whole-wall R-value: Average *R-value* of a wall, taking into account the *thermal bridging* through wall studs.

Wind farm: Electricity-generating windmills grouped together to improve operation and maintenance efficiencies and economic performance; typically comprised of large windmills; the power is usually fed into the utility grid.

Wind power: Use of wind to generate electricity.

Worm bin: Alternative to a composting bin for kitchen scraps; worms digest organic waste, converting it into a rich soil.

Xeriscaping: Type of landscaping that requires little if any irrigation; suited to dry climates; generally relies on regionally adapted native plants.

Index

About the Author

ALEX WILSON IS THE PRESIDENT OF BuildingGreen, Inc. in Brattleboro, Vermont and executive editor of *Environmental Building News* and the *GreenSpec® Directory*. A biologist by training, he has written about energy-efficient and environmentally responsible design and construction for more than 25 years. Prior to starting his own company in 1985 (now BuildingGreen, Inc.), he was executive director of the Northeast Sustainable Energy Association for five years; before that he taught workshops on the construction of solar greenhouses in New Mexico in the late '70s. Alex is coauthor of the *Consumer Guide to Home Energy Savings* (ACEEE, 8th edition, 2003) and the Rocky Mountain Institute's comprehensive textbook *Green Development: Integrating Ecology and Real Estate* (John Wiley & Sons, 1998). He has also written hundreds of articles for other publications, including *Fine Homebuilding, Architectural Record, Landscape Architecture,* the *Journal of Light Construction,* and *Popular Science*. Along with writing about design and construction, Alex has written four guidebooks on quiet-water paddling in the Northeast for the Appalachian Mountain Club.

Alex served on the board of directors of the U.S. Green Building Council for five years and he is currently a trustee of The Nature Conservancy — Vermont Chapter. He lives in Dummerston, Vermont with his wife and two daughters, and in good weather commutes by bicycle to work.

If you have enjoyed *Your Green Home*
you might also enjoy other

BOOKS TO BUILD A NEW SOCIETY

Our books provide positive solutions for people who want to
make a difference. We specialize in:

**Environment and Justice • Conscientious Commerce
Sustainable Living • Ecological Design and Planning
Natural Building & Appropriate Technology • New Forestry
Educational and Parenting Resources • Nonviolence
Progressive Leadership • Resistance and Community**

New Society Publishers

ENVIRONMENTAL BENEFITS STATEMENT

New Society Publishers has chosen to produce this book on recycled paper made with
100% post consumer waste, processed chlorine free, and old growth free.

For every 5,000 books printed, New Society saves the following resources:[1]

28	Trees
2,528	Pounds of Solid Waste
2,782	Gallons of Water
3,629	Kilowatt Hours of Electricity
4,596	Pounds of Greenhouse Gases
20	Pounds of HAPs, VOCs, and AOX Combined
7	Cubic Yards of Landfill Space

---

[1]Environmental benefits are calculated based on research done by the Environmental Defense Fund and
other members of the Paper Task Force who study the environmental impacts of the paper industry.

For a full list of NSP's titles, please call **1-800-567-6772** *or check out our website at:*

www.newsociety.com

NEW SOCIETY PUBLISHERS